What Women Want from Work

York Studies on Women and Men

General Editors: **Haleh Afshar** and **Mary Maynard**

Alison L. Boden
WOMEN'S RIGHTS AND RELIGIOUS PRACTICE
Claims in Conflict

Nikki Craske
GENDER AND THE POLITICS OF RIGHTS AND DEMOCRACY IN LATIN AMERICA

Myfanwy Franks
WOMEN AND REVIVALISM IN THE WEST
Choosing Fundamentalism in a Liberal Democracy

Shirin M. Rai (*editor*)
INTERNATIONAL PERSPECTIVES ON GENDER AND DEMOCRATIZATION

Carmel Roulston and Celia Davies (*editors*)
GENDER, DEMOCRACY AND INCLUSION IN NORTHERN IRELAND

Yvette Taylor
WORKING CLASS LESBIAN LIFE
Classed Outsiders

Ruth Woodfield
WHAT WOMEN WANT FROM WORK
Gender and Occupational Choice in the 21st Century

York Studies on Women and Men
Series Standing Order ISBN 0–333–71512–8
(*outside North America Only*)

You can receive future titles in this series as they are published by placing a standing order. Please contact your bookseller or, in case of difficulty, write to us at the address below with your name and address, the title of the series and the ISBN quoted above.

Customer Services Department, Macmillan Distribution Limited, Houndmills, Basingstoke, Hampshire RG21 6XS, England

What Women Want from Work

Gender and Occupational Choice in the 21st Century

Ruth Woodfield
University of Sussex

First published 2007 by
PALGRAVE MACMILLAN
Houndmills, Basingstoke, Hampshire RG21 6XS and
175 Fifth Avenue, New York, N.Y. 10010
Companies and representatives throughout the world

PALGRAVE MACMILLAN is the global academic imprint of the Palgrave Macmillan division of St. Martin's Press, LLC and of Palgrave Macmillan Ltd. Macmillan® is a registered trademark in the United States, United Kingdom and other countries. Palgrave is a registered trademark in the European Union and other countries.

ISBN-13: 978–0–230–54922–7   hardback
ISBN-10: 0–230–54922–5   hardback

This book is printed on paper suitable for recycling and made from fully managed and sustained forest sources. Logging, pulping and manufacturing processes are expected to conform to the environmental regulations of the country of origin.

A catalogue record for this book is available from the British Library.

A catalog record for this book is available from Library of Congress.

10   9   8   7   6   5   4   3   2   1
16   15   14   13   12   11   10   09   08   07

Printed and bound in Great Britain by
Antony Rowe Ltd, Chippenham and Eastbourne

For my boys: Richard, Jess, Kim & Davy

Contents

Acknowledgements

A big thank you is due to all of the participants who took part in this project. They were voluntary contributors and I am extremely grateful for their efforts and their willingness to discuss ideas and opinions as openly as they did. Although all had constraints on their time, the teachers and firefighters were particularly pressured, and I am therefore doubly indebted to them for agreeing to be interviewed. The research left me much clearer about what their respective work roles involve and all the more impressed that they carry out their public service with the dedication and humour that they do.

Various researchers and individuals who didn't duck fast enough helped enormously: Emma Sims-Fielding and Jacqui Shepherd are deserving of particular mention for the skilful production of several hours of interview data each; Wendy Bishop and Lucy Solomon also produced some excellent data, albeit on a smaller scale; Wendy Bishop undertook a very helpful literature search and proved to be a first class proofreader; Brenda Whatmore undertook some invaluable data entry on the Fire Service project, which is not directly used here but formed the backdrop to the interviews; James Ravenhill was an expert transcriber of many of the interview tapes; Hetty Meyric Hughes kindly checked my teacher 'facts'; Hattie Judson and her friends helped clarify a theme towards the end of the research by good-naturedly providing supplementary interviews.

The Equal Opportunities Commission (EOC) deserves separate mention. It has proved, once again, to be an invaluable resource in this research. David Perfect, in particular (again!) has been especially helpful in his advice and explanation.

Thanks are also due to the British Academy who provided funding for many of the teacher interviews, some of the student interviews and the transcription costs. East Sussex Fire & Rescue Service provided funding for the firefighter interviews, for most of the student interviews and for time to analyse the data. They also provided background information on the firefighter role. All of my dealings with the Service – but especially with Des Pritchard, Chris Large, Sue Johnston and more recently, Cheryl Rolph – have been positive, open and helpful.

I would like also to thank Jill Lake at Palgrave Macmillan, for her support and patience during the writing of this book; staff of

Macmillan India, for careful proofing and advice; and Jane Henderson of Indexplorations for her speedy and excellent index work.

On a more personal level, I would like to say thank you to colleagues in the Sociology Department, and the School of Social and Cultural Studies, at Sussex University for clearing the decks and allowing me to finish this project; to my first sociology teachers, Mr Green (for his inspirational teaching) and Ms Ingledew (for the same, and for patiently introducing the idea of feminism to a sceptical audience); and to my family, especially my mother, Kathleen Holness, and brother, Andrew Woodfield, for support and for providing another perspective. This latter, crucial, contribution was, of course, most effectively provided by my three wonderful sons: Jess, Kim and Davy Whatmore.

It is not an exaggeration to say that this book would not have been written without Richard Whatmore, whose love and support, once again, have been immeasurable.

1
What Women Want from Work – An Introduction

The role women play in the paid-employment sector changed dramatically in the closing decades of the last century. More women joined the workforce, they worked for longer before having children and increasingly returned to work afterwards. Women entered occupations that were once considered closed to them, often in considerable numbers; and they climbed to positions previously thought impossible. It is, nevertheless, the case that gendered-occupational segregation, whereby women and men are concentrated into different areas of work (horizontal segregation), and at different levels (vertical segregation), remains a global phenomenon. Women have made some remarkable inroads, but they are still overwhelmingly concentrated in comparatively few occupational areas, and remain under-represented in the highest-paid and most senior and powerful positions.

How can we to best explain this? When surveyed, most children and adults – and especially girls and women – expressly support an individual's right to choose the jobs that most please and satisfy them (O'Brien & Fassinger 1993; Lightbody & Durndell 1998; University of Wisconsin Survey Center, 2003; McQuaid, Bond & Robinson 2004; EOC 2005a; HMSO 2005). Yet there is substantial evidence that these same adults maintain segregation through their own practical occupational choices. For some, in the context of extensive equal opportunities legislation, and girls' and women's considerable educational successes, the most persuasive explanation is fundamentally individualist, claiming that occupational patterns must be reflecting intrinsic differences and desires in individual men and women. There are less women construction workers, plumbers and sailors because less women actually want to undertake these employment roles. Similarly, there are fewer women in the boardrooms of major businesses, fewer women politicians, judges and police chiefs because women simply have less strong desires to climb up career ladders, less evident abilities, or both. Given women's recent educational achievements, explanations that rely on their inferior abilities have lost some of their critical force, ceding ground to beliefs that women must *want* the work roles that they end up in. If this is the case, it is suggested, then academic researchers and policy makers need not expend so much time and energy chronicling and attempting to correct gendered employment imbalances.

This view is integrated into both our academic and common sense ways of talking and thinking about occupational decision-making (Padavic 1992). The touchstone image of much of the discussion around occupational 'choice' is the unfettered individual making a well-informed selection of their target job from the range of roles that match their abilities and desires. In the context of these assumptions, and the decline of critical perspectives to challenge them, some uncomfortable facts resist easy explication. How can we explain the gender gap in wages, for instance, whereby women earn less than men, even for the same kinds of work and in female-dominated sectors? Similarly, how can we explain some women's claims that they are victims of discrimination within the workplace, and have their career desire thwarted by factors external to them? Are individual workplaces and managers, with anomalous cultures and attitudes, to blame? Or are there wider, systemic and powerful aspects of modern society that conspire to maintain a gender regime that persists in privileging men's interests above women's? Is it the case that, although many formal barriers to greater occupational choice and progression have been removed, many informal ones remain and these restrict women's employment patterns? These questions require an examination of structural factors within society to assess the role they are playing in producing segregation patterns.

It is one of the paradoxes associated with occupational-segregation research, that literature focusing on individualist explanations rarely derives evidence for its arguments from talking to people directly. Much of the literature that assumes that extra-individual factors are key determinants of work patterns does not do this either, but the approach is more centrally embraced within this broad perspective. There is, nevertheless, a lack of literature that examines how women understand and account for their own occupational choices, including how and why they orient towards gender-atypical careers, as well as how and why most orient away from gender-atypical roles, and very senior and well-paid careers. There is a need to examine in more depth how women account for their own agency in the decision-making process, for the influence of micro-sociological factors such as parental expectations and peer pressure, and the effects of macro-sociological factors such as equal opportunities policies and media representations.

This book seeks to address each of these lacunae, and the research questions that emerge from the currently uncertain social context of occupational segregation, through an analysis of a large and original data-set that comprises accounts from 186 girls and women. The book focuses exclusively on female participants for a number of reasons. It follows the research tradition that has developed since the 1970s in so doing, reflecting the fact that it is this group who have historically been the most restricted in terms of employment patterns (Hensley 1998). Moreover, it is the changes in women's employment that represent the most significant shifts in overall segregation patterns over recent decades, against which men's employment has been comparatively static, suggesting that the specific attention is warranted (Proctor & Padfield 1998). Girls and women are also particularly interesting when considering occupational segregation and choice. It has been argued that they are simultaneously *more* expressive of vulnerability to stereotype pressure, *less* likely to stereotype jobs themselves and *more* likely to go into atypical occupations than males, although the overwhelming majority of girls choose not to (O'Brien & Fassinger 1993; O'Brien, Friedman, Tipton and Linn 2000; McQuaid, Bond & Robinson 2004; EOC 2005a). Notwithstanding this, the book is conceived of as the first of two, with the second focusing exclusively on boy's and men's employment choices.

Just under 100 of the interview participants were still in full-time education, and were therefore still at the stage of formulating their occupational preferences. Interviews sought to explore their views on a range of employment-related issues via general questions and specific examination of a gender-atypical occupation – firefighting – and the gender-typical role of teaching. Both of these occupations, but especially firefighting, have been neglected within the literature to date. These interviewees' contributions have been teamed with interviews from women in both of these occupations. This design is aimed to ensure adequate cognisance of the perspective of those still engaged in making their initial occupational choices, as well as those who have already chosen a specific occupation. It therefore captures data during the initial identification of a career, a period that is crucial because, 'once people have chosen an occupation, it becomes incredibly difficult to change to a new one . . . the choice of first job is very important' (HMSO 2005: 7), and allows for analysis of this data alongside the more experienced reflections of seasoned women workers.

The initial part of the book comprises an extensive literature review of research examining gendered-occupational segregation, within two chapters. The first, Chapter 2, deals with individualist and more socially focused explanations of segregation that are based on information sources other than directly accessed accounts. Chapter 3 then focuses on the smaller sample of research which centrally deploys qualitative interviews to understand segregation, focusing on the contribution this methodological approach can make to our comprehension of segregation phenomena, before introducing the data presentation that will follow in the subsequent three chapters. Although this original data derives from the UK alone, the literature it reviews, and within which its empirical findings are contextualised, is international.

The second part of the book comprises an introduction and three data presentation chapters. Chapter 4 examines views on atypical work generally and through the lens of views on the role of firefighting. It explores the perspective of those still in full-time education, and of those already in the firefighter role, or attempting to become firefighters. Chapter 5 examines views on gender-typical work generally and through the lens of views on teaching, as evinced by both those in full-time education and teachers themselves. Chapter 6 examines all the participants' commentary that relates to the phenomenon of vertical segregation, how those in education see themselves in relation to ambition and career progress, and how female teachers and firefighters understand their own experience of advancement opportunities and costs.

Finally, the book ends with Chapters 7 and 8, and an analysis of the key findings from the empirical data, how they contribute to the existing literature base and to our understanding of women's work choices in the UK and elsewhere. These chapters confirm that the individualist approach, focusing as it does on women's 'choices' in relation to work, has experienced an ascendancy that is premature, and, indeed, will probably never be opportune, ignoring as it does the still-extensive, extra-individual factors that shape and inhibit women's employment desires and career outcomes, and the probability that they will always do so. To be sure, we need to account for an individual agent negotiating her way in the context of these factors towards what is experienced as a personal biography in relation to work, but the accounts examined here confirm that she is far from unfettered in her choices, and that what women want from work is, ultimately, as much a function of forces beyond immediate experience, than it is of desires from within.

2
Gender and Occupational Segregation – Setting the Scene

Occupational segregation in the UK and elsewhere

Introduction

This chapter begins with a review of literature focusing on gendered occupational segregation in order to delineate the extent and nature of this employment feature within the UK and elsewhere. It will then consider the various accounts of what causes segregation patterns, and the issues and debates that emerge from the different explanatory modes adopted.

A great deal has been written on the subject of occupational selection and segregation, and this review is by no means exhaustive. Only literature that has a clear gender dimension is examined here, for instance. A key aim is to cover the most pertinent themes to emerge within the literature over the past few decades.

Horizontal and vertical segregation

Three decades have passed since the landmark Sex Discrimination Acts of the 1970s that outlawed discrimination on the basis of a person's sex in educational and occupational settings. In the intervening years, there have been significant changes in the gendered composition of many occupational sectors and roles, and women's participation in the paid work economy has increased substantially. Despite this, gendered occupational segregation of some sort and to varying degrees persists in all countries (Elder & Schmidt 2004; Miller *et al.* 2004; Charles 2005; Blackburn & Jarman 2006).

Commonly, two types of interlinked segregations are described in the available literature: horizontal and vertical. The term 'horizontal segregation' refers to the phenomenon whereby women are disproportionately concentrated within particular occupational sectors while being significantly under-represented within others. 'Vertical segregation' refers to the phenomenon whereby women are disproportionately present at certain levels of all occupational sectors, and disproportionately under-represented at other levels.

Along with the general nature of occupational segregation, there are some salient global trends in female employment. One is the significant growth of female participation in the labour force, but this growth has developed in tandem with features that put women at a disadvantage as compared to men. On average, women are paid less than men, even for the same type of work, and even in female-dominated sectors. They are more likely than men to be employed within an informal economy, to be in receipt of irregular wages or be unsalaried, and to be in employment that is highly vulnerable and with inferior conditions. Women are far more likely to work part-time; such employment brings with it more vulnerability, poorer career prospects and even larger pay gaps (Elder & Schmidt 2004; Miller *et al.* 2004; EOC 2006).

The majority of research into segregation has identified both horizontal and vertical types as mutually reinforcing determinations of gendered inequality. The employment features that differentiate women's work have therefore been linked to segregation of both kinds.

Horizontal segregation

Various analytical techniques have been utilised to measure the unequal distribution of men and women across different occupational sectors (DeLeire & Levy 2001; Blackburn & Jarman 2006). A commonly adopted definition for an occupation being considered gender-typical or atypical as far as women are concerned, however, is whether they comprise more than 75 per cent or less than 25 per cent of its incumbents, respectively. Analysis of occupational compositions has shown that the scale of skewed distribution has declined in past decades but remains remarkably persistent and somewhat fixed in its fundamental characteristics.

Recent estimates suggest that 60 per cent of UK women workers are employed in just 10 out of 77 occupations, with most employed within the '5 Cs: Caring, Cashiering, Catering, Cleaning and Clerical' (HMSO 2005: 6). The UK is by no means alone in this pattern. Women's near-global association with domesticity, and its related tasks, means that occupational sectors and roles that are identified as reproducing these tasks are almost always female-dominated, from national contexts as diverse as Japan, the US, Switzerland, Portugal, Sweden, Italy and Iceland (Proctor & Padfield 1998; Elder & Schmidt 2004; Miller *et al.* 2004; Charles 2005).

Indeed, the substantial increases in female labour force participation over the past decades have dovetailed with the burgeoning of service and clerical occupational sectors, with many women taking employment roles in these areas. More specifically, women in the UK comprise 79 per cent of those in the Health and Social Work sector, and 73 per cent of those in Education (EOC 2006). In terms of roles, they account for 84 per cent of 'Personal Service' workers, 95 per cent of receptionists, 88 per cent of nurses and care assistants, and 80 per cent of 'Administrative and secretarial' workers (EOC 2005b). Female concentration looks set to continue in the immediate term if we take the gendered distribution of the current pool of trainees as an indication. Girls and women represent 97 per cent of those taking apprenticeship training in Early Years Care and Education, 91 per cent of those in Hairdressing, 87 per cent of those in Health and Social Care and 69 per cent of those training in Customer Service (EOC 2006).

Conversely, female under-representation in many sectors and occupations characterised by manual work (for example, construction), as well as professional scientific and technical occupations (for example, Information Technology work), is also marked in the majority of countries (Rees 1998; Roger & Duffield 2000; Woodfield 2000; Sian & Callaghan 2001; Miller *et al.* 2004).

To be sure, some remarkable inroads have been made by women into occupations previously dominated by men, and across the globe (Davey & Lalande 2004; Elder & Schmidt 2004). In the UK, some sectors that were male-dominated have become far more balanced or have even achieved gender equity, such as public administration (EOC 2006). Many key sectors, however, remain heavily male-dominated (EOC 2006; Woodfield 2006a). Although there are important variations according to the level of work (for example, professional/non-professional; graduate/non-graduate), the evidence consistently shows that women are significantly under-represented in agriculture, industry, financial services and science, engineering and technology (SET) occupations (Rees 1998; Miller *et al.* 2004; EOC 2005a). As with female-dominated sectors, the situation in relation to pre-entry qualifiers for these areas does not herald change in the immediate future. Women have, for instance, comprised less than a quarter of those undertaking Computer Science degrees in the UK since the 1990s (Woodfield 2006b). Figures on apprenticeship recruits in the UK show that only 1 per cent of those for construction and plumbing are currently female. This is despite, in the case of the latter occupation, the work's reputation as skilled and well-remunerated.

This ghettoised pattern has been identified as a key factor in perpetuating women's disadvantage in the paid labour force. Recent assessments have identified occupational segregation as a major factor behind the persistent gender pay gap (Elder & Schmidt 2004; ILO 2004; EOC 2005a; HMSO 2005). Female workers in the UK, on average, are paid 17 per cent per hour less than males for comparable full-time work. The pay gap is significantly wider for women who work part-time – they earn 40 per cent less per hour than full-time male workers (EOC 2007) – and in the private sector where it reaches 22 per cent (ILO 2004: 30). The status attached to work associated with women is also lower than that associated with men.

> The areas of work within which women traditionally tend to be concentrated, are generally those with lower average pay and lower status. . . . For women to obtain better paid (and higher status) work, it is usually necessary for them to consider working in occupations typically perceived as male.
>
> (Miller *et al.* 2004: 22)

As well as the pay and prestige, horizontal segregation is also damaging to women's employment and personal prospects insofar as it limits their opportunities. This could equally be said of men's opportunities for working in areas traditionally associated with women. The difference being that, when men do enter female-dominated sectors, they are more likely to enter at higher levels, be promoted with relative speed and generally receive higher than average wages. By contrast, women who enter male-dominated occupations may fare better than they would in female-dominated work in terms of status – although this is by no means unproblematically conferred – and sometimes initial pay benefits, but they enjoy mixed fortunes in terms of the longer-term pay gap, and have lower retention and promotion rates as compared to men in the same field (Davey & Lalande 2004; ILO 2004; Miller *et al.* 2004; EOC 2005a; Woodfield 2006a). Moreover, this mixed picture holds for male-dominated *professional* work; in skilled and semi-skilled manual work, women fare even worse than they do in gender-typical areas (ILO 2004).

This gendered occupational segregation has also been highlighted as damaging to the economies concerned insofar as markets are not recruiting employees from the widest possible pool of workers, and 'there is a clear correlation between employment sectors where men predominate and skills shortages' (Miller *et al.* 2004; HMSO 2005; EOC 2005a: 11; see also, EOC 2006).

Vertical segregation

As with horizontal segregation, vertical segregation has been eroded considerably since the Sex Discrimination legislation of the 1970s. At that time, in the UK, approximately one in ten professional workers was female, whereas the figure now is two-fifths (EOC 2006). Despite this upward trend, the UK still does not compare well against many other countries in this regard. In North America, Australia and New Zealand, women comprise more than 50 per cent of professional workers (ILO 2004). More generally, women's inroads into professional work are further decisive – around 60 per cent – in some Eastern European and South American countries.

The presence of women in senior and managerial positions has also increased (Crompton 1997; Holton 1998; Wacjman 1998; Jones & Goulding 1999; Miller *et al.* 2004; HMSO 2005). It is nevertheless the case that women in the UK comprise less than 40 per cent of workforces in 'high-paid' jobs. They account for 34 per cent of managers and senior officials, 29 per cent of marketing and sales managers and 17 per cent of directors and chief executives of major organisations (EOC, 2006). At the other end of the scale, they account for over 70 per cent of workforces in very 'low-paid' jobs, including 96 per cent of school midday assistants, 72 per cent of sales and retail assistants, 76 per cent of cleaners and domestics and 73 per cent of kitchen and catering assistants (ibid.).

Women in the UK are still under-represented in the most powerful public positions – they comprise only 39 per cent of public appointments, 8 per cent of senior judges, 15 per cent of university vice-chancellors, 10 per cent of senior police officers, less than 1 per cent of senior ranks in the armed forces and only account for 35 per cent of workers in all government departments (EOC 2005b; EOC 2006). In addition, there is evidence that women have less likelihood of being successful in senior managerial roles (Holton 1998). To pick up on a point made above, it is further noteworthy that men occupy a disproportionate amount of senior positions even in occupations and sectors where women are concentrated, such as Health and Social Service. Less than 6 per cent of managers are employed part-time, but the majority of these are women (ibid.).

The pattern whereby women are under-represented in managerial ranks is evident elsewhere. In 2002, women only accounted for between

20 and 40 per cent of managerial positions in the majority of countries surveyed by the International Labour Office for its *Breaking Through the Glass Ceiling* report (ILO 2004). In the US, women comprise 46 per cent of administrative and managerial workers, but only 12 per cent of actual managers, and are 'particularly under-represented in higher positions' (ibid.: 17). In Japan, Bahrain, Pakistan, Bangladesh and Saudi Arabia, females represent less than 10 per cent of administrative and managerial workers.

Moreover, in only one – Costa Rica – of the 48 'Group 1' countries surveyed women held more than 50 per cent of the most senior and powerful positions – legislators, senior officials and senior managers. In all countries, bar four, the number of women in senior positions is below 40 per cent, and in half of these countries is below 30 per cent (ibid. 2004). The global average for female representatives in national governments is less than 16 per cent, although women have made inroads into cabinets in many countries, albeit, again, in gender-typical areas such as Health, Education and Social Affairs (ibid.: 22).

In terms of top positions in the private sector in particular, women fare even worse. In Australia they comprise only 8 per cent of board members. The percentage is higher in the US, where female board membership with the Fortune 500 list has reached 14 per cent (ibid.: 20). Even in Sweden, usually identified as a beacon country in terms of its egalitarian policies, it is noted that 'far more men than women occupy top positions' (Dryler 1998: 375; see also ILO 2004). This pattern is not simply a function of female workforce participation rates. The ILO survey found that 'after several years of work, a woman is more likely to be found in a lower position than a man with the same qualifications who joined the labour market at the same time' (2004: 17).

Gender-based vertical segregation affects all sectors. To build on points made above, even within the female-dominated sectors, women are disadvantaged by vertical segregation. In the service sector, for instance, women are concentrated within social and personal services work, and far less likely to be found in financial and business service work; in the education sector, they are far more likely to stay in the junior ranks than male counterparts (Elder & Schmidt 2004; Miller *et al.* 2004; Charles, 2005).

As we might expect, vertical segregation has also been, somewhat truistically, cited as a cause of the gender pay gap (ILO 2004: 30). What is of greater interest is the fact that even women who achieve top positions receive less pay than their male comparators, and the average pay gap in the higher echelons is bigger than the national average; indeed it further widens the more senior the position (EOC 2002; ILO 2004: 31; Miller *et al.* 2004).

Occupational segregation and inequality revisited – the overall picture

As has been indicated, the majority of research characterises both horizontal and vertical segregation as phenomena significantly associated with occupational gender inequality, and with female disadvantage. In relation to both types of segregation these claims have been challenged, and the case made for a more sophisticated, empirically accurate and operationally useful deployment of segregation concepts.

It is suggested that, while all occupational segregation entails some inequality, the degree to which this is *always* to female disadvantage, and male advantage, has been overplayed (Blackburn & Jarman 2006). Although the systemic and systematic disadvantages to women are acknowledged within this perspective, what is also highlighted, therefore, are the heterogeneous gender effects of segregation (ibid.: 291).

A major point to emerge from this approach is that, if we take into account the *overall* diverse and complex effects of both horizontal *and* vertical segregation, occupational segregation, as it has developed over the last three decades in the UK, holds some advantages for women. Notwithstanding the very considerable opportunity costs to both sexes in relation to their restricted choices, women fare better than men within this framework in certain important respects.

In terms of vertical segregation, they are advantaged because they are concentrated in the middle and above-middle occupational ranks, in non-manual occupations, albeit with far great frequency in the lower echelons of these roles. Their employment is focused in 'Professional', 'Associated professional and technical' and clerical and service and sales occupations (Charles 2005: 296; Blackburn & Jarman 2006). Although many of their jobs are low-paid, as a group, women are not frequently found in the very lowest occupational categories of 'Process, plant and machinery operatives' and 'Elementary occupations', which are characterised by the lowest levels of required skill.

Men, as we have seen, are undoubtedly dominant when it comes to the top occupational categories, and consequently are better remunerated overall, but they are a polarised occupational group and so are also dominant at the bottom of the occupational ladder, in skilled, semi-skilled and unskilled and manual work. It is suggested that 'the net result is the slight advantage to women' (Blackburn & Jarman 2006: 305). This is reported to currently be the case in the US, Canada, Japan, Belgium, France, Sweden, West Germany, Italy, Portugal and Switzerland (ibid.; Charles 2005), and the 'strong similarity across country groups' is taken as evidence of a general and fundamental shape of sex segregation patterning (Charles 2005: 298). This patterning represents an improvement on the picture in the 1970s. Then, the same polarised pattern of male employment, versus the comparatively homogenous and bunched pattern of female employment, was noted (Shinar 1975; Gottfredson 1981), but it was concluded that 'employed men and women have the same occupational prestige on the average' (Gottfredson 1981: 553). The dangers of overlooking the overall picture of segregation by focusing only on male domination at the top end was equally highlighted then as 'misleading about sex differences' (ibid.: 553).

There is certainly a tendency in the available literature to deploy the term 'dominated' when referring to sectors where men are concentrated, but not when referring to those where women are over-represented. This tendency has obviously grown out of a desire and need to reflect the qualitative dominion of masculinity within the occupational sphere, and not simply men's quantitative advantage, and this requirement remains very much a live one. Equally, however, the researchers cited here are right that we need to keep the overall segregation patterning in mind if we are to understand the complexities of its relationship to inequality.

In this light, Blackburn and Jarman have also reviewed horizontal segregation and reconsidered its disadvantages to women alongside possible advantages. Indeed, the claim is that, contra the common assumption that vertical and horizontal segregation are inextricably bound up with each other and mutually reinforcing, there is a 'striking' tendency for them to move in opposite directions (Blackburn & Jarman 2006: 300). Horizontal segregation, when more effectively and systematically developed, reduces the opportunities for the occurrence of gender discrimination within gender-typed occupations. Overall, it is argued, women will be less discriminated against within male-typical work as there are fewer of them in it, and, more importantly, they will be less disadvantaged within female-typical work as, with fewer men, they will have more even opportunities of reaching the upper echelons. Blackburn and Jarman state that the best-case scenario would be low horizontal *and* vertical segregation, but also that 'this is not what we have observed' (300).

Sweden is taken as an example in point. It is very heavily horizontally segregated. Although, as we have seen, women are still under-represented at the highest occupational levels (Dryler 1998: 375; ILO 2004), vertical segregation is comparatively low as compared to many other countries, most notably the UK and North America. According to Blackburn and Jarman, women suffer fewer disadvantages on four key variables designed by the United Nations to measure women's empowerment: proportion of seats in parliament, proportion of women in key managerial positions, proportion of women in professional and technical posts, and proportion of women who share earned income (ibid.: 295). They conclude that segregation causes and reflects inequality, that we should not be misled into thinking women in any country have gained equality, but the picture with regard to female disadvantage needs to be examined alongside the elements of advantage (Blackburn & Jarman 2006: 305).

Blackburn and Jarman have, in particular, challenged the use of the terms 'horizontal' and 'vertical' segregation, and have argued that they can be misleading and analytically problematic. These terms will, nevertheless, still be used here, as they are used in the majority of existing research on segregation, although it is also acknowledged that they are contestable, and that the overall perspective is crucial.

Key explanations of occupational segregation patterns

Introduction

A variety of explanatory modes have been proposed to account for gendered occupational segregation patterns. The process of categorising them is both challenging and open to contestation, not least by the authors of the research being categorised. The range of approaches are commonly classified, on the one hand, as those giving emphasis to the 'individual' (these have also sometimes been grouped as 'supply', 'actor' or 'choice' factors), and, on the other hand, as those emphasising extra-individual factors, or, what might loosely be referred to as the 'social' (these have also sometimes been grouped as 'demand', 'organisation', 'materialist', 'structural', 'cultural' and 'institutional' factors). This broad and necessarily somewhat crude typology will be adopted here, despite its bluntness, as it highlights key underlying assumptions on each side which, in turn, point to particular conceptions of occupational 'choice' and its limitations, and different perspectives on the need, or not, for 'solutions' to address perceived occupational imbalances.

The differences in perspective between 'individual' versus 'social' accounts lie, not *necessarily* in the overall fundamental ontological assumptions of the positions – beliefs about what the human world is composed of – but where analytical and explanatory priority is granted. An important point of distinction is, for instance, the locus of the primary attribution of agency. Broadly speaking, 'individual' approaches tend to theorise, either implicitly or explicitly, the individual as the primary site of occupational choice, and the most rational focus of academic enquiry. Those that emphasise extra-individual factors conversely tend to attribute agency primarily to forces outside of the individual, which act upon the individual, and therefore which should be the primary focus of study if we are to understand occupational segregation patterns.

Explanations that posit segregation as primarily a function of individual choice do not necessarily, however, claim the 'social' is of minimal importance, or that 'choice' is completely unfettered. Some of the individualist literature that takes the individual as the primary unit of analysis also assumes, often explicitly, that they are a product of early socialisation, or biological influence, both of which may be taken as important factors in shaping 'choice' processes and outcomes. The distinctiveness of this research, however, lies in the researchers' decision to place the primary analytical emphasis on the individual, and all that this implies: that, to understand crucial decision-making about work, the focus needs to be on the processes taking place within the individual, even if these are partly expressions of extra-individual influences, and that research needs to identify the 'effects' of these individual processes on work outcomes. Many individualist approaches derive from an attempt to critique alleged 'social determinism', or perspectives placing primary emphasis on social factors such as employers' attitudes, discrimination, disadvantages in education etc. These approaches, while they might admit of structural, institutional or organisational constraints on individual decision-making processes, usually fail to delineate in any detail what these might be and how they might operate; sometimes their effects are not addressed at all and the individual is posited as relatively fixed or given. Conversely, while some 'social' perspectives may, implicitly or explicitly, admit of a role for individual agency, they often fail to delineate or explore of what this might consist, or largely sideline it in their analysis. Even when focusing on individuals and how they generate their decisions, therefore, they are largely seeking to identify the 'effects' of the social.

One of the most important issues to highlight is that most of the research on segregation is based on methodological approaches to data that do not involve actually engaging with individuals in an in-depth manner. Somewhat paradoxically, this is especially the case with research taking a more 'individualist' perspective. Here, at most, individual-level data are derived from test instruments, or from national labour surveys that pick up on indicators of employment activity without engaging directly with individuals at all. Those accounts that treat social, extra-individual factors as the primary units of analysis are far more often deployers of genuinely *individualised* accounts.

The remainder of this chapter will review the key research that has attempted to explain occupational segregation from both 'individual' and 'social' perspectives, but which also has deployed methodological approaches that do *not* involve accessing individual women workers' narrated accounts directly, although it may involve eliciting individual information via questionnaires, including open-ended questionnaire items in some cases. Chapter 3 will then focus on those far fewer examples of research that are based on directly accessed accounts of women workers narrating their occupational decisions, and which use qualitative methodologies to ensure in-depth descriptions from participants.

Modes of explanation giving primacy to individual factors

Individualist perspectives usually take as their starting point the assumption that broad, underlying and fixed differences between men and women exist, which are reflected in their employment choices and behaviour. This is most obviously the case in literature that seeks to demonstrate that a significant part of occupational segregation is a function of biological or 'brainsex' differences between the sexes.

'Brainsex' approaches

Doreen Kimura has been a key advocate of the 'brainsex' approach. In her influential book *Sex and Cognition* (2000), she summarises research on the relationship between basic sex differences and the production of cognitive effects, arguing that differences in both prenatal and life-course sex hormone levels are the chief factor in determining adult levels of spatial ability, mathematical reasoning, verbal ability, as well as other cognitive abilities (ibid.; see also Kimura 2006). These ability differences, she suggests, manifest themselves very early on in the development of children, notably before exposure to major differences in life experience, and remain regardless of different cultural gender norms that might exist in varying national contexts, and across changing historical periods (Kimura 2006). Women's roles have changed radically since the 1960s, in terms of their access to previously male-dominated educational and employment opportunities, for instance, and yet, she argues, their measured cognitive differences have not. Our sex differences, in this sense, parallel those found in non-humans where social influences are deemed less determining of behaviour, or are artificially minimised (such as in laboratories) (ibid.).

What should be noted here is that this research does not claim that *all* men are superior to *all* women in terms of, say, mathematical reasoning. Rather, that the average man is superior to the average woman in this regard, and that, despite there being a lot of overlap between many men's and women's abilities, there will be far more men who 'naturally' fall at the top end of the ability spectrum, and far more women who fall at the bottom end. Furthermore, ability differences dovetail with interest differences, so more men than women will be attracted by mathematics. Similarly, it is argued that women's innate cognitive composition and abilities naturally predispose them to more interest in animate rather than inanimate phenomena, and in particular, in people, nurturance and verbal memory and expression (Kimura & Clarke 2002; Kimura 2006). We should expect occupational segregation patterns to reflect such differences, and eschew perspectives that misrecognise these patterns as a function of social determination. Women will be attracted to nursing in far higher numbers than men, although some men will want to undertake nursing work, and men will be attracted to engineering in far higher numbers than women, although some women will excel in this field. However,

> We need to face the fact that men and women may be disproportionately represented across a wide range of occupations and professions, without the inference that there must have been either deliberate or systemic obstacles being put in the way of either sex. Rather, it appears that self-selection on the basis of talents and interests now largely determine such career choices. Engaging in coercive social engineering to balance the sex ratios may actually be the worst kind of discrimination. It also serves to entice some people into fields they will neither excel in nor enjoy.
>
> (Kimura 2001: 3)

On the basis of the evidence she surveys, Kimura condemns much of the debate on occupational segregation that has taken place since the 1970s. The use of terms such as 'under-representation' and 'discrimination', she views as preventing an appropriate level of rational discussion (2006). Although she does acknowledge that some significant contextual variations (national variations, for instance) exist in the numbers of women participating in 'male' fields, such as engineering, and that these are due to *some* social amplification of natural differences, she concludes that the basic, widespread patterning of male and female occupations (as well as, in some cases, men in very senior positions) reflects *natural*, fundamental sex differences and should not therefore be unduly concerning or challenging.

There are less robust positions on the 'brainsex' basis of occupational choice, positions that are more admitting of social influences, including those of researchers such as Govier (1998) and Holdstock (1998). Here, '"brainsex" influences our job choice but . . . it does not follow that all males will want to follow the same set of occupations and females another set' (Govier 1998: 1–2), and the match between sex and educational field and occupation is 'sex related and not sex determined' (Holdstock 1998: 63). What is maintained, however, is the primacy of the individual as an expression of significant natural gendered inclinations, that overly socialised accounts of occupational segregation belie the evidential scientific base from biology and psychology alike, and that social 'solutions' to perceived imbalances will have natural limitations:

> Initiatives like WISE are attempts to encourage *categories* of young people to take up a specific occupation . . . all these initiatives seem to have been pursued with enthusiasm rather than any knowledge of psychology. All occupational psychologists know that *selection must be by the individual and a balance achieved among several kinds of information.* . . . To discuss the success or otherwise of the WISE campaign purely in terms of equal numbers in categories could be irresponsibly naïve.
>
> (Holdstock 1998: 63)

Psychological and developmental approaches – the self-concept

Although some psychological approaches to explaining occupational segregation assume fundamental differences in 'brainsex', many do not. What they share, however, is a belief that certain gendered differences, which can be linked to work decisions, are created early on in an individual's development, and remain relatively stable for the periods during which key work choices are made. Many take their starting point from Super's early, influential research work where he claimed that, 'in choosing an occupation one is, in effect, choosing a means of implementing a self-concept' (1957: 196). The self-concept, or self-identity, of an individual is both a reflexive and premeditated understanding the individual holds about their self – their personality, beliefs, abilities, inclinations, attitudes, image, actions and behavioural tendencies. Individuals, so it is argued, will seek to identify occupations that match most well with their self-concept in a variety of respects. The psychological and developmental research on gender and occupational selection has consequently focused on supposed differences in the self-concept between men and women as a primary source of segregation.

Circumscription and compromise. Gottfredson's landmark 'Circumscription and compromise: A developmental theory of occupational aspirations' (1981), stands out as unusual within this body of research insofar as it places the individual firmly at the centre of the point at which a job role is actively selected, yet attends in substantial detail to the social and psychological forces that create the individual up until that point. For this reason, and because it holds much interest, it will be reviewed comparatively closely here. The focus of Gottfredson's work is the preliminary psychological stages of childhood development, and how each is negotiated through interaction with complex social messages. The 'Circumscription and compromise' monograph is based around a meta-analysis of empirical data, through which she develops an account of work choices that posits the adult individual making selections that are experienced as 'natural', and automatic, but are the result of the long and complex development of the pre-adolescent self-concept.

Gottfredson claims that all the key attraction characteristics of particular occupations – interest area, status, desirability and sex-type – are substantially agreed upon, and firmly attached to various roles, by the time individuals reach the adolescent stage, and that they remain relatively stable and intact thereafter. At the very earliest ages of development, she suggests, nearly all occupations are positively valued in children, but there is a gradual cognisance of differential prestige differences so that by early adolescence individuals perceive a clear prestige hierarchy that is highly correlated with that held by fully grown adults (ibid.: 550).

The characteristics associated with an occupation produce, and are produced by, stereotypes of its incumbents, including perceptions of the latter's likely social class, gender and personality traits. These are almost universally held, and seem not to depend on direct or detailed knowledge of the tasks and skills associated with the work, so that incumbents, novices *and* individuals with no involvement in the occupation at all, share the same beliefs about it and its workforce. Teachers, for instance, are perceived by all as 'sensitive, unselfish, underpaid and friendly' (Gottfredson 1981: 550). Gottfredson also summarises research that shows that these beliefs are based on very little knowledge of the actual occupation, *or how to join it.* They are based upon impressionistic ideas: 'occupational images deal almost exclusively with the lifestyle that occupations afford an incumbent and the type of person that he or she is' (ibid.: 551). A key exception to this, Gottfredson claims, is the detailed information that individuals obtain about their father's occupation.

Gottfredson is clear that one of the strongest characteristics that define an occupation is its sex-type. An awareness of this, she claims, develops in very early life, in the pre-school years, so that by ages 4–5 children are aware of key gendered differences of adult roles, for example, the belief that only men have roles involving violence or danger. By adulthood, the sex-type of an occupation is generally correlated with its actual sex-typing with .85 accuracy (ibid.: 551). Notwithstanding this, perceptions remain vague as to why particular occupations should be inhabited by one sex rather than another. There are features of the perceptual sex-typing of jobs that Gottfredson reports that are of particular interest here. Fewer jobs are typed as female than are typed male, and male jobs cover a broader range of prestige levels, so that, as jobs are perceived to be female, they are also perceived to be more moderate in prestige (ibid.: 553). Using Holland's (1973) categories, Gottfredson delineates a sex-typed work map: 'Investigative' (science, technology and medicine) work is 'somewhat' masculine and ranked 1st in terms of prestige; 'Realistic' (manual) work is perceived to be masculine and ranked lowest in terms of prestige. 'Enterprising' (business and management) work is also masculine and is ranked 4th, but is ranked very closely with two fairly 'neutral' areas: 'Social' (social service and education, ranked 2nd), and 'Artistic' (aesthetic and literary, ranked 3rd). 'Conventional' work is the only clear feminine-typed area and is ranked 5th in terms of prestige (ibid.: 553).

Dovetailed with the growing awareness of the status and broad characteristics of different work roles, is the awareness of the individual's own status and characteristics, and how these might be best matched with a 'suitable' job. When choosing occupations, individuals assess the compatibility of work with salient images of who they are and who they would like to be: 'those occupations that are highly compatible with one's sense of self will be highly valued: those that are highly incompatible will be disliked' (Gottfredson 1981: 548). Information about occupations will, as noted before, be impressionistic at best, will be strongly influenced by an individual's immediate social setting, and will be accepted more easily and often if no effort is required to access it (ibid.: 570).

Through a process of 'circumscription' and 'compromise', the 'social space' where individual background and awareness interacts with collective knowledge thereby produces a range of 'acceptable alternative' occupational roles that the individual perceives to be suitable for themselves and would be appropriate to their status and characteristics in the eyes of teachers, family, peers and society more generally (ibid.: 546). As indicated above, occupations are ruled in or out on the basis of gender through childhood development (ibid.: 559). This is not just according to broad work area, but prestige and seniority. In terms of prestige, girls' original aspirations are much higher than those of boys in the early grades (ibid.: 563). However, boys' occupational preferences rise considerably over their development, and they make a significant shift away from blue-collar work and towards major professional and executive work before adulthood. Conversely, girls' preferences increasingly move towards lower-prestige work (semi-professional and clerical work) and away from their target higher-prestige jobs in the lesser-professional ranks (nurse and teacher). Both genders finally fix on work choices that may be different from their original desires, but are arrived at through a gradual matching of the self-to-work process.

This is an important part of Gottfredson's message. Equally important is her underscoring of the fact that the 'cognitive map' of occupations that individuals develop over time plays a significant part in their understanding of themselves and the world and '*the social identity conferred by occupations is clear and of great concern to people* [my emphasis]' (ibid.: 550). The extent to which Gottfredson showcases research demonstrating that, broadly speaking, *people share very similar perceptions of occupations*, regardless of their own sex, social class, education level, ethnic group, residential area, age, political persuasion and traditionality of beliefs, and regardless of the decade of the study, is significant (ibid.: 550). There are some countervailing trends to this rule, however. Although jobs are ranked in the same way for all socioeconomic groups, lower groups tend to see jobs as more strongly sex-typed. Additionally, Gottfredson identifies a 'homophily bonus' insofar as social groupings, such as ethnic minorities, and class-based groupings, rank the occupations associated with their own social group more favourably.

This rule extends to gender groupings, according to Gottfredson. She argues that, although we could assume that women's flow towards moderate-level work is a function of 'options being foreclosed and women accepting their less favoured status' (ibid.: 560), there is far more evidence to support the view that women – like men – actively prefer their own gender, and its representation, and believe it to be superior. It is no surprise, she argues, that men and women favour own-gender-identified work.

Gottfredson's conceptual development of gendered occupational 'preferences' is more complex and sophisticated than we find elsewhere. Preferences are not simply taken as somewhat unchanging or underdeveloped 'givens' that find free expression in employment outcomes. They emerge as a result of a process of negotiation and compromise and are rather 'one's likes and dislikes and they range from what is more desired to what would be least tolerable' (546). Individuals can hold particular basic preferences but, given the need to compromise, end up with differently expressed aspirations, and different employment outcomes.

Although few provide Gottfredson's level of process analysis, other psychological or developmental accounts of gendered occupational selection share with her the aim of describing how particular, early established and often comparatively stable, individual gender traits produce particular work patterns. Much of this work differs from Gottfredson's, however, insofar as it is more often focused on horizontal segregation primarily or exclusively. It also tends towards the use of quantitative data collected from individuals via instruments and/or surveys, hypothesis-testing regarding identified aspects of an individual's intra-psychic make-up that may be linked to the selection and de-selection of particular occupations and roles, and ultimately seeks to provide less of a descriptive, and more of a, 'causal model' by way of explanation of occupational patterns (O'Brien & Fassinger 1993). Gender has been demonstrated to be a strong predictor of occupational choice in this body of research, and it tends to focus on the attempt to refine this finding by identifying, from a range of intra-psychic variables, precisely what about men and women is both different *and* can predict choice. Taken as a whole, partly due to its tighter focus and hypotheses-testing formula, this body of research tends also to produce somewhat confusing and contradictory findings.

Sex and gender roles.   Some sex and gender role research has attempted to explain the patterning of men's and women's employment. In this context, the term 'role' refers to the perceived characteristics that are attached to being female or male within society, and from which we expect certain attitudes, beliefs and behaviours to flow.

In the 1970s, Sandra Bem developed the *Bem Sex-Role Inventory* (BSRI),[1] a psychological test instrument designed to measure an individual's perception of their own sex role. It allows for an individual to be typed as masculine, feminine or both – 'androgynous', rather than assuming males are automatically masculine and females automatically feminine.

Some individualist research has utilised the *BSRI* when exploring occupational patterning to assess the links between measured sex role and occupational orientation, to a somewhat confusing effect. As might be expected, we can find research that links 'feminine-typed' females with gender-typical work, and 'masculine-typed' females with gender-atypical work. There is, however, also evidence linking more 'androgynous-typed' females to both typically feminine areas *and* to typically masculine fields such as mathematics. In Steitz' study (1997), a group of cosmetology (cosmetics) students' *BSRI* scores were contrasted with a group of upper-level mathematics students, with the finding that the former were significantly more androgynous (rather than feminine) than the latter. There is also evidence demonstrating that 'feminine-typed' females may have higher-career aspirations than 'androgynous-typed' ones. Finally, there is evidence that sex roles, as measured by the *BSRI*, have no particular effect on career aspirations (Steitz 1997; Wulff & Steitz 1997; Hensley 1998).

Related research has argued that women are overwhelmingly more likely to believe family pursuits are more important than careers because of their gendered self-concept, and that they are more likely to choose traditional and less challenging careers if they have more home-than career-orientation (O'Brien & Fassinger 1993). Fassinger (1990) hypothesised that a number of sex role variables would predict higher career orientation, including instrumentality, feminist orientation and family orientation. Her findings revealed that liberal sex-roles, as well as instrumentality and high ability predicted general career focus and ambition, and orientation to gender-atypical careers specifically (see also, Fassinger 1993).

Work values.   Other researchers have followed Super and focused specifically on the concept of 'work values' as a way of conceptualising how gendered individuals end up being oriented to particular work roles and away from others. Values, in this context, are beliefs experienced by the individual as guiding standards for how they should function. They are cognitive, behavioural and affective structures (Brown 2002). Work-value research argues that values are a critical part of our self-identity and we must therefore expect them to play a key role in our selection of an occupation. We will tend to select work roles that fit our self-concept but are specifically also matched to our value system, how and what we prioritise in our lifestyle, and what we perceive to be socially acceptable for someone with our particular identity. Selecting an occupation consonant with our values consequently contributes to our sense of work satisfaction.

Research in this area has shown that social values, such as the value of altruism, are powerful drives in women when they are selecting work (Davey 2001; Davey & Lalande 2004). They are more likely to hold a 'collectivism' social value than an 'individualism' one (Brown 2002). This is why, it is argued, they are more likely to enter roles such as teaching and nursing. More generally, echoing approaches reviewed above, it has been claimed that women seek work that is focused on the animate and shy away from that which is focused on the inanimate (Lightbody & Durndell 1998[2]). It is for this reason that they are under-represented in science education and over-represented in language education (Trusty, Robinson, Plata & Kok-Mun 2000). Equally, it is for this reason they are under-represented in scientific and technical careers, and over-represented in teaching, nursing, carework and so on. Males, conversely, are more likely to select occupations that are consonant with an instrumental value – the need to match their intrinsic interests (Davey 2001).

This position allows for women having strong aptitudes in the scientific and technical arena, and for them being welcomed within these arenas, but also for their usual selection away from related careers on the basis that they simply do not want to undertake work that does not match their core-value orientations. Lightbody and Durndell (1998) have called this the 'we can, but I don't want to' (37) explanation of segregation, pointing out that this explanation makes sense of both the recent educational successes of females in previously male-dominated arenas, and with the lack of evidence of overwhelming pressure on girls to conform to female stereotypes in terms of educational and occupational choice. It thereby moves away from the 'deficiency mode' of assuming women's under-representation in SET is due to lacks on their own part (Sian & Callaghan 2001). It is argued that female under-representation in SET is therefore best viewed 'in terms of opportunity costs', that women are selecting more highly paid professions, or professions that are more appealing (ibid.: 93): Female under-representation in SET 'should be viewed in the context of well-qualified young women as active mistresses of their occupational identity' (ibid.: 93).

Some research has fundamentally queried whether such value differences exist between men and women at all. Johnson (2001) found smaller differences between men and women, but also that the development and expression of values may be context-, time- and information-dependent. Davey (2001) has suggested that value differences may exist but women may be less influenced by them than men when choosing work roles. She argues, for instance, that both women with an individualism social value *and* those with a collectivism social value enter a more restricted range of professions than men at both ends of this value spectrum, suggesting that values are weaker predictors of job outcomes than other traits and factors. More specifically, it has been claimed that women are more likely to consider others' needs when selecting employment, marginalizing personal values (Betz 1994). Furthermore, women and men within particular professions may share measurable values, but there is evidence that the meanings they attach to them differ (Davey & Lalande 2004).

Moreover, Rowe and Snizek (1995) in a very large-scale study utilising data from 12 national samples and from 7,436 full-time male and female workers across all major occupational classifications and sectors, report no consistent or robust evidence for any significant differences between their work values. Work values were more likely to be a function of an individual's age, educational achievements and the prestige of their occupation. Rowe and Snizek critique the persistent focus of research on gendered values, arguing that this tendency simply reinforces traditional gender-role stereotypes.

Self-efficacy and fear of success.   Although there is significant overlap with sex role and work values literature, research into the phenomenon of perceived self-efficacy and the role it plays in influencing gendered-work orientations has developed as a distinct strand of exploration. Perceived self-efficacy refers to an individual's belief that they can accomplish what they desire and seek to accomplish (O'Brien & Fassinger 1993). In others words, it refers to the individual's sense of effective agency and to whether they can translate their interests, desires, predispositions and abilities into their goals. This is obviously a crucial part of an individual's make-up, and its potential links to occupational choice are clear. Indeed, self-efficacy has been linked to the undertaking of more challenging work roles and higher earnings (Hakim 2002: 433). Researchers have consistently found that females have lower levels of self-efficacy in general and have identified self-efficacy as a constraining factor on women's occupational choice (O'Brien & Fassinger 1993; O'Brien, Friedman, Tipton & Linn 2000; Davey 2001). More generally, women reportedly experience significantly more role conflict than men in anticipation of their career (Anderson 1998: 153).

Bandura[3], Barbaranelli, Caprara and Pastorelli (2001) studied 272 children to model the relationship between perceived self-efficacy, achievement and occupational choices. They concluded that perceived self-efficacy was 'the key determinant of their perceived occupational self-efficacy and preferred choice of worklife' (187). It ranked above the children's actual academic achievement and abilities in determining occupational choices in terms of both work area and level. Overall, their findings indicated that the higher an individual's self-efficacy levels, the more likely they are to consider a wider range of career options (ibid.: 188). Significant gender differences were found. Males judged themselves to be more efficacious in work areas associated with SET, regardless of the fact that girls matched their academic achievements in these areas. Conversely, females believed themselves to be more efficacious in relation to social, educational and health work. Bandura *et al.* argue that, because individuals have very little incentive to pursue goals they believe they will fail to achieve, the differences in these underlying self-efficacy levels explain why girls avoid SET work areas.

O'Brien and Fassinger's work (1993) echoes these claims. They argue that, notwithstanding other differences, young women who are identified as more ambitious than average are also found to be higher in their sense of agency, and in their ability. Girls higher in agency are also more likely to be higher in career-orientation and to be more likely to choose gender-atypical careers. A strong and positive sense of self-efficacy therefore is implicated in a complex set of interrelationships that, nevertheless, augments the chances of such women doing well in their chosen career and selecting careers from a wider range of options. Conversely, they argue, women who are less oriented to achievement in the paid employment sphere are more likely to be lower in their sense of agency and are more likely to orient to gender-typical work (1993: 466).

Linked to this research are claims that a 'fear of success' limits female choices and chances of achievement. First coined by Horner (1968), the concept refers to women's alleged greater motive to avoid success because of the negative consequences associated with attainment. This includes being viewed as unfeminine and the consequent fear of social disapprobation. Women therefore self-select out of challenging work and work associated with men, even if they are qualified for it.

'Fear of success' denotes the mirror image psychological process to the 'fear of failure' that underpins low self-efficacy, yet the resulting effects are the same for women: they are less likely to take risks in relation to their occupational choices; and are more likely to choose a role that is gender-typical and that is consonant with their own and others' expectations.

There are counter-claims to this evidence, however. Krishnan & Sweeney (1998) found 'Fear of Success' imagery on a medical programme to be slightly higher for men than women, despite this field being traditionally associated with men. Hensley (1998) has argued for a separation of traditionalism in career choice from commitment to success, suggesting that women who choose gender-typical careers may be no less ambitious, or have lower beliefs in their own agency (see also, O'Brien, Friedman, Tipton & Linn 2000). Nauta and Epperson (2003) have also challenged the claim that self-efficacy is the central component of area-orientation, suggesting that it may simply be a reflection of actual ability, rather than an independent intra-psychic resource (454).

Preference research

There are clear overlaps between research that posits women's work values, interests and sex role, for example, to be primary causes of their different occupational outcomes from men, and research which posits these outcomes as primarily a function of gendered preferences. What distinguishes preference research further is the extent to which, as the term 'preference' suggests, segregation patterns are seen to result from largely unfettered choices on the part of the individuals seeking work, as well as the extent to which there is almost no attempt to model either the social *or* the intra-psychic realm that may be playing a role in the production of these inclinations. Furthermore, preference research tends to focus as happily on providing an explanation for gendered vertical segregation as it does for explaining horizontal differences. Whereas much 'brainsex' and developmental research concentrates almost exclusively on explaining horizontal segregation, and fights a little shy of utilizing their approaches to explain hierarchical differences between men and women in the workplace that are not a function of this, preference approaches are more explicit about the implications of their positions for our understanding of overall segregation patterns.

Under the heading of preference research, I am including traditional Rational Choice Theory approaches, Human Capital approaches, as well as those overtly investigating 'preferences' – the researcher whose work is mostly focused on here is Catherine Hakim. Indeed, although Hakim distances herself from Human Capital and Rational Choice positions, she also builds on the assumptions of both, arguing that key aspects of gendered-work patterns are basically the result of utility optimising positions held by individual workers.

Human capital differences – the differences between men and women's educational and temporal investment in employment qualifying 'capital' – have been cited as major causes of gender pay gaps (ILO 2004: 30). Women, it is alleged, are less willing to invest their time and energy into building up their human capital as they are oriented to family as well as to their career. They therefore seek out less-skilled and less-prestigious roles, and employers' preference for male workers is often simply a function of their rational decision-making regarding the best-qualified worker at the point of hiring. Similarly, Rational Choice Theory research claims that women select work that holds less penalties for child-rearing duties, career-breaks and so on (Becker 1985; DeLeire & Levy 2001; Hwang & Polacheck 2004). It is claimed that such personal investment differences between men and women can account for up to two-thirds of gendered occupational segregation (Hwang & Polacheck 2004: 30). In each of these positions, individual applicants, as well as the employment market, are assumed to operate rationally and efficiently, rather than around inherent biases towards men.

According to Hakim, her analysis of gendered occupational patterns differs from much Human Capital Theory and Rational Choice Theory research because as she does not assume 'preferences are stable and homogenous enough not to require direct empirical investigation and that preferences are revealed through behaviour' (2002: 429–430). Her analysis, although 'empirically based in that it was built up from a review and synthesis of hundreds of social science studies in several disciplines using a huge variety of research methods' (ibid.: 439), is directly based on work with large-scale, longitudinal or snapshot datasets. More specifically, it is often based on the selection of answers to a small number of 'parsimonious' (ibid.: 439) survey questions regarding aspirations and outcomes in relation to work and family life; these, Hakim claims, represent key issues previously identified 'most effectively by qualitative studies based on in-depth interviews' (ibid.: 439).

Hakim comes to a number of significant conclusions in her articulation of 'Preference Theory'. Arguing for the positioning of 'choice', and individuals making choices, at the heart of our understanding of gendered job selection, she suggests that work patterns – women being over-represented in part-time work and in less well-remunerated work for instance – reflect not external constraints, such as discrimination, but the existence of fundamentally different types of women. She claims that feminist readings of such patterns have ignored this fact and have treated women as a homogenous group all desiring the same things from work (Hakim 1995, 1996, 2002). Instead, Hakim identifies distinct groups: work-oriented women and home-oriented women (1995) and, more recently, adaptors (2002). As the terminology suggests, each group's members are classified by their different levels of work commitment. Hakim states that, generally, women's commitment is not equal to men's (1995, 2002), as less women than men state that they would work even if they had no financial need to (1995, 2002). Intra-gender differences for women are further significant and impact on career choice. Women who are work-oriented invest in 'training and qualifications, and generally achieve higher-grade occupations and higher-paid jobs which they pursue full-time for the most part' (1995: 434). Home-oriented women do not invest in 'human capital, transfer quickly and permanently to part-time work as soon as a breadwinner husband permits it, choose undemanding jobs with 'no worries or responsibilities' when they do work, and hence are found concentrated in lower grade and lower paid jobs which offer convenient working hours with which they are perfectly happy' (1995: 434). The third category of adaptors, those who prefer to combine careers and families as well as those with 'unplanned' and drifting careers (2002), account for the majority of women according to Hakim's later work, and prefer to combine employment and domestic commitments without giving fixed priority to either. They want to enjoy the best of both worlds.

As indicated above, Hakim believes we can access women's preferences from their measured attitudes and values – 'these "psychological" variables are too often omitted from research, so their importance has been overlooked' (2002: 432) – and that these are strongly predictive of work patterns in the sense that they can forecast choices relating to job type, hours worked and so on. It is further claimed that, in a context in which 'today, genuine choices are open to women' (ibid.: 433) and where women have 'obtained equal access to all positions, occupations and careers in the labour market' (434), values associated with women, such as preference for 'friendly' and 'social' work settings rather than challenging work settings (433), exert powerful influences and explain much of gendered pay, status and investment differentials. Such preferences can be expressed early and yet still prove to powerfully predict later work outcomes. Modelling their effects is a falsifiable exercise, and therefore, according to Hakim, far more worthwhile than the post hoc, vague and biased treatments of other segregation researchers which either impute women's agency from outcomes without the requisite evidential basis for doing so, *or*, ignore it altogether:

> We must stop presenting women as 'victims' or as an undifferentiated mass of mindless zombies whose every move is determined by other actors and social forces . . . women are responsible adults, who make real choices and are the authors and agents of their own lives.
>
> (Hakim 1996: 186)

It is not that Hakim completely denies 'the impact of social, economic and institutional factors' but that she argues they are secondary to 'women's motivations and aspirations', which are 'independent factors with causal powers that must be investigated more thoroughly' (2002: 454). Furthermore, they do not affect women's equality of access to the employment market.

Hakim's framework offers an explanation of many of the characteristics of women's work, but not necessarily of the sector women choose to work within (2002: 450). To explain horizontal segregation, she argues, we need to 'rely instead on benign social processes, such as the tendency for people to choose same sex friends and hence also to prefer same sex work groups' (2002: 454).

Some researchers have, however, argued that we can explain horizontal segregation patterns with reference to underlying gendered preferences. DeLeire and Levy (2001), for instance, have argued that women are significantly more likely to select occupations that maximise their chances of addressing home-centred needs. They will, therefore, be more risk-averse in their occupational choices and will select less-dangerous work roles. A significant relationship therefore exists between risk factors associated with occupations and female representation – women are densely populated within the safest top ten occupations (including administrative, clerical and secretarial work, teaching, some computer-related work and sales) and men in the most dangerous (including construction, protective services and engineering and science technicians) (ibid.: 10). Women's safety-orientation increases if they become mothers, and pregnant women's return to work is less likely if their job is either dangerous or very physical.

DeLeire and Levy note in their review of gendered-preference literature that 'there is very little consensus on methods, results and interpretation' (13). They further suggest that different preferences may not be reflected in employment outcomes. In particular, women's preferences for safe and people-oriented work are not necessarily met in their current employment or in their expressed experience of it (see also Reed & Dahlquist 1994). Risman, Atkinson and Blackwelder's (1999) analysis of survey data also produces findings that challenge the claim that earlier attitudes relating to work and family roles are more predictive of employment outcomes than adults' experience within *actual* family and work contexts (339).

The origins of individualist approaches

It is clear that 'brainsex' researchers locate the origins of gender variation, and of concomitant employment outcomes, in innate biological differences. As we have seen, this leads them to reject the problematisation of occupational segregation that informs much of the sociological literature on the area. It is less obvious where the other individualist approaches reviewed here locate the primary origins of the gender differences they cite to explain segregation patterns. Despite Gottfredson's careful emphasis on the interaction between the self and the social, for instance, it would be a mistake to misrecognise her underlying model of the self as primarily social in origin, or as indicating gendered-work choices as primarily a function of social gendering processes. Her reference to Kohlberg's (1966) Cognitive Development Theory suggests some significant biological input to expressed gender differences, and she does say that women's occupational preferences for the middle-, rather than high-, ranking work may be a function of their basic family orientation (1981: 569). She also says that both men and women end up where they broadly *should* be and that women's gradual lowering of aspirations is a natural corrective as: 'In a sense, girls' aspirations start out "too high" and boy's "too low"' (ibid.: 563).

Indeed, taking Gottfredson's corpus as a whole, it is clear that she has strong affiliations with those researchers described above who have emphasised 'brainsex' differences in their explanations of occupational segregation. It is clear that she considers higher-level work as demanding higher-level cognitive reasoning functions, and believes the latter to be largely genetically endowed. She also considers sex differences to be basic traits, 'evolutionary facts', and that women are biologically committed to both careers and caring (Gottfredson 2005; 2006). Women's position in the labour market is, then, the right one, and any social correctives to perceived imbalances are ultimately self-defeating:

> Genetic differences in a population create a dilemma for democratic societies. Social inequality is inevitable when a society's members vary genetically in a trait . . . that is highly useful and rewarded by the society. Equal opportunity to use one's talents will guarantee unequal results.
>
> (Gottfredson 2006: 20; see also Gottfredson 1994)

The putative origins of roles, values and self-efficacy are often not explicitly discussed in the research cited here, but it is clear that elsewhere self-efficacy differences have certainly been attributed to biological origins (Bellingham-Young & Adamson-Macedo 2003), and the origins of fear of success to deep-rooted psychological development are related to basic feminine and masculine types and their 'healthy' and 'unhealthy' trajectories. Similarly, research has suggested the origins of work interests, values and predispositions can be biological.

Far more research, however, does not make such claims, and concentrates instead on the socialisation process that has produced the child and its development towards particular orientations. Bandura's basic approach lies in Social Learning Theory, and his work makes it clear that no claim is being made for gendered differences in ability influencing the development of the self-efficacy resource. Brown (2002) has argued that gendered values are a function of different socialisation processes for girls and boys. It is generally the case that parents are seen as key players in this development process[4]. Again, however, research focusing on this relationship has produced contradictory findings, with the greater likelihood of selecting gender-atypical employment being variously claimed to be both linked and not linked to parental attitudes, parental aspirations, parental levels of support for choices, and so on (Marjoribanks 1987; Fassinger 1990; O'Brien & Fassinger 1993; Dryler 1998; Hensley 1998). Moreover, there is little in the way of analysis of the origins of parental traits, beliefs and behaviour.

Hakim shares the tendency towards obfuscation in relation to the origins of her imputed female preferences, but the evidence would seem to point clearly to some form of innate origin. Certainly, her insistence that preferences persist in a context where equal opportunities legislation has done its work, would seem to support this conclusion, as does the suggestion that choices are now 'unfettered', with the clear implication that in different historical periods they existed in a fettered form, and so manifested differently. The obscurity of their origins in and of itself points to these and other conclusions – that preferences are not factors that require adjustment, that they are probably therefore in their unfettered form somewhat fixed, and consequently fundamentally 'natural' or 'biological'. As Crompton and Harris suggest, it would seem that preferences are 'psychobiological' at base (Crompton & Harris 1998b, 1999b). Hakim's work thereby chimes with that of Human Capital Theory and Rational Choice Theory insofar as an uncritical perspective on current labour market patterns is adopted, and the normal, if not natural, nature of underlying causes is assumed (Crompton & Harris 1998b).

Other preference researchers, such as DeLeire and Levy (2001), make no explicit statement about the origins of preferences and, indeed, allow for them to be a function of discrimination *or* sex differences. Moreover, they ascribe more overt flexibility to them, demonstrating, for instance, that the risk-averse behaviour noted in women's occupational choices can also emerge in men. Single fathers' risk aversion is elevated above that of married fathers, for example. They also, however, argue for 'a consistent difference in men's and women's preferences that is independent of family structure' (ibid.: 2), and adopt the stance of uncritical observers of gendered trends whose origins are not, in actual fact, of essential interest.

Modes of explanation giving primacy to social factors

Introduction

Much of the individualist literature is organised, in part, around an attempt to critique what are seen as less effective explanations of occupational segregation provided by accounts that marginalise the individual's role and provide overly social, overly determinist perspectives. Conversely, much of the literature that emphasises extra-individual factors is organised around a critique of the particular explanatory lacunae and limitations within the individualist literature. Many sociologists have long argued that there are fundamental problems with taking the individual as the primary unit of analysis. One is the relationship between attitudes and actions, which can be anything but linear or rational (LaPiere 1934; Ajzen & Fishbein 1977). Instead, it is suggested that we need to attend to the general sweep of gendered patterns of behaviour and to the array of gendered structural and personal constraints and facilitators, within which individuals are but one part, in order to begin to understand what women and men, and their decisions and actions, are comprised of.

For many researchers, attitude and preference data, and, indeed, individual attitudes and preferences, constitute no more than the essentially descriptive starting point of any meaningful analysis of occupational decision-making; their relationship to outcomes is a comparatively superficial finding that belies a densely complex interaction between people and the positions they end up occupying. The dominant methodological approaches associated with individually focused research are frequently the target of criticism. Data derived from instruments that measure attitude, preference, trait, and personality differences between men and women draw criticism for, as Hakim herself has noted, 'their notorious volatility' (2002: 429). Despite her subsequent protestations that such data are highly reliable and yield significant associations with work outcomes, there are areas of concern. Firstly, there is the lack of emerging associations where we might expect them.

For instance, in the current context, how do we make sense of the fact that in an Equal Opportunities Commission (EOC) survey (EOC 2005a; see also UWSC 2003), over 90 per cent of adults expressed the view that occupational segregation was not a good thing, if women are generally having their preferences met, as preference theories would suggest? Similarly, what are we to make of the finding that women are more supportive than men of policies designed to promote gender equity (O'Brien & Fassinger 1993: 510), if they are happy with their occupational choices, and are not experiencing themselves as *disadvantaged*, as Hakim (2002) suggests? Similarly, how do we make sense of the finding that individual's make work-related decisions in the absence of any real idea about the consequences of their decisions (see, for instance, Allen 1999)? How does the finding that women seek out comparatively poorly paid part-time work, viewing this work as demanding less commitment from them, sit with the finding that the majority of women are ignorant of pay-rate differences (EOC 2005a)?

The work of sociologists such as Rosemary Crompton and others (Breugel 1996; Ginn *et al.* 1996; Crompton 1997; Crompton & Harris 1998b), for instance, provides a powerful case for moving away from attitude data as the primary focus of research, and towards the production of a sociological account of how such attitudes and preferences were constructed in the first place, how particular choices are facilitated by extra-individual factors, and others constrained, and how tortuous the journey can be from the expression of values, interests and inclinations to behavioural outcomes.

To accept the basic tenets of this more sociological approach, is also to accept that the key assumptions of many of the more individualist perspectives, as well as their over-reliance on the preferred methods of survey and instrument testing, are flawed; they are inadequate to the task of explaining occupational choice and segregation. Even those 'social' approaches deploying such methods, maintain the position that individual choices are, in some essential sense, the expression of extra-individual forces, and provide an explanation of what these might be. In doing so, they challenge the basic understanding of choice in the individualist model, as well as redrawing the parameters for exploring the causes of occupational segregation. Critically, in stressing the importance of the social shaping of the context in which occupational choices are made, proponents of this approach open up the question of whether segregation patterns could and more importantly, *should*, be different.

As has been noted above, some of this literature is based on qualitative research involving direct contact with girls and women themselves with the emphasis being on processes whereby research participants can provide a meaningful account of their decision-making and its outcomes. This will be discussed in Chapter 3. What follows in the rest of this chapter is a review of literature that does not directly access the accounts of individuals making decisions about their employment, or, in some cases, the quantitative elements of accounts that use mixed methods, and those writings not directly discussing empirical findings.

The individual as a product of the social

Socialisation, stereotypes and the development of gender identities

As we have seen, early socialisation patterns have been identified within the individualist literature as having a strong influence on the developing self-concept, and in tandem with this, the development of occupational preferences. Whether these patterns are fixed, or subject to development in the adult phase, or arise as a function of fundamental biological differences between men and women, is often not explicitly addressed. The claim from those researchers emphasising the role of socialisation as a clear cause, and demonstration, of social forces on the individual, and of their decision-making around occupational choice, is a distinct strand of research. Although privileging similar reference points, it tends to be more discursive and critical, and broader in its theoretical and methodological framework. Within this literature, links are drawn between socialisation and the kind of work women are oriented to, the level at which they want to work, and the extent of their career commitment. Interactions with significant others – parents, peers, teachers, for example – are highlighted as playing a crucial role in the development of femininity and determining gender-typical or gender-atypical occupational choices (Roger & Duffield 2000; Turner, Bernt & Pecora 2002; Miller *et al.* 2004).

Some who stress the importance of sociological factors in determining gender differences question whether documented sex differences exist at all. Evidence has suggested that girls are identified as different from boys from early babyhood and are encouraged by adults to behave in a gender-appropriate manner, to be less aggressive, less physical and less demanding of attention (Smith & Lloyd 1978). Duveen and Lloyd have presented the case for why gender differences must, therefore, be viewed as forming one of the fundamental categories of social life. Gender, they argue, is 'a ubiquitous dimension of social organisation, its influence is apparent in every social encounter' (1986: 222). Individuals are given a gender assignation according to the binary system of male and female sex categories at birth and this ascription takes place in accordance with observed genital differences. They remain tied to that categorisation for the duration of their lives, unless surgical intervention takes place; and even then, initial gender ascription may persist. It is argued that 'the elaboration of systematic gender characterisation is a product of social life employing biological sex differences as signifiers in a semiotic system in which social representations of gender are signified' (222). These signifying practices determine specific life trajectories in societies as particular meanings are attached to these universal physical sex differences.

The gender system is a hierarchical one. Allied to male and female categories are 'activities, attitudes, symbols and expectations', the precise nature of which may vary according to different cultural contexts, but the value of which do not: 'we note that this is not a balanced opposition. Everywhere . . . gender categories are hierarchically arranged with the masculine over the feminine' (Cucchiari 1981: 32).

Of particular interest here is the link socialisation is claimed to make between femininity and the domestic sphere, and between certain work-related traits. Instead of accepting that girls, when making occupational decisions, are reflecting their given preferences, it is suggested that they are reflecting internalised, socialised notions of femininity and masculinity. Rather than stating that girls make decisions about future occupations based on anticipated domestic roles, we should be asking why girls consider domestic commitments more readily than boys. Rosemary Crompton argues that such assumptions are shaped by prevailing notions of masculinity and femininity that are demonstrably historically contingent. Ideas about what constitutes a 'suitable' job for each gender are determinations of these notions (1997: 41). 'Suitable' work dovetails with the almost universal and persistent ideology that assigns the domestic sphere to women and, more specifically, primary childcare to mothers. Treas and Widmer's cross-national survey (2000) of attitudes to working mothers provides a window on these prevailing gendered norms and values transmitted to children. In the US, although 84 per cent think women should work full-time before having children, only 11 per cent believe they should continue to do so with pre-schoolers. In the UK, the figures are 88 per cent and 6 per cent, respectively; in Italy they are 59 per cent and 5 per cent (2000: 1411). It could be argued that, although the figures are all broadly comparable, the significant national variation points to such attitudes being more a function of social interpretations, rather than *reflections*, of biological difference. It has been suggested that children are exposed to attitudes to women and employment that also vary in accordance with other background factors, including ethnicity and class. Research has revealed, for instance, that children from lower-income households are less often in receipt of encouragement to try non-traditional careers (HMSO 2005; Francis, Osgood, Dalgety & Archer 2005) although elsewhere it is suggested that stereotypes are no more solid in lower-income and ethnic households than they are anywhere else (EOC 2005c: 16).

It is not just parents and family that take part in this socialisation process. As well as the education system (see below), the media is considered to be a powerful secondary socialisation factor (EOC 2001b; Skelton & Hall 2001). It is further maintained, especially in more recent analytical developments, that children are not simply acted upon by socialisation agents from the outside, and emerge finished and fixed gendered beings, but that children themselves actively construct their own gender identities and produce stereotypes when it comes to how they perceive men and women and suitable occupations (Messner 2000; Skelton & Hall 2001; Francis *et al.* 2005). This conception of gender socialisation, as well as assuming that children are more active in their own socialisation, also assumes that gender categories themselves are fluid rather than fixed, and that the overarching gender regime within which they develop is more of a complex and often contradictory process, than a consistent and static monolith. Gender is not here perceived to be something we can identify in individual people, or in individual attributes, but is instead something that develops within the interactions between various agential players and through discursive practices. The level of analysis is not the individual, but the group life, and the group processes whereby both adults and children perform and produce gender in everyday life (Messner 2000: 766). Individuals here do not automatically act in a gendered way because that is the only way they have learnt to act, but because they perform according to one gendered script or another at any given point in order to live and present a meaningful identity to the world. They can perform both typically, atypically and comparatively neutrally by turns; 'gender varies in salience from situation to situation' (Messner 2000: 766).

Whichever model of gender socialisation is adopted, and whichever socialisation factors are deemed most influential, it is commonly accepted that children are fully cognisant with prevailing gender stereotypes at a very young age and that these have a 'huge' (EOC 2001a: 1) influence on their emerging identities and future lives. The impact on their views of men and women's abilities and desired employment roles is particularly pronounced, and the evidence suggests this is in place by primary school age. School-age children are, for instance, clear about what gender-appropriate tasks are, and what they are not. In an Equal Opportunities Commission survey (2001a), 95 per cent of boys thought that car repairs should only be conducted by men, while 85 per cent of girls thought that washing and mending clothes should only be done by women. They also believed that childcare in the paid employment sector should be largely undertaken by women, whether this is in a caring or educational role (Skelton & Hall 2001). In terms of occupations, girls commonly express an aim to be an actress or dancer, health professional, hairdresser, teacher and secretary, while boys commonly aim to be pilots, firefighters and scientists (EOC 2001a; Miller *et al.* 2004). Boys are also far more likely to express the belief that they will end up in a skilled manual role (EOC 2001a: 7). Such stereotyping affects self-esteem and self-efficacy levels that are often the focus of more individualist research. Although there is evidence that children's attitudes to men and women taking gender-atypical work loosen as they grow, what is more significant is evidence that this has limited or no impact on the decisions they make about their occupational choices (EOC 2001a; Miller *et al.* 2004). Moreover, as children grow older, they are less likely to express confidence that girls and boys will be treated the same within family life (EOC 2001a).

Formal education

It is widely claimed by those stressing extra-individual factors that formal education is a key part of the mechanism whereby girls are channelled into certain roles and occupations. To be sure, children enter school-age with already strong ideas about masculinity and femininity, as well as which aspects of the curriculum are sex-typed male and female and which are neutral, but it is argued by some that the schooling process itself, instead of challenging this early stereotyping, both augments and cements it.

Academic subjects are 'gendered' in the sense that they are sex-typed by children and adults and gendered preferences for particular subject areas exist across a wide range of countries and cultures (Holdstock 1998; EOC 2001a; Sian & Callaghan 2001). Usually, men are associated with engineering, computer science, physics, economics, maths and business; and women are associated with biology, English, sociology, psychology, languages and education. The generalised nature of this phenomenon is often cited by researchers as proof of a biological basis to the expressed interest pattern. However, an array of school-based factors is alternatively identified by research as being part of a fundamentally *social* process whereby subject gendering takes place. Teachers and their teaching styles have been described as potentially problematic agents insofar as they may assume a natural propensity for certain subjects by one gender or the other, encourage gendered interests to develop, and communicate unchallenged stereotypical images of study areas (Francis 2000; Turner *et al.* 2002; Miller *et al.* 2004). Particularly targeted for its implications for gendered-occupational segregation is the stereotyping of maths and SET, as male, and the subsequent orientation of girls away from it (Miller *et al.* 2004). According to Roger and Duffield (2000), primary teachers can be key 'change agents' in this regard. Due to the highly gender-segregated nature of this educational level, and the fact that many women 'have limited experience of science and especially technology' themselves (ibid.: 370), primary teachers are more likely to read off a lack of interest in science from girls' behaviour, and attribute this to their sex. Furthermore, girls lose out significantly from having such poor role models. It has been argued that proactive attempts to change the way girls and boys view the opportunities of SET are contested by dominant social processes within schools that shape the way it is presented, and interactions about and around it. These reinforce the area as suitable for males rather than females (Henwood 1998).

Often highlighted is the age at which students make critical subject choices in the UK, and elsewhere (Dryler 1998; Roger & Duffield 2000; Miller *et al.* 2004). When UK students select down from the full array of national curriculum subjects to the ones they want to specialise in – at approximately 14 years old – the orientation of girls away from SET becomes consolidated and expressed. At each selection stage, there is a substantial 'leak' of girls away from subjects generally associated with masculinity. This is not merely linked with horizontal segregation in the occupational sector, but also with vertical segregation, as careers requiring maths- and science-related qualifications are often among the most prestigious.

The leakage of girls out of 'male' subjects is despite the fact that their educational achievements in these areas now surpass that of their male counterparts (McQuaid, Bond & Robinson 2004; EOC 2006; Woodfield 2006b). Girls perform better in science, before an age when curriculum choice is permitted. Furthermore, although fewer of them take science once they have choice, those that do, continue to surpass boys' achievements in the area. Higher proportions of girls now gain an A–C grade pass in their General Certificate of Secondary Education (GCSE) examinations in chemistry and biology and physics (EOC 2005b). In terms of A levels, the qualifications usually taken at the end of the first two-year period of non-compulsory education (and during the ages of 16–18 years), girls also proportionately achieve more A–C passes in these subject areas (EOC 2004).

It is argued that this process of self-selection out of particular sex-typed subject areas is more likely to happen in early-to-mid adolescence (Roger & Duffield 2000; Miller *et al.* 2004). Boys and girls in this period undergo a process of re-examining their established gender identities and a related period of instability and exploration which, somewhat paradoxically, often results in a desire to signal a highly fixed gender identity to the outside world (Erikson 1980). Selecting gender-typical options is one way of doing this, but this symbolic value is not unconnected to projected careers – pupils are clear that they are choosing subjects they believe will be of use in their later employment (McQuaid *et al.* 2004). Both before and after this period (say, by age 17–18), pupils are more willing to consider atypical interests and ideas *if* they are exposed to them (Miller *et al.* 2004; HMSO 2005), but during this time they are exceptionally sensitive to others' views and more risk-averse than they have previously been, and will become.

By the time girls are selecting their tertiary-level educational subjects, or their desired occupational areas, key educational decisions have already been taken that have placed them on particular trajectories and excluded them from others (Miller *et al.* 2004). For those individuals who want to re-evaluate their occupational interests and goals a little later on in life, there is little state support for retraining (EOC 2005a).

It is claimed that biological explanations for subject choices sit rather uncomfortably with female performance in 'male' areas, as well as with the fact that this performance has changed quite rapidly in recent years (Woodfield & Earl-Novell 2006; Woodfield 2006b). Sian and Callaghan (2001) suggest that biological explanations cannot easily explain why women are markedly under-represented within physics, maths and engineering (PME), but very well represented within medicine and biology (ibid.: 89), which are also sciences, and require very similar pre-entry qualifications. They conclude, however, that, rather than cultural aspects actively dissuading women from furthering their PME studies, it may simply be the case that these areas may not offer sufficient attractions to improve female entry (ibid.: 91). This conclusion has been contested by other researchers who claim that to understand female self-selection out of 'male' subjects, we cannot ignore the 'chilly climate' that girls and women encounter in these subject areas if they do select them (Millar & Jagger 2001; Lee 2002; Woodfield 2006b).

It has also been argued that even activities designed to build awareness occupational choice within school pupils – such as work placements and careers guidance – often do more to reinforce gendered
choices than they do to challenge them. Work placements, which are
undertaken by the vast majority of school children in the UK and
remain very influential in occupational decision-making, are heavily
segregated by gender (Miller *et al.* 2004; Francis *et al.* 2005). The influence of teachers, careers advisors and, to a lesser degree, parents is
strong, and there is evidence that, even when children have expressed
interest in a non-traditional career, this does not translate into an atypical work placement (EOC 2005c; Francis *et al.* 2005). Evidence suggests
that key adults are slow to challenge gender occupational stereotypes or
pick up on atypical interests, and are generally unclear themselves
about opportunities for cross-gender work (Roger & Duffield 2000; EOC
2001a; Miller *et al.* 2004; EOC 2005c; EOC 2005a). Francis *et al.* (2005)
found that of 43 girls given childcare placements, only 29 had expressed
an interest in pursuing a career in this sector (iv). Girls are three times
more likely to be placed in traditional female positions, such as clerical
and administrative work, and five times more frequently placed in
social service work. Conversely, boys are 12 times more likely to be
placed in engineering work and 30 times more likely to find construction placements (MacKenzie 1997).

As well as the role played by education in the formation of horizontal segregation, it has also historically been argued that girls have been
persuaded by educational experiences that they are less able and less
suited to the top jobs than boys (Spender 1981). The former claim is less
easily accepted in the current climate, where girls are outperforming
boys in terms of measured achievement at almost every level of education.
What is still claimed, however, is that girls are subjected to subtle
school-based socialisation that reinforces gender roles within which
women are associated with domestic labour as much as, if not more
than, paid employment. This creates a situation in which women are
pressurised to maintain a precarious feminine identity incorporating
academic successes within traditional female sex roles, both at school
and after their education has been completed.

Some researchers have queried the utility of work that focuses primarily
on demonstrating the effects of socialisation and education on children
and young adults when trying to understand occupational segregation.
The problem resides in the assumption of some socialisation theorists that
individual choice, once expressed, can be more or less directly linked to
occupational outcomes. An important strand of sociological research has

attempted to show, therefore, that such preferences have to be understood in the context of significant, and often overwhelming, 'demand-side' restrictions to their actualisation.

The individual versus the structural

The importance of labour markets and regulatory regimes

Some sociologists have stressed the importance of labour markets and national regulatory policies and regimes in determining female work preferences and outcomes (O'Reilly & Fagan 1998; Crompton 1999; Blyton & Turnbull 2004). Padavic (1992) has claimed that 'gender is a multilevel system of differences and disadvantages that include socioeconomic arrangements and widely held cultural beliefs at the macro level' (219). Labour market theorists echo this and analyse the aspects of markets and regulatory regimes to demonstrate their gendered determinations.

Legislative changes in the 1970s and 1980s have clearly made a significant difference in eroding barriers to women's entry into the full spectrum of paid employment, and to facilitating progress within them, but, as we have seen, we still have substantial levels of both horizontal and vertical segregation. Research focusing on labour markets and their regulation has provided analyses of macro-level policies that claim that, while not legislating for segregation, they often support particular patterns of gendered-employment activity. This research serves to underscore the importance of these phenomena for the individual worker's experience, what they feel their choices are, and how they are facilitated or denied by the wider social context. It is argued, for instance, that if countries have welfare policies that support full-time work for women, including the provision of good childcare options, then women will feel more easily that full-time work is an option; if this context doesn't exist, they are less likely to feel this. This can result in women being confined to part-time work ghettos that have often developed alongside, instead of within, the mainstream employment economy, and which are characterised by poorer pay and conditions. A lack of national policies and strategies designed to tackle segregation is thus identified as undermining of equal opportunities legislation (Yeandle 1999; Crompton & Harris 1999a; Treas & Widmer 2000; Werum 2002; Jacobs & Gerson 2004; EOC 2005a).

Labour markets also develop in particular ways that affect women's opportunities, and, in the context of a strong system of gender relations, mitigate against the effects of equal opportunity legislation. As has been outlined above, women have long been associated with the domestic sphere, with domestic tasks and roles (Crompton 1997; Charles 2005). This association has historically developed to dovetail with labour market needs – women are credited with particular domestic characteristics that particular forms of employment require. Crompton's work has therefore claimed that, although women do have choices, which their individual attitudes can influence (Crompton & Harris 1999a: 119), we need to keep focused upon the 'disparities in power and resources between men and women in the labour market' (1997: 18) that create structural and interpersonal constraints on how these choices are formed, and how effective women are at realising their goals. Such constraints are determinations of (in the dual sense of being both determined by and determining of) a widespread, powerful, gender regime that influences an individual's life path from early socialisation through to how we fare in our chosen occupation and beyond, and which, crucially, usually advantages men over women.

Using data from ten industrial market societies, Charles (2005) has also argued that occupational segregation is primarily due to economies developing within the context of particular gender ideologies in which women are distinct from men by virtue of 'functional or symbolic' links to traditional female roles (306), and that these ideologies are not neutral. Work identified as being associated with feminine spheres of influence and skill is also identified as less valuable (Phillips & Taylor 1980; Miller *et al.* 2004; Charles 2005). In this context, Charles argues, post-industrialism, and the widespread move to service work, has augmented a 'pink collar ghetto', and has simultaneously drawn women further into non-manual occupations *and* low status roles within them (Charles 2005: 304). Horizontal segregation is thus higher in post-industrial countries, and, as mentioned before, is found alongside stronger vertical segregation within the non-manual sector (304). Charles argues that 'these effects offset, and in some cases, exceed, the integrative effects of modern gender egalitarian cultural principles' (306), and explain the 'seeming disjunction between the slow, uneven declines in overall levels of sex segregation and the frantic improvements over the past three decades in other typical indicators of women's status' (306).

Within this body of research, even those who employ very similar methodological techniques dispute the assumptions and outcomes of individualist approaches such as Hakim's. Jacobs and Gerson's *The Time Divide* (2004) provides a good example in this regard. Jacobs and Gerson utilise a large number of items from US national-scale survey data in their quest to understand issues related to work, family and gender inequality. They conclude that we cannot simply look to individuals, their values, interests or preferences to explain gendered occupational patterns. Taking the example of the increase in household work time over the past decades (Americans now only take an average of 11 days of holiday per annum per Full-Time Equivalent), the authors contest explanations for the increase that cite US citizens' penchant for over-work. For a more accurate explanation, they argue, we need to look at the rise of the dual-earner couple model and the expansion of this family type into middle-class and professional households. This rise has been supported by a number of national trends, government initiatives and workplace practices, and is therefore a function of structural forces rather than individual differences.

Jacobs and Gerson argue that we cannot assume outcomes are a func-tion of choices, nor that we can ascertain '"true" preferences from sur-veys or work outcomes', and stress that more work needs to be done to access 'how workers *feel*' about their experience of work and family life (ibid.: 62, 73).

The working patterns of women specifically cannot be explained with reference to underlying preferences as expressed in survey data. Instead we must look to policies that produce particular employment outcomes. Despite increases in female paid work hours in the US, Jacobs and Gerson cite evidence demonstrating that women, nonetheless, still undertake the lion's share of domestic work in the home, and that trends in parenting styles have become more intensive and committed. We might, they argue, consequently expect women to experience their increased participation in paid employment as negative. In Hakim's model, we remember, many women, and especially mothers, elect to work part-time and accept comparatively poor conditions associated with that employment form in order to keep a manageable work-life balance. Jacobs and Gerson, however, illustrate how workers, including mothers, do not actually *experience* their households as time- and energy-'greedy'. Indeed, *The Time Divide* demonstrates that most people 'agree that work and family are equally important life commitments that need to be combined and integrated, not avoided' (78).

The key factor that mitigates the pressure produced by longer average workweeks for women, according to this research, is control – a degree of flexibility regarding when and where hours are worked – and, although this is an accepted panacea by many suffering from 'time binds', Jacobs and Gerson claim it is particularly hard to come by for women. Women are awarded control as a benefit associated with senior-ity less readily than men, and when they get it by dint of maternity leave or parental status, its advantages can all too often be offset by draconian financial and rank costs. Even when working hours are maintained, women sustain an average of 7 per cent income drop for each child they have, and those who opt for part-time work can expect substantially reduced hourly wages and minimal benefits as a consequence.

Jacobs and Gerson thus suggest that, in respect of this issue, serious dislocations between what workers claim they want in terms of work conditions and what employers are willing to offer result in employment outcomes precisely *not* flowing from expressed preferences. This dislocation is a result of policy lags whereby government legislation and strategies are yet to catch up with broad-based social changes. In contrast with Hakim's view that we are already living in societies marked by equality of opportunity, Jacobs and Gerson claim that in US and European societies alike, we are a long way off from achieving this scenario, and the models that privilege preferences consequently have little explanatory power (see also, Breugel 1996; Ginn *et al.* 1996).

Employers' attitudes and organisational constraints

As we have already seen, survey results have found that employers' expressed attitudes to equal opportunities issues are rather liberal (see, for example, EOC 2005a). It is claimed, however, that, on entering employment, women workers meet significant challenges to any initial aspirations they might have held. The individual and organisational constraints they encounter occur from recruitment through to retirement.

Human Capital Theory, we should remember, attempts to explain the difference between male and female employment patterns in terms of women's lesser investment in 'capital' education, training and experience goods. It is claimed that this is difficult to square, not only with the recent reversal of male and female fortunes in terms of measured educational achievement, but also, as Padavic (1992: 224) suggests, with skills shortages and the operation of market economies. The increasingly competitive needs of employers should see the disintegration of occupational selection if this model is to be credited as persuasive. What the evidence cited here suggests, however, is that employer attitudes and perceptions of female applicants and workers reproduce segregation patterns regardless of human capital developments.

At the stage of recruitment, it is argued not simply that 'individuals choose occupations, but occupations also choose individuals' (Scott & Creighton 1998: 127). Some job descriptions or formal requirements remain quite clearly biased towards men, such as the Fire Service physical test, or height restrictions for police forces (Scott & Chreighton

1998: 127; Woodfield 2003). These are increasingly rare in the UK, however. Nonetheless, researchers claim that there are still significant 'demand-side' factors discriminating against women that are either identified as causing self-selection out of areas and roles, or that more actively block female entry and progress.

Although there is minimal empirical evidence to support the contention that employers actively discriminate against women when recruiting (Miller *et al.* 2004; England 2005), there is indirect evidence that something inherent within employing organisations forms a barrier to female entry. The IT industry provides a good illustrative example here. It is undeniable that girls' under-representation within the lower-educational levels of the IT field is a contributory factor in their under-representation within the field. As the vast majority select out of educational IT, the vast majority are not overtly qualified for IT employment. If this were the only, or indeed even *primary*, reason for the female participation and progression rates in IT employment, however, we should expect to see women with professional-level IT qualifications present within the IT sector in terms broadly proportionate to comparably qualified men. IT-qualified women, it should be noted, have bucked the gender trend and demonstrated their commitment and interest in the field. The 'first destination' figures for men and women leaving UK universities with a degree that should qualify them for professional IT work demonstrates that this is not the case, however (Woodfield 2006a). These women fail to enter professional IT roles with anything like the same frequency as we would expect, and at about half the frequency of comparably qualified men. Moreover, over a quarter of all women with this qualification end up in an occupation within non-professional 'Administrative & Secretarial' work, double the proportions of men who do this. Indeed, women with a Computer Science degree are *more* likely to go into 'Administrative & Secretarial' work than they are to convert their degree into a professional-level job within IT (ibid.).

It might still be held that women are choosing to self-select out of IT, rather than this pattern being a function of employer discrimination. There are several other findings that point otherwise, however. For those women that persevere and continue to seek employment in the sector, there are fewer rewards than for men. They are less likely to secure employment, despite their greater likelihood of securing a higher degree class in their science, and to have achieved more qualifications more generally (ibid.). Indeed, at times, female computer scientists have provided the sole exception to the current rule that sees women UK graduates more likely than male graduates to secure employment after graduating (Millar & Jagger 2001). For those who do secure employment in the sector, women are likely to receive less pay for comparable work and be promoted less often (Millar & Jagger 2001). Retention levels, including among senior ranks, are also far worse than those of males. Some reports suggest that the industry has at times been losing more female staff than it can recruit (Grey & Healey 2004), which is all the more remarkable in the context of its persistent skill shortages.

Unsurprisingly, there are indications that women understand these dynamics, however impressionistically, and that this understanding forms a part of their occupational decision-making. In this case, it may still be claimed that the self-selection thesis provides a key plank of the explanation for women's under-representation in IT. In the context of female educational achievements, the negative perception of IT work could play a critical role in determining the numbers of women choosing courses that qualify them for it. It is also claimed, however, that such an account belies the role employers play in pursuing organisational policies and cultural practices (of an either implicit or explicit nature) that are inimical to women, or, in some cases, actively block women's entry. In the case of IT, there is evidence of demand-side activity favouring male entrants to the field that operates regardless of female will. The success rate of suitably qualified females converting their degrees into professional-level IT jobs is far lower than it is for females converting engineering degrees into professional-level engineering jobs.

Engineering, as with computer science, is heavily male-dominated both at the university and occupational level; indeed it is more so. It has an image that is at least as masculine as IT, again, if not more so. It also shares the characteristic of having a reasonably clear vocational link between degree-level study and professional work in the field. It is the case, however, that 10 per cent more women engineering graduates successfully make the transition to professional-level work that women computer science graduates (Woodfield 2006a). Supply-side arguments alone cannot explain this variation. One key demand-side problem that has been highlighted is the fact that movement into IT work is still often based upon informal contacts and networks, especially in the context of the field's serial contract culture. Indeed, it has been claimed that most senior IT professionals are appointed through networks (Flood 2005), and that personal knowledge is also a key factor in determining promotion.

The tendency of women to fail to convert their superior qualifications into top jobs is often amplified when women select to work in gender-atypical sectors. In the context of general graduate-level skill shortages, three times more women graduates end up in low-level jobs than they did ten years ago, and 10 per cent of them stay in low-level jobs throughout their working lives (EOC 2007). Again, one way of explaining this is the self-selection thesis. This surely stretches credibility, however. Why would so many women pursue a degree in order to work in a bottom-quartile role for the rest of their working life? Can the desired joint pursuit of family commitments and work really explain this outcome? Although there is evidence that women more than men hold these joint desires (EOC 2007), it is only by a considerable elision that we may conclude that women are satisfied with poor remuneration and conditions (Crompton 1997: 48).

Generic versions of the kind of problems facing women in the IT sector have been claimed to mar the whole paid employment sector. Over and above macro-level policies that disadvantage women, there are meso- and micro-level practices and attitudes, as well as individual actions, which create systemic difficulties. It is claimed that male networks operate to advantage men and exclude women from initial entry to organisations (Werum 2002). Rennenkampff's (2004) examination of perceptions of 'leadership' qualities in potential applicants found that photographs of women were perceived to indicate less authority than photographs of men, and to signify less leadership competence. Physical appearance, and gender, were also both demonstrated to be powerful elements in decision-making around hypothetical appointments. Photograph-based perceptions were demonstrated to act as a basis for the development of different types of questions being formulated for hypothetical interviews with candidates, with women being asked more 'negative' questions, confirming of previously established negative stereotypes, and men being asked more positive questions designed to confirm previously established positive images (6).

It is suggested elsewhere that 'glass ceilings', 'sticky floors' and 'concrete walls' exist to keep women in prescribed roles and prevent both vertical and horizontal mobility within organisations, and that these operate from micro-level everyday interactions to senior management policies (Kanter 1977; Hall 1993; Dryler 1998; Woodfield 2000; EOC 2002; Miller *et al.* 2004; HMSO, 2005). Ascribed characteristics and associations with the domestic sphere function at this level too and provide discursive rationalisations for operational biases. Skills held by men, regardless of their 'objective' worth are privileged (Phillips & Taylor 1980; Henwood 1987; Padavic 1992). This is the case with demonstrable skills, skills that are underpinned by qualifications, and by the less tangible and indeterminate skills (Atkinson & Delamont 1990; Woodfield 2000). 'Unsympathetic' or even 'downright hostile' workplace environments are claimed to be evident across many non-traditional areas (HMSO 2005: 16). Senior roles are established according to a pattern whereby anyone with outside commitments will struggle to meet the demands of long hours (EOC 2002). Where women persist and secure employment in male sectors, or positions, they can suffer tokenism, isolation and marginalisation (Werum 2002). Individual women can secure reasonable conditions seemingly as a result more of serendipity than anything else, as the paid employment sector as a whole is uncoordinated and inconsistent about its attitude to 'non-standard' working practices (Crompton 1997; Blyton & Turnbull 2004; EOC 2005a; HMSO 2005; EOC 2007).

Indeed, it is argued that there is very little difference between men and women in terms of originating career ambitions, but that demand-side factors prove to be the determining features of career differences (Jones & Goulding 1999). It is suggested that there is far more overlap between male and female focus on the domestic *and* employment and that women only feel themselves to be 'slightly' more restricted by family and social ties (ibid.; see also, EOC 2007), but that this differentiator, however small, is enough to bifurcate their occupational successes.

The prime origins of gender systems that disadvantage women

As with individualist research, when reviewing socially focused explanations of occupational segregation and choice, it is important to try and identify the assumed prime causes of the social forces under investigation. What are the main origins of occupational systems where women seem to be disadvantaged? From its inception until the present day, Marxism has provided a strong explanatory trend, claiming that labour markets disadvantage women because Capital and, more latterly, *capitalisms*, operate more effectively with a divided labour force (Walby 1986; Hall & Soskice 2003; Blyton & Turnbull 2004). By contrast, it has been argued that the balance of available evidence suggests the profit motive is not strong enough to offset essentially patriarchal gender causes and effects of occupational segregation; a case in point being the continued exclusion of women from sectors with potentially profit-limiting skill-shortages. The operation of patriarchy is thereby also cited as a prime causal agent, whether this is conceptualised in terms of systemic legacy regimes, disadvantaging both men and women, or as men actively pursuing their advantage (Hartmann 1981; Reskin & Roos 1990; Walby 1990; Padavic 1992). In both streams of literature, however, there is a clear materialist challenge to the claim that occupational segregation and choice are functions of biological differences between the sexes, although, equally, it is often the case that a comparably essentialist implicit assumption is made regarding women and men's inherent differences (Crompton 1997; Crompton 1999).

One issue linked to the emergence of the 'gender as process and performance' model is its chronological and analytical relationship to the decline of grand narratives. More fluid and relational models of gender emerged in the wake of overarching accounts of occupational differences in which one group is seen as the witting, and to some extent, wilful agents of social, political and economic advantage. Many researchers in the newly emerged stream do not explicitly stake their colours to the mast when it comes to identifying the origins of male privilege. There is an emphasis on developing multi-faceted frameworks that can best account for the complex of intermediate causal agents, including, in some cases, an eclectic mix of biological, individual and social factors because, 'recent developments in our understanding of human learning processes suggest that asking whether gender differences are caused by socialisation or biology is unhelpful as it is almost impossible to disentangle the two' (Skelton & Hall 2001: 5).

3
Accounting for Occupational Segregation – The Perspective of Girls and Women

Introduction

Chapter 2 reviewed a wide range of explanations for why gendered-occupational segregation might be shaped in the way it is. None of the research discussed was based on the accessing of narrated explanations for occupational choices direct from girls and women themselves. Although many of the findings discussed in Chapter 2 resurface in the literature focused on here, the latter has the distinction of deriving its data solely or partly from direct accounts, and within a methodological framework that therefore deploys only or primarily qualitative approaches. The threshold for including work in this discussion was that research designs *had* to involve qualitative interviewing techniques, and usually as a primary focus, to allow for some access to girls' and women's accounts of their experience of occupational decision-making. The chapter will also concentrate on relevant research published in the last decade or so.

The chapter will end with a summary of the issues of choice that have emerged from the literature reviews of this and the previous chapter, followed by a methodological introduction to the data presentation chapters.

The utility of accessing direct accounts and deploying qualitative methodologies

Although much of the literature reviewed in Chapter 2 provides rich and insightful findings for researchers of gendered-occupational choice, significant issues arise from the lack of direct accounts. It should be reiterated that this perspective is different from that found in the *individualist* approach. Although much of the research previously discussed is *individualist* in focus, it is almost exclusively based on methodological approaches to data that do not involve actually engaging directly with individuals in an in-depth manner.[1] A lot of sociological, or socially focused, work also neglects this perspective, but such research forms the majority discussed here.

Acknowledgement of the pitfalls of non-qualitative approaches within this research area, along with frequent recommendations that more qualitative work needs to be undertaken, comes from a range of sources, including those whose own work is individualist in stance or solely quantitative.

DeLeire and Levy (2001) freely admit, for example, that their finding that women are more risk-averse in their search for suitable work, does not extend to understanding the origin of this trait, or even that such risk-aversion is a trait. Indeed, they 'cannot distinguish between demand and supply factors that might be driving the differences between men's and women's occupational choice' (ibid.: 14). Others have noted that, although we might observe differences between men's and women's survey answers, in relation to, say, work values, or job characteristics, we may still not know whether named values or characteristics connote the same meanings for men and for women (Reed & Dahlquist 1994; Crozier & Dorval 2002; Davey & Lalande 2004). As we shall see in what follows, it is not uncommon for assumptions about the meaning of individuals' answers on a survey to be subsequently challenged by research utilising interviews (Crozier & Dorval 2002).

As this suggests, one of the most significant concerns that arises from the lack of directly accessed, individual accounts is the difficulty of understanding the meanings that research participants might hold. Key issues remain unclear once we have considered indirect accounts. Among them are: What, or who, do girls consider to be the most important influences in relation to their occupational selection? How much information about both typical and atypical occupations do girls and women actually possess, and what are the most important knowledge sources? How much of a concern are actual or projected domestic commitments for girls and women when making their occupational choices? How free do girls and women feel when making occupational choices? Or, put differently, how do they feel their preferences are formed, and how much agency do they feel in relation to actualising them? Do girls and women view themselves as being members of fundamentally different groups of either home-centred or work-centred individuals?

Some researchers have suggested that 'the way forward may be to utilise a totally qualitative approach', of group and single interviews (Anderson 1998: 145), to avoid the pitfalls of the unknown or 'fantasy' elements in survey responses, and in order to maximise the chances of achieving a hermeneutic understanding of how career choice develops 'meaningfully within the context of a person's entire social experiences' (ibid.: 146). While it is not necessary to argue that all research needs a qualitative, individual dimension, it does seem clear that a significant research effort has to be driven by these characteristics for a fuller, more appropriate picture of gender and employment choices. As we will see, 'qualitative research . . . refers to the meanings, concepts, definitions, characteristics, metaphors, symbols and descriptions of things' (Berg 1995: 3). Qualitative accounts address the individual 'process' questions in more detail. Although neglected in this field, they have the potential to open the blackbox of occupational decision-making to allow the individual participant to unpack, reflect and explore the meanings and experiences which formed their occupational choices, and how these meanings are constructed, reproduced and changed, and to allow some of the subsequent complexities of the processes to be given fuller expression (Halford, Savage & Witz 1997; Jones & Goulding 1999; Crompton & Harris 1999b; Crozier & Dorval 2002; Blustein, Kenna, Murphy, DeVoy & DeWine 2005). In focusing on examples of research utilising these approaches here, the aim is to access the viewpoint of girls and women themselves.[2] More specifically, the aim is to access information on how they perceive their abilities, experiences and achievements in relation to their occupational choice, how they identify desired opportunities and reject others and so on.

What have directly accessed accounts revealed?

Pathways towards work

McQuaid, Bond and Robinson (2004), interviewed 85 mixed-sex children alongside the collection of survey data to explore the role played by gender stereotyping in career choice. By contrast with the survey's findings that pupils choose educational subject areas on the basis of enjoyment rather than ability or interest, interviews revealed that both boys and girls justified their own choice of targeted careers in terms of the latter two factors, as well as on the basis of having a known role model already in the post. They did not view these selection criteria as gendered, however. Pupils reported that they excluded careers on the basis of a lack of ability or interest, but rarely on the basis of their gender (ibid.: 10). As is the case with other research, however, although participants, especially female participants, expressed beliefs that both women and men could work in most occupations, including gender-atypical ones, their target occupation was usually gender-typical. The main reason both boys and girls provided for believing men or women are better suited for particular jobs was the association of particular gendered characteristics with work types. Women, it was reported, were associated with good communication, caring and helping skills, and men with physical, technical and practical prowess (ibid.: 9).

Francis's (2002) work with 100 secondary school pupils confirmed that boys and girls were more likely to orientate to gender-typical work. In line with other research, girls' choice of possible jobs showed more diversity than that of the boys', although, interestingly, they were also more conservative in terms of the gendered attributes they ascribed to occupations (ibid.: 84). Many of their choices were informed by the media (ibid.: 77), and revealed a distinct lack of knowledge about what qualifications occupations might require (ibid.: 86). Girls were likely to describe a desire to secure a 'caring' or 'creative' job, by contrast with boys who highlighted scientific, technical or business oriented occupations (ibid.: 77), and in so doing highlighted the continued salience of fundamental 'binary dichotomies' of gender: rationality/emotionality; science/arts and so on (ibid.: 83), in which femaleness is always the 'other' and 'substandard'. Francis concludes that her participants' choice narratives, in continuing to reflect these deeply embedded dichotomies 'demonstrate little recognition of changes in the adult employment market' (ibid.: 75). The study further demonstrated that girls' aspirations were, nevertheless, ambitious and they were generally more likely to choose a 'professional' job as their desired target, by contrast with boys and with participants in qualitative studies of girls' aspirations from the 1970s and 1980s (ibid.: 75–77).

Francis discusses the cases of some interviewees who buck the gender trends and appear to be choosing atypical work. She argues that they do so by drawing on 'alternative discourses, such as those of gender equity and individual freedom, to construct an alternative outlook' (ibid.: 83). The research also indicated that 'girls now see their chosen occupations as reflecting their identity . . . rather than as reflecting their future roles as wives' (ibid.: 83), which Francis claims is due to 'various economic and social changes' over previous decades (ibid.: 84): 'girls' increased ambition, coupled with an awareness that opportunities in the workplace are skewed against them, has provided girls with new motivation for achievement in the workplace' (ibid.: 84).

Other research on participants still in full-time education has revealed that the meanings males and females attach to job characteristics may differ on further examination. Crozier and Dorval (2002) cite evidence demonstrating the centrality of work values for women's occupational identity across a number of different and divergent samples of participants. It is shown that women seek to satisfy relational impulses at work and through work. They value communication, teaching and work that satisfies altruistic impulses for individuals and the world in general (ibid.: 3).

Crozier and Dorval have challenged the findings of some value-based research using quantitative methodologies, and which has produced varying results for associations of relational and altruistic characteristics and women workers. Using their qualitative data, they attempt to uncover the meanings attached to work values as they are expressed in surveys. They found that the values that female students' answers had initially categorised as non-relational, did in actual fact connote relational meanings. Relatively good wage levels, for instance, were discovered to connote a better ability to provide for children (ibid.: 5). 'Achievement' at work was also best understood in relational terms for women, the authors argue. Participants made it clear that achievement had relational connotations too. It was understood to mean 'achieving good relationships' and helping people 'to lead happy healthy lives', to achieve trust, concern and responsibility for others (ibid.: 5). It was concluded that by contrast with the 'male' lens, relational values are salient for women across a wide range of their thoughts and feelings about work, and that, although this was the case for all women, it was particularly so for those in gender-typical employment (ibid.: 7).

The origin of career-related information has been analysed using qualitative techniques. In this research, the influence of significant others in occupational decision-making has been confirmed. Interviews conducted by Schultheiss, Palma, Predragovich and Glasscock (2002), for instance, indicated that siblings 'are a significant and overlooked influence' (ibid.: 302) insofar as they provide information and support during the work-identification process. Qualitative accounts have revealed gender differences in the receptivity to familial messages. MacKenzie's (1997) interview work with school children has revealed that girls are much more likely than boys to be influenced by parents and other non-school adults when considering their career choices, and that they are less likely to be influenced by teachers (ibid.: 4).

Buldu's (2006) Turkish research supports the existence and importance of strongly gendered images of work attributes, and points to the key role of television in the provision of initial stereotype templates for children (130). His findings suggest that stereotypes about work attributes may have less power to affect career choice in adolescence than is thought elsewhere, however. Although occupational images, such as those of scientists, can have a 'powerful affect on future plans' (ibid.: 122), he found that they had weakened between ages 8 and 15. The study also revealed that socio-economic background has a significant effect on the level of stereotyping of occupations and their attributes, with children from higher Social-Economic Status (SES) backgrounds being less 'traditional' in their image reproduction (ibid.: 122).

Erwin and Maurutto (1998) have examined the in-depth accounts of women who are considering a less traditional career and, indeed, who are already undertaking a science degree at undergraduate level. As has been noted in Chapter 2, it is commonly expected that crossing into gender-atypical educational or occupational territory bespeaks a very strong commitment to the selected area or role, as the individuals concerned have to battle against social expectations on both a direct and indirect level. The authors note that in research utilising other methodological and analytical approaches this commitment has been assumed to emerge from women's measured differences from other women, and from men:

> be it academic ability, self-confidence, attitudes, expectations of discrimination etc. . . . While there is support for each of these factors, the findings are often ambiguous, what is found in one study is frequently contradicted in another, and the difference that gender makes continues to be a source of controversy and speculation. What is missing in many of these accounts is the standpoint of the women themselves.
>
> (ibid.: 54)

After analysing individual accounts, the authors confirmed that women believed themselves to be more oriented to science because they had indeed done well academically in this area in the past, but they, nevertheless, reported anxiety about their abilities, and perceived the 'hard' end of science – physics, for example – to be too difficult for them. This was despite evidence that their performance was demonstrably better than that of others, including comparable men (ibid.: 58). Participants also reported selecting an atypical area because they had felt themselves to be supported in this decision by parents and significant others, such as teachers and known role models. Their accounts otherwise highlighted a general paucity of information and support, indicating, again, a basic lack of knowledge about what specific careers involved. Less than 20 per cent reported 'adequate' careers counselling. Unfortunately, it was also the case that participants were often fixated with a narrow set of roles and 'had given very little thought to alternative occupations if the first choice failed' (ibid.: 59).

There were clear findings in relation to the respondents' reported beliefs about their gender identity, and its impact on their future. Participants firmly did not believe that structural factors could affect their performance within 'male' areas, or that sexism would play a role in determining their careers. Perhaps relatedly, less than a third considered themselves to be feminists, and less than 4 per cent believed their own gender would influence their occupational choices. Following on from their performance anxieties, respondents reported their beliefs that failures in relation to meeting their desired occupational targets would be due to poor luck, or their own inadequacies (ibid.: 59–63). Twenty per cent of them did, however, indicate that they were vaguely aware of discrimination instances on their courses (ibid.: 62). Finally, although more than 80 per cent believed that juggling motherhood and a professional career would prove very difficult, few had given more than a cursory thought to how this difficulty may be addressed in their own lives.

Paradoxically, the identification of clear career targets, coupled with firm assumptions of open access to them, was expressed alongside what Erwin and Maurutto identify as a growing cleavage between participants' career hopes and expectations as time progressed. This tacit awareness of foreclosing opportunities was not linked in participants' minds to gendered constraints. For the authors, these contradictory elements in the narratives of occupational decision-making were symptomatic of powerful discourses of individualism and meritocracy which,

> shaped the worldviews, subjective interpretations and social practices of the women. In these discourses the self was valorised; it is personal drive, ability, will-power and resourcefulness that shape experiences and determine outcomes. Even when structural forces are acknowledged, they are constructed as obstacles that – with sufficient motivation and effort – can be overcome.
>
> (ibid.: 60)

Erwin and Maurutto conclude that women in science tackle a complicated system of competing and contradictory discourses and realities while making career decisions and identities.

Proctor and Padfield's (1998) study underscores both the importance of *post*-school experiences in forming employment outcomes, but also another aspect of what they claim to be the currently contradictory nature of women's experiences of choice. The research comprised longitudinal interviewing with 79 young adult women of two distinct types and aimed to explore their aspirations in relation to work and family. The first were 'single workers' (full-time paid employment, no partner or children) and the second 'early mothers' (partner, children and no paid employment).

The interview data revealed that, despite similar experiences at school, those with positive experiences of further education and training were more likely to commit to full-time employment trajectories. The 'early mothers' often had poor experiences in this regard (ibid.: 245). 'Early mothers' also had youthful experiences of somewhat traditional relationships with male partners. This research identifies the importance of 'fateful moments' in participants' accounts, times within their lives when the framework of opportunities and constraints shift significantly (ibid.: 246).

The authors highlight the existence of a high agential group of women, who are very effective at realising their ambitions, but simultaneously contest the concept of 'choice' in relation to women's general experience of paid employment, arguing that: 'for real choices to be exercised, work and family need to be socially organised for women to permit either one or both to be lived, as is the everyday experiences of men in society' (ibid.: 7). They emphasise that for all women, the domestic sphere acts as a constriction. The limits on work choices of either actual children or anticipated children are consequently 'experienced in ways which are similar, despite differences in . . . class location' (ibid.: 3).

This research contests the utility of individualist approaches, and in particular, Preference Theories' analytical categories. Women are seen, 'rather than hopelessly failing to make necessary choices', as being in the midst of an historical period that locates them as expected workers *and* as primarily responsible for the home sphere (ibid.: 6). It further argues that any identified commitments 'first and foremost to family responsibilities' cannot best be understood as a family-orientation (ibid.: 247). 'The 'single workers' group were in full-time paid employment at the time of the research but not because of an expressed 'career orientation': 'very few of the group displayed a clear commitment to work *over* family . . . our analysis conceptualises young women as "living a contradiction"' (ibid.: 247). The majority of 'single worker' respondents, therefore, maintained both family and career trajectories as potential futures 'because it was not possible to predict the configuration of agency and structure in the future' (ibid.: 247). Proctor and Padfield argue that this was a function of women's roles being so ambiguously constructed in the current social context. Similarly, 'early mothers' orientations were not expressed as stable or innate, and many saw future trajectories as including a 'career'. Proctor and Padfield conclude that

> Hakim's concepts seem inapplicable at the descriptive level. In emphasising the agency of the actor through her 'orientations' and neglecting the interaction of agency and structure, Hakim also neglects the complexity of causation in the social world.
>
> (ibid.: 6–7)

The important longitudinal study *Growing up Girl* (Walkerdine, Lucey & Melody 2001) further underscores the contradictory nature of girls' realities as they progress through education and towards paid employment. It is specifically argued in this study that, although these contradictions are ever-present for all girls and women, they affect different sub-groups in different ways. Especially prominent are class differences. The move into paid employment 'has gained importance since the early 1980s as a powerful signifier of adult status for young women, as it previously was for young men' (ibid.: 57), and many girls focus on their future working careers with a high degree of anticipatory verve. Indeed, many girls feel their future opportunities to be limitless, especially in the context of good educational performances. The researchers demonstrate, however, that participants' life chances are, in actual fact, highly structured and the transition to work is problematic for all young women (ibid.: 56). Class location was, however, 'the most efficient predictor' of how participants' negotiated this transition (ibid.: 58).

Growing Up Girl analyses participants' 'dreams of a working future' (ibid.: 78) and note that middle-class girls were far more focused on a professional life and expected a good level of reward. By contrast, working-class girls, who often started their working lives earlier as they were more likely to leave school at 16, tended to be 'more vague' about the shape of their future' (ibid.: 79). Such findings resonate with other work reviewed here insofar as they highlight the precarious and contradictory nature of female identity in the face of discourses that present limitless life-course choices, and experiential realities of more traditional perceptions of gender. In terms of the former, 'individuals are increasingly held accountable for their own fate' but in the context of 'old patterns of gender politics' remaining firmly entrenched (ibid.: 81). The 'necessity for self-invention is imposed in extremely contradictory economic, social and individual landscapes' (ibid.: 81), where, for instance, girls are expected to do well academically, even in traditional male subjects, but can be perceived as challenging when they do so (ibid.: 56).

The book finds that some groups of women – middle-class women for instance – over the course of their life-time, have been provided with a range of both internal and external resources that frame the possibilities of a successful and rewarding working life more definitely, form a stronger sense of self-efficacy to achieve it, and remove any constraints that may impede it. This echoes Proctor and Padfield's identification of highly agential women, but is part of a more materialist analysis insofar as socio-economic differences are deemed to be salient in the production of agency. As has been indicated above, however, the movement of *any* woman towards employment is not represented as unproblematic by any means. The transition may be difficult and it may not be what women necessarily '*want*'. Indeed, some participants clearly feel themselves to be disadvantaged by the trajectory they are presented with, even if it involves a 'successful' career. What distinguishes say, middle-class girls, however, is that they can more readily imagine this future as an option, and consequently can more easily tread the expected path, or something akin to it, or they can actively reject it. This is contrasted with 'people who cannot imagine things being different, cannot reinvent themselves' (ibid.: 68).

Hanson and Pratt's (1991) study comprised in-depth interviews within a representative sample of 620 households and concentrated on identifying what individuals look for when seeking employment, and how they seek it. A significant finding is that the majority of both men and women respondents had 'fallen into' their current work through informal contacts, rather than having actively searched for it. The interviews further revealed significant gender differences in the ways men and women identify work opportunities, differences that can help explain gender-based occupational segregation.

Women revealed that they had different patterns of social networks, which were strongly oriented around other women, and were more community and family related. It was via these networks that they elicited most of their occupational information, and accordingly most of it was derived from other women. This was especially the case with women in female-dominated occupations where community-based information was most dominant. Conversely, men tended to get their occupational information from other men. Interestingly, women in male-dominated occupations were even more likely to use personal contacts to secure work than other types of workers, but this was usually oriented around male family contacts (ibid.: 240–241). Participants' accounts suggested that these types of contact could often be associated with upward mobility (ibid.: 241). Following on from this, a key finding of Hanson and Pratt's research is that women are a heterogenous group who have different interests and different ways of approaching work searches (ibid.: 251), but that for those in female-dominated work spheres, their contacts are limiting.

Hanson and Pratt argue that 'the gendered nature of social life' funnels women towards certain occupations and away from others, and once women are in these occupations, their employment choices are reinforced by their gendered networks outside and inside the workplace (ibid.: 240). They further argue that this situation augments differences between the characteristics men and women value most highly in occupations. Women reported looking for proximity to home, children and flexibility, while men reported focusing more on wage and prestige levels. These differences were, however, reinforced in female-dominated occupations and by female-dominated social networks (ibid.: 246).

The authors claim that their research challenges over-simplified explanations of occupational segregation that either prioritise supply- or demand-side explanations, and demonstrates that 'individuals come as fully-embedded agents' (ibid.: 250). They find support for Preference Theories in the sense that they can identify a clear association between labour force position and women's association with the home, and for women entering the occupations they do as 'an active' process: 'in a meaningful way, they slot themselves into these occupations' (ibid.: 251). They claim, however, that this positioning is a 'not unconstrained process' (ibid.: 251), and that their qualitative treatment has demonstrated that the nature of the link between employment and the domestic sphere 'is very different' to how it is presented in individualist approaches (ibid.: 250). Women end up in female-dominated and low-paid work because of their reluctance to commute as far as men, and because of the occupational information flows that they are networked into, and, ultimately, the phenomenon of occupational segregation itself, but not because they are 'making rational, long-term, life-long income-maximising decisions' (ibid.: 251).

Pathways within work

Rosemary Crompton's critique of preference-oriented explanatory frameworks is partly derived from the findings she has obtained utilising individually focused research. With Harris (1999a, 1999b), for instance, she conducted over 150 biographical interviews from women in medical and banking work in five countries. These were focused on exploring women's choice-making in relation to employment and home. From this data-set, she concludes that, while women make decisions which are then 'reflected in aggregated patterns of employment' (1999a: 118), these are not a function of an underlying female typology but of women actively constructing their 'work-life' biographies in the face of externally located 'available opportunities and constraints' (ibid.: 119). These biographies are diverse, reflecting the fact that women are heterogenous and adopt different strategies for managing their career trajectories. Crompton and Harris use their qualitative evidence to show, for instance, that women who work full-time and have 'successful' careers, and therefore could be identified as being among Hakim's committed, work-oriented individuals, as distinct from the compromising 'adaptors', in actual fact often also experience their work-orientation as a compromising one. Female doctors, for instance, describe 'satisficing' behaviour – planning to meet their family and career needs in equal measure, via selecting particular specialities that favour flexible hours, for instance (1999a: 123). Crompton and Harris argue that their 'bottom up' approach to understanding segregation runs directly counter to Hakim's movement from the 'macro-categories she identifies to the micro-level' (1999b: 132), and allows them 'through an analysis of the *processes* through which women arrive at different combinations of employment and family biographies, [to] . . . demonstrate how both "choice" and "constraint" play their part' (ibid.: 132). They argue that the fixed nature of Hakim's analytical categories is also contested in their data as 'women's intentions and actions change, and vary over time and with circumstances' (1999b: 132).

What this research indicates strongly is that women in various employment categories are often more similar than different. Some in full-time employment originally had less commitment to their career than those in part-time employment, and vice versa, but circumstances have pushed them along alternative paths to the ones they initially envisaged. Echoing Proctor and Padfield's accounts of 'fateful moments', Crompton and Harris note that over three-quarters of the participants described an 'epiphany' moment during which their work-life biographies were disrupted and changed significantly due to 'external' factors, such as bereavement or overt discrimination (ibid.: 139).

They also demonstrate, however, that there was 'systematic variation in the kinds of constraint and opportunity offered by banking and medicine' (ibid.: 144). The varying demands of different occupational roles in these sectors (different options for flexibility and part-time work, for example), played a significant part in determining how the women lived their working lives in terms of their domestic relationships and their gender identities, 'and thus in the way in which men and women "do gender" in a practical sense' (ibid.: 136). This included how likely women were to experience biographical disruption for family reasons, and how likely they were to experience it for non-family reasons. Doctors were more likely to do the former – to, for instance, scale down work commitments because of children – and bankers, the latter. Crompton and Harris acknowledge that it could be suggested that these groups differ because they were fundamentally different *before* they entered their chosen occupations; that this is why they selected the type of work they did. They contest this explanation, however, arguing that 'an examination of the background of the women interviewed suggested a remarkable similarity of social origins and early experiences' (ibid.: 141). Both groups experienced higher-level professional fathers, working mothers, academic encouragement from home and school and so on, to a similar degree. They conclude that their data 'do not lend support to the self-selection hypothesis as an explanation of occupational differences. It would seem that occupational context has had an important impact on employment/family career choices' (ibid.: 142), adding that the fact the finding was robust across different national contexts, and varying macro-economic formations, underpins the findings (ibid.: 144).

Paralleling the work of several other researchers explored here, Crompton and Harris emphasise that one group 'stand out as individuals' (ibid.: 143) in this study. 'Maximisers' – those who have sought to 'maximise their goals in respect of both employment careers and family lives' (ibid.: 137) – are distinctive because of their higher than average sense of personal efficacy:

> Maximisers shared a dynamic approach to both their employment and their family lives. It would seem reasonable to assume that, whatever these women had chosen to do, and wherever they had chosen to do it, they would have effectively made the most of their opportunities and achievements.
>
> (ibid.: 143)

Crompton and Harris suggest that these individuals are not distinct by virtue of innate differences, but because of 'their childhood experiences' (ibid.: 143) – they were far more likely to receive parental encouragement, and more likely to have school encouragement too. They were also far more likely to be aware of work-related discrimination issues, and to claim personal experience of discrimination at work. The authors conclude that such differences are therefore 'deeply rooted in early patterns of socialisation . . . on how the *social* structure affect individuals – without in any way seeing individuals as entirely "determined" by structure' (ibid.: 145). Neither individualist nor overly structural explanations provide an adequate framework for understanding women's choices around work:

> Certainly women can and do make choices – although in aggregate, their lack of power and resources relative to men means that both today and in the past they have been less able to do so than the opposite sex. Women – and men – can choose but are also constrained, a fact that lies at the root of sociological explanations of human behaviour.
>
> (ibid.: 147)

Other research has demonstrated that pre-entry expressions of work interests or values can be undone in the face of within-work 'material situations' (Padavic 1992: 224). Padavic's study combined questionnaire and interview data and explored women's willingness to transfer from female-dominated white-collar work, to better-paid male-dominated blue-collar work in the same location. She contested traditional reasoning that stipulated that women 'voluntarily' avoided traditional 'male' blue-collar work because they held normative preferences for white-collar work attributes, such as that it was clean and allowed for social interaction (ibid.: 217). Padavic found that, although women did value these features (ibid.: 223), such 'preferences' were unable to predict their willingness to transfer, nor could gender attitudes, or a history of holding atypical interests in childhood (ibid.: 224). As such, 'aspirations toward sex-appropriate jobs and their accompanying working conditions are unstable and are only weakly connected to occupational outcomes' (ibid.: 218). What was persuasive for women was higher pay, but this was held in check by anticipated, and largely structurally driven, problems of juggling work and home life (ibid.: 226). Padavic concludes that we 'need to acknowledge the malleability of work-related attitudes' (ibid.: 226), and 'must look to demand-side explanations to understand women's underrepresentation' (ibid.: 227).

Aveling's (2002) qualitative study of women interviewed in 1986 and again in 2000–2001 is of particular interest as it looks at the development of women's employment decisions longitudinally. It also supports the contention that work formations play a primary role in determining women's trajectories, but further suggests that work experiences can alter expressed beliefs and can cause women to retrospectively alter accounts of decision-making processes. In their early interviews, Aveling's participants followed those from other research examined here, and expressed the view that gender was not an issue for them in terms of career choice. This was irrespective of the type of career they ultimately chose. They also denied that career choice was influenced by the future prospects of marriage and children, and seemed to have thought little about how possible work and family commitments might be managed (ibid.: 274). Many maintained educational links with maths or science in order to keep alive the option of an atypical career, and most believed that they were under a societal obligation to pursue a career. Participants also felt themselves to be active agents constructing their own futures, and controlling their destinies (ibid.: 277).

Despite this optimism and feeling of control, the second interviews often revealed a different life-course had emerged for participants than the ones first envisaged. Although, most still claimed that career choices had been unaffected by projected concerns about juggling family and work, participants' labour market positions at the time of the second interviews reflected their maternal status. For the participants who had become mothers, regardless of initial educational achievements and commitment to work, their primary orientations were now to the home and they reported that 'birth had made them rethink equality and what it meant to be female' (ibid.: 273).

This tendency to retrospectively interpolate later realities, and feelings about them, into earlier narratives of expectation and choice, also affected participants' accounts about their particular job choices. For instance, 'even those women who, at the time of the first interview, said that they didn't really know what specific occupation they wanted to follow, had gone on to find employment in a field in which they said they had always been interested' (ibid.: 272).

Despite the evidence that participants had adjusted their expectations and narrative accounts in line with their lived experiences of both occupational and domestic spheres, like Erwin and Maurutto, Aveling concludes that her evidence points to participants actively constructing and reconstructing their work-life narratives from within a range of competing, contradictory discourses, but that feminist and collective identity discourses, among these, did not 'speak' to them (ibid.: 273).

Meiskins and Whalley's *Putting Work in Its Place* (2002) comprises interview work with an unusual set of comparatively powerful participants. They interviewed 127 successful (99 per cent of who are women) technical professionals – hi-tech engineers, software programmers and so on – in the US. The study's central theme was to explore precisely the experiences of individual workers negotiating their way through the strictures of long, demanding and fixed working weeks towards more 'customised' schedules in order to better manage their work-life balance. Their sample was such that we should expect the task of negotiating new working styles to be easier for this group than for others. They were professional, highly skilled and sought after, and their core business often lends itself more easily to home-working than many occupations. For decades, commentators have heralded a revolution in how we work that would see Information Technology (IT) at its core, given it affords the spatial and temporal flexibility required if non-standard workweeks are to become more commonplace. Equally, however, many workers in this sector have been identified as actively constructing an occupational culture where extremely long workweeks, to the exclusion of outside life, are the norm.

Meiskins and Whalley's book finds that, despite, or perhaps because of, the competitive workaholism that characterises this male-dominated sector, women are far more successful than men at negotiating reduced working hours in an organisational context. They normally do so after the birth of children, and in the context of ongoing parental responsibilities. Meiskins and Whalley found that maternity leave presented an accepted window of opportunity during which women, and their employers, could recognise the benefits of a reduced workweek.

Such research demonstrates how much latitude women workers have when they are in a comparatively powerful position to negotiate from, and questions whether a move into what is often part-time work, necessarily brings with it the characteristics normally associated with such a transition: reduced pay, status and benefits, and less challenging and satisfying roles. Their conclusion is that some women incurred costs in terms of some lost opportunities for promotion and pay rises, but that this group manages to achieve a 'customised' work schedule while retaining the same level of pay and while maintaining stimulating and rewarding work.

The qualitative evidence from the participants also clearly indicates, however, that, in reducing their hours, these women are not shifting focus from work to home, and do not report experiencing any associated shift in identities. Equally, in their continued commitment to paid employment, they are not 'fleeing' the family. What they are seeking, and what they claim to achieve, is a role that reflects a resistance to choose one sphere over the other, and an identity that can embrace equally their activities and priorities in both. Once work is 'in its place', they report a greater enjoyment and satisfaction within both spheres; neither overwhelms.

What the study also makes clear, however, is the lack of fit between individual preferences in this regard and the social, legislative and organisational context. The greatest obstacle to participants' negotiations is the absence of adequate frameworks to facilitate non-standard work time. In this situation, permissions are at the discretion of individual organisations, and, in practice, at the discretion of individual managers. Thus, what should be a relatively impersonal decision turns on the contingencies and whims of personal relationships, and nearly all part-timers reported persistent labelling as 'deviant' and pressure to return to the 'norm'.

Stacked against these facts is considerable evidence indicating employers will reap as many benefits from a bigger uptake of a reduced workweek as the employees who seek them. Part-timers reported increased loyalty to their organisations, and claimed to be more productive. They report taking uncompleted tasks home, checking emails regularly during non-work hours and labouring with an intensity that doesn't allow for standing 'around shooting the breeze' (ibid.: 40).

Meiskins and Whalley's samples are particularly interesting insofar as they typify the highly agential and achieving group of workers identified in other qualitative studies. They can be contrasted with less internally resourceful, focused and efficacious groups, or groups with strong structural constraints. The Halford, Savage and Witz study (1997) of the gendered-career narratives of a more diverse sample of male and female workers found that, on the whole, the majority in each group did not 'adopt instrumental narratives of their careers' (ibid.: 190), and reported perceptions of contingency and constraint, rather than of strategic 'planfulness'. The authors noted that narrations of careers elicited 'more complex emotional issues of belonging (to the organisation, to their working colleagues, to their families etc.) and/or detachment' (ibid.). Individuals tended to see their careers primarily in terms of the organisational context in which they worked, and not in terms of themselves as *individuals*. The researchers identified an important distinction between the two genders, however, insofar as organisational 'constructions of opportunities' differed so that men were privileged and women, especially women with children, were not (ibid.: 190). Halford *et al*. concluded that 'the success of the majority of senior men in banking and local government was strongly linked to their gender but not to any sense of masculine strategic behaviour' (ibid.).

I have also argued this elsewhere – *Women, Work and Computing* (2000) – after analysing qualitative interviews and observation data from a powerful, highly educated and skilled group of men and women IT scientists, and in the context of a 'cutting-edge' organisation. The latter's management explicitly claimed that the opportunity costs of gender bias were too high for its staff to indulge in, and that the organisation was 'skill-shopping' and not 'body-shopping'. Members of staff were recruited because they represented 'the cream of the cream' (ibid.: 71) in terms of available human capital, and so questions about their qualifications for the role had already been answered. So pervasive was this claim that members of the organisation sometimes refused to discuss individuals in terms of their gender, arguing that this was outmoded and obsolete (ibid.: 169). In this context, reference to formal rules regarding gender equity was muted.

Female participants reported themselves to have entered the organisation committed to a career in IT and optimistic about their futures having previously overcome considerable difficulties to secure their position. Despite this, the women reported the emergence of significant differences between themselves and men in terms of their opportunities and treatments within the organisation once they had joined it. These experiences were at odds with the pervasive discourse of successfully implemented equal opportunities and gender-blindness. Analysis of 'alternative discourses' operating within the organisation, such as the strong and persistent association of men with technical skills, and with skilled work *per se*, as well as powerful definitions of technical skill in terms of indeterminate, and intangible 'dispositional' differences more often identified in men than women, revealed that discriminatory perspectives competed with equal opportunities perspectives for primacy. More often than not, women were disadvantaged by the primacy of the former over the latter. The evidence suggested that 'the careers of male and female technical employees seemed to follow differently configured paths through the allegedly meritocractic system' (ibid.: 122), a feature that left female staff feeling themselves to be underutilised and undervalued (ibid.: 129), and less committed than they once were. Many reported thoughts of leaving, not just the organisation, but the field of computing altogether (ibid.: 121). Their accounts could be linked to verifiable material differences in male and female promotion prospects, pay rises and retention rates. It is concluded that, in the absence of firm and highly visible gender equity policies and procedures, informal gender systems, that carry assumptions regarding women's suitability to high-level technical work, persist. In this context, it is therefore over-optimistic to expect gender equity to follow from each individual's 'neutral' appreciation of a worker's skill.

What have these accounts added to our understanding?

The findings of the directly accessed individualised accounts elicited via qualitative approaches are critical to our understanding of the occupational-choice process in girls and women. This is not to say that the findings from the literature reviewed in Chapter 2 are less valuable. Indeed, many highlighted here speak directly to those elicited via non-qualitative methods, or from findings not derived directly from empirical research. It is the case, however, that these individualised accounts are less often added to the research picture, and, as these findings testify, this is a mistake. Those of a particular interest here are highlighted below.

The data examined here confirms that girls and women, in the current climate, see themselves as comparatively free agents at the point at which they are making decisions about the kind of work they wish to pursue, and often as highly efficacious in this pursuance. Participants feel themselves to be *actively* selecting some roles and de-selecting others. They deny that gender is a factor in their own selection of a work role. On the whole, they do not perceive that their experiences are marred by sexism, gender-based hierarchies or by external obstacles in relation to their own case, although they may be aware of discrimination within the workplace as a possibility. They believe their particular life chances are essentially a function of a meritocratic social order. Feminist discourses, or discourses based on any recognition of a collective experience or treatment, do not, therefore, speak to them. Participants sometimes indicate internal anxiety barriers with regard to their own abilities. There is little evidence from the interview data that girls consider that problems related to combining domestic responsibilities with paid work will impact on them, or that it is a primary issue that they need to think through when selecting a career.

These accounts have also confirmed that choice is, nevertheless, highly gendered when it comes to girls making their own occupational decisions. The majority select gender-typical work for themselves, and before this, gender-typical academic subjects may be selected because they are perceived to place individuals on the right general path for a chosen gender-typical occupation. The role played by altruism, as well as other socially oriented and gender-typified values, in selecting and deselecting occupational areas, is confirmed in this work. What is also identified in these accounts, as well as other literature, is that the gender-typing of an occupation is very clear, but equally that this identification, and subsequent selection, is framed by very little detailed and accurate knowledge of what it involves or even what precise qualifications are required to become a viable applicant. Family, immediate social community and the media are identified as particularly important influences in filling this information void. Teachers and careers advisors were experienced as less significant.

The individualised literature has also suggested that, once women are faced with the realities of work, and later of combining paid work and parenthood, their accounts change in certain respects. Women of working age are more reflective of the constraints domestic responsibilities place on them. The expectations of others were noted to be part of the circumscription process in some accounts. The expectations, or lack of them, of co-workers, social contacts and boyfriends were noted in relation to both employment and home. On the whole, however, this shift co-existed with a persistent narrative of equal opportunity, individual agency and preference in which women are self-selecting out of certain roles and into others. Women did not usually report experiencing any shifts or adjustments to their original or ongoing hopes and plans as the result of structural inequalities or as even necessarily oppressive. The feminist or collective discourses still did not 'speak' to them. Indeed, there is some evidence that women who experience a radically different trajectory to the one they once envisaged and voiced, nevertheless, maintained much of their original identities in their adjusted identity, and certainly more than we might expect from observation of their movement from an aspiring or actual full-time worker, to a part-time worker, or to being employed full-time within the home.

Indeed, somewhat paradoxically, because the equal opportunities discourses are so prominent in the individual accounts, there is ostensibly little data that speaks to the operation of oppressive or exclusionary structures or practices in general, although these may be identified in the course of the researchers' analyses as influencing work decisions, but also as suppressing the articulation of systemic biases. It is often the case, therefore, that researchers focusing on the individual's perspective are more likely to find strong evidence of non-individualist explanations of occupational choice, and are therefore more confirming of the role of external facilitators and constraints on the individual, but also, that the data they describe, the narrations of the individual women, are often as, if not more, confirming of individualist accounts of agency, constraints and choice. This can be attributed to the fact that individuals do indeed possess and experience agency in the face of such external constraints; the sense of personal autonomy and effectiveness is central to experience. The irreducible nature of this is clarified within individualised accounts, and stands as a corrective to any assumption that women experience complete passivity in the face of any kind of external force.

This seeming paradox can also be attributed to the inability of individual girls and women to identify a collective shape to their gendered experience, the shape that may become manifest to researchers when hearing a critical mass of narrated experiences.

What these researchers have drawn attention to, is the belief that structural positioning, and subsequent differences in individual characteristics and agential properties, better explains segregation than independent or pre-existing socialisation, behaviour, traits or preferences. Kanter, of course, made this point best in *Men and Women of the Corporation* (1977), where she highlights the relationship between the structuring of work opportunities along key power axes, and the ordering of individuals' and groups' behaviour in relation to where they are placed within and in relation to these opportunities. Work-related resource allocation is, therefore, largely a determination of formal structural relationships and informal alliances (ibid.: 247). Kanter therefore warned against 'individual models of behaviour', in which it is assumed that 'the factors producing inequities at work are somehow carried inside the individual person' (ibid.: 261). Indeed, Kanter argues that when women are treated the same way as men in employment situations, and have access to the same resources and opportunities, they will behave in the same way. Hence, there is nothing intrinsically 'female' about their work-related values, approach and aims. They will want the same things when they perceive that these are available to them in the same way that they are available to men. The findings here chime with another early piece of qualitative research. Gerson's (1985) study concluded that women who had positive experiences of paid employment were pulled into this sphere and those who had negative experiences were pushed back into the domestic realm.

Despite this emphasis, a finding of considerable interest across several studies is the identification of a highly agential group. Importantly, in terms of the latter, this group is decidedly *not* simply oriented to work, as Hakim might suppose, but can be identified as very effective in combining work and domestic responsibilities. These women seem to be able to better actualise their 'preferences' than others. People who can more effectively plan their futures and have social support to do so, as well as the capacity to reinvent themselves when their plans do not go smoothly, are also highlighted as more likely to progress to making 'successful' employment decisions. Although it is sometimes indicated that a more 'planful' trajectory may in actual fact merely be a middle-class artefact, and a potentially constricting one at that, the imputation of a higher agency, and therefore freer group of women, is maintained. Such women are more likely to select professional work, to pursue it more planfully and to seek adjustments in the face of other calls on their time that do not always mean inevitable compromises in the work arena. Perhaps counter-intuitively, they are more likely to perceive structural constraint and discrimination in their paths.

Also of significant interest is the identification of key transitional periods, such as those from school to work, and 'epiphany' or 'fateful' moments, such as bereavement, motherhood, personal experience of discrimination. These are emphasised as times when the further pursuance of a particular career, or even of any career, can be consolidated or changed, in a relatively quick space of time, and sometimes in a context of new, unusual or unpredictable experience. The successful negotiation of these periods, in which the targeted outcome is met, is linked to individuals high in agency.

The literature review underscores the dangers of developing 'one size fits all' analyses and terminology for understanding female occupational choice, especially in relation to the role of the domestic sphere, but also in relation to women with very different occupational interests. It does, however, point to shared experiences that are not best understood by overly disaggregating the women into analytical sub-groups.

Perceptions of 'choice'

What prevailing concepts of choice emerge from the literature reviewed here, and in Chapter 2? The first point to make is that the conceptual and practical role of occupational 'choice' is still very unclear in much of this research. Some research argues that we best understand occupational decision-making in terms of individuals freely selecting from a full range of alternatives, regardless of their gender. Other research emphasises that, on the contrary, we should understand decisions are strongly determined and circumscribed, and an individual's gender, for whatever reason, is key in determining how they select jobs but also how jobs select them. Here the terminology of 'choice' is jettisoned in favour of discourses of 'occupational fate' (Anderson 1998: 146; see also, Allen 1999: 323; Rowe & Snizek 1995).

As has been seen in Chapter 2, it is important to identify the assumed prime causes of occupational segregation, as these can be revealing of the general understanding of how and when choice occurs, and how choices are linked to correlative outcomes, even if neither causes nor outcomes are explicitly stated. It is clear that 'brainsex' theories posit biological origins as prime causes. A hidden hand of 'natural' differences is also detectable in much of preference theory's contribution. If markets are rational and fair, and individuals unfettered, where else can we look for a cause of the current structuring of segregation than to innate, or at least fixed, differences between men and women? Some difficulty is produced here in terms of developing adequate explanations of the actions of individuals who make up the part of the variance *not* explained in the research models underpinning much individualist research, or areas of segregation where preferences and outcomes cannot be statistically associated very clearly. In terms of the latter, the explanations of horizontal segregation are patchy and unclear. DeLeire and Levy (2001) have argued that this phenomenon could be linked to natural differences *or* social factors. Hakim (2002) assumes that it must be explained with reference to 'benign' social factors. Such a claim fails to address potentially critical differences between women who choose typical work roles, as well as between these women and those who choose atypical roles, which is odd given her arguments against unwarranted presumptions of female homogeneity in the research field. By the same token, preference models do not fully engage with the overall pattern of segregation as elaborated by researchers such as Blackburn and Jarman (2006), in which women's labour force participation is demonstrated to be skewed against manual work and the very lowest occupational levels.

In both these areas, and despite the model's emphasis on female agency, there seems to be little attempt to account for women's selection away from certain forms of work. In terms of the latter area, it has to be said that there is only a limited attempt in the literature to account for female de-selection of manual and low-skilled work.

Anderson, in her discussion of choice discourses, has argued that we need to keep a clear analytical distinction between individuals exercising occupational choice – in an unfettered manner – and those who are merely occupational incumbents (1998: 144). In this she is joined by Hammond and Hammond (2002), who argue we should differentiate between 'high-choice' situations and 'low-choice' ones, the former relating to decisions where the selector has total autonomy to act in accordance with innate preferences, and the latter to situations where externalities are distorting these preferences. These possible adjustments could not save the preference model, however, as they merely defer questions as to the origins of choices as well as precisely how and why some individuals become fettered and end up in jobs they have not freely chosen. Moreover, although the general sweep of gendered employment patterns are all broadly comparable across a variety of different national contexts, any significant variation would seem to point to such attitudes being more a function of social interpretation, and amplification, rather than being genuine *reflections* of biological difference.

More socially focused approaches contest the significance of any 'natural' differences, arguing that the prime causes of segregation are to be found in social structures and processes that are either external to the individual, or have become internalised within it. These positions, however, often fail to explain how some girls and women buck the trend and select gender-atypical work, or manage to overcome constraints and achieve unexpected and unusual occupational levels. Assuming that girls and women experience choice, but within a seriously constrained framework, is more persuasive, but questions are still begged as to why some women seem to rise above any expected trajectory than we would expect them to take given their social positioning.

The critique of models prioritising 'choice', we should remember, is not only on the basis that they ignore, or are too optimistic about, external constraints, but also that they may be too optimitistic about the capacity for individual agency, and fail to acknowledge our limited understanding of it. What is it about the experience of some women that cuts across the influence of socially produced constraints? The identification of groups or individuals seemingly higher in agency is an important starting point, and the further identification of associated background factors, such as class position, and parental and school support for achievement, is also welcome, but this needs further scrutiny. This is equally the case with the identification of 'epiphany' or 'fateful' moments. What makes some individuals crumble at these times, and others utilise them to achieve an altered, but equally 'preferred' set of life goals? We need to move beyond voluntaristic explanations towards more detailed accounts of what agency is and how it is developed or thwarted.

Types of assumed prime causes also influence views on whether occupational segregation is seen as problematic or not, and whether and how we frame the necessity and nature of any possible solutions. Those positing a strong biological basis think segregation patterns are a natural reflection of innate differences and specifically argue against their problematisation, and against any proposed corrections. For those assuming over-riding social origins, society and organisations need to change (Kanter 1977: 261).

Eclectic, multi-causal models or those that shirk identifying prime causes, would seem to be a problem. Although sometimes this approach generates a complex and sophisticated model of gender and segregation, the issue of male advantage still requires attention and explanation. In relation to occupational choice, research not only needs to explain why women prefer certain roles and sectors, and not only how these preferences are linked to occupational disadvantage, but also why. Anderson has pointed out that the discourse of occupational choice involves an inherent presumption that people are free to choose, and implies 'some kind of deficiency on the part of those who appear to restrict their selection to specific fields' (1998: 144), an assumption which clearly dovetails with a resistance to identifying deficiencies in the 'system'. What emerges from multi-causal models and that remains important, however, is the positing of an ongoing choice process. In this vein, Anderson has commented that: 'Choice cannot be considered simply as one event occurring at a particular point in time'. Instead it can only 'be seen meaningfully within the context of a person's entire social experiences' (ibid.: 146; see also, O'Brien & Fassinger 1993). It is in view of this complexity that Anderson offers the term 'occupational fate' as an 'alternative label' (Anderson 1998: 146):

> Fate is usually viewed as predetermined which is partly appropriate when used in the present context as we cannot control our sex . . . nor can we intervene in how we are socialised . . . also in line with most instances when fate is applied to the human condition there is invariably as aspect of self-determination . . . the term may not incorporate the degree of self-determination that people bring to occupational choice and in this sense is not wholly appropriate . . . however if we conceptualise a continuum from choice to fate, the reality of occupational behaviour is closer to the fate end of the scale.
>
> (ibid.: 146)

Such terminology is surely as laden with discursive impetus as the language of 'choice', however. The term 'occupational fate' is usually invoked in relation to groups that have notable disadvantages over and above their gender, such as health issues (Eckstein 1978; Vogel, Bell,

Blumenthal, Neumann & Schuttler 1988). Its use does more than convey constriction, and sidesteps the necessity to address the issue of prime causes, and again, specifically the issue of male advantage.

A further note on method

All of the research here, as well as that which forms the basis of this book and is examined in the following three chapters, utilise qualitative approaches to data collection and analysis. Just as quantitative approaches have been criticised, qualitative approaches have been subject to scrutiny, especially in the past, although even now they are often read as having less authority. Where criticisms have been raised, they are on the basis that this approach allegedly lacks precision, objectivity, repeatability and generalisability. Quantitative methods have always been represented as being substantially different from qualitative counterparts in that their focus and concern is the acquisition of precise knowledge, precisely codified and therefore comparable knowledge, precise factors, precise steps for the researcher to take, precise conclusions. Quantitative approaches are designed to produce testable, replicable findings, which are more a result of objective enquiry than subjective interpretation. By contrast, qualitative methods, precisely by being so obviously bound up with the processes of meaning production on the part of the participants *and* the researchers, produce fuzzier, less accurate and less disinterested truths.

Some qualitative researchers have defended their techniques on the basis that they are accessing somehow essentially *more* truthful accounts than those that merely produce associations between, say, the superficial expressions of preference in survey data, and subsequent employment outcomes. There is a long-standing tradition of deploying qualitative approaches to elicit and explore data relating to gender issues, and this can be directly linked to the debates about the relative merits of quantitative and qualitative methodologies. One important strand of this tradition is the development of feminist methodology as distinct from mainstream social enquiry, which privileges its own form of enquiry above others (see, for example, Oakley 1981; Stanley & Wise 1983). In their various guises, feminist methodologists have assumed that women's consciousness and experience has been largely ignored in mainstream social enquiry (Smith 1974; Stanley & Wise 1993). A consequence of this marginalisation, and of a patriarchal gender system more generally, is that social enquiry lacks accurate knowledge about women's experiences, as do male researchers. Challenges to the 'scientific' and 'objective' claims of quantitative techniques are made on the grounds that traditional approaches are only accounting for the distorted semi-experience of being male.

In some cases, the ontological and epistemological independence of women's consciousness is assumed, and distinct feminist methods are justified on the grounds that only this approach will access this consciousness effectively (Stanley & Wise 1983; Harding 1986). Standpoint theories take their lead from Hegelian understandings of the master–slave dialectic, and the assumption that 'slavish' consciousness is always able to be more knowing than masterful consciousness due to its ability to recognise its master's experience *and* its own, as well as the necessity of so doing. It has been specifically argued that accessing women's accounts produces more 'objective' (less partial) forms of social knowledge (Harstock 1983; Harding 1986; Harding and Norburg 2005).

Feminist standpoint theory has been rejected by postmodernist feminist writers, among others who have claimed that all knowledge is partial, a privileged position is unobtainable, and any denial of this constitutes an attempt to invoke an epistemological *deus ex machina*, or 'God-trick' (Haraway 1988) in order to shore up a particular and partial truth-claim.

As standpoint theory has developed, however, it has moved away from the more 'problematic modernist assumptions about truth and reality' (Harding 1997: 382), but maintains an argument for a recognition that 'not all social situations are equally good ones from which to be able to see how the social order works. Dominant groups have more interests than those they dominate in not formulating and in excluding questions about how social relations and nature "really work"' (ibid.: 384). In doing so standpoint theory has come closer to the position of the critics of its earlier incarnations. Critics have, nevertheless, argued that standpoint theory still requires the drawing of distinctions between accounts of the dominated and the dominators, which amounts to an essentially arbitrary exercise, and one that can only be undertaken on the basis of political commitment to one side or the other, rather than either's intrinsic veracity (Hekman 1997: 400).

The precise delineation of what feminist methodology is ideally comprised of cannot be addressed fully here, but what is clear is that it generally involves the use of qualitative, participatory techniques, a challenge to the power relationships between the researcher and the researched, and overt political engagement. What is of particular relevance here is the widespread claim that qualitative techniques, and direct engagement with individuals and their accounts, comprise a privileged methodological approach.

Feminist methodologists are not alone in claiming this; many 'mainstream' qualitative methodologists have made similar assumptions. In the 1970s, Howard Becker noted sociologists' 'penchant for exposé . . . the intention . . . to get "the real story" . . . hidden behind the platitude of any group . . . to discount heavily any expressions of the "official ideology"' (1970: 103). Van Maanen has suggested that the assumption that the qualitative approach automatically produces more truthful data presupposes that direct contact in itself is enough to guarantee what he calls 'immaculate perception', a less biased and distorted account than would have been produced by other research methods (cited in Hammersley 1990: 23). Similarly, feminist writers maintain that 'interviews can give a deeper, more complex knowledge of the issues. . . . For example, if we are faced with a chocolate, we can see from the outside that it is a chocolate, however we must delve deeper to discover whether it is hard or soft, has a hazelnut or an orange centre, and so on. It is this inner knowledge that is gained by interviews' (Westmarland 2001: 8).

Hammersley has identified this general form of defence of qualitative research as indicative of underlying realist assumptions about the nature of the social world and how we might access it (1992: 44). In acknowledgement of this, a few words need to be said here on the assumed truth-claim of the qualitative accounts discussed earlier in this chapter, as well as those that provide a key part of the empirical data discussed in the following three chapters of this book. The selection of directly accessed individual accounts of gendered occupational choice are not here taken as providing a definitive statement on the subject. They are, however, seen as providing critical information of a neglected sort, and from a neglected source.

Language is central to the processes whereby individuals and groups interpret the world. Listening to, and reading, participants' accounts constitutes an attempt to map the web of meanings they give to various phenomena and experiences. When people talk, they do not neutrally reflect the world, but re-present it in ways that have developed in the context of the culture they are part of. Individuals produce and maintain contradictory truths because they adopt different positions in different contexts in the course of their lives. Among other things, the speech content of participants is comprised of what Mills (1940) called 'a vocabulary of motives' and, as such, should not be expected to ultimately point to a single coherent version of experience that the researcher can identify and expose. In accessing women's accounts in relation to their occupational choice-making, researchers cannot, and *need* not, make the claim that they are accessing more truthful accounts than would be produced by asking male employers what women want from their work. It may well be true that the disadvantaged or 'slavish' consciousness of women within a patriarchal gender regime will ensure access to a fuller perspective on social phenomena insofar as, in relation to their gender, they can more readily appreciate both the perspectives of the advantaged and disadvantaged. We have no epistemological grounds for underpinning this claim with the legitimacy of a 'Truth', however. Deciding we want to privilege one account over another is an ethical and political decision, and a no less powerful and committed one for that.

We do not need to make decisions about the relative veracity of competing accounts that emerge from a particular individual or whole samples of participants, and this would not represent the most fruitful or interesting approach to such data. It is not necessary to claim that participants do or even can express the 'real' or univocal version of their experience, in the light of which other versions can be jettisoned, and that such a version is accessible to the expert or neutral researcher's gaze. This gaze is far from neutral, as can be seen in the discussion of the qualitative accounts earlier in this chapter. Participants' accounts are subject to partiality, contradiction and change. Equally, it would be a mistake to assume automatically that some groups of individuals, usually those disenfranchised or disaffected in some manner, express the truth about some social phenomenon by virtue of their marginalisation. Moreover, we cannot assume that particular expressed meanings neatly dovetail with particular positions of power and interest. The most 'critical' perspective on social phenomena is not automatically the most truthful, and cannot be assumed to be held by the most disenfranchised. Manifest interests, material or otherwise, are not simply mirrored in descriptions of evaluations of experiences. Informants have access to a variety of ways of speaking and representing their experiences and they often adopt positions which seem mutually exclusive, or out of step with descriptions and forms of representation that a more superficial appraisal of their position would lead one to expect them to adopt. The association of qualitative techniques with the revelation of deeper truths needs to be considered in this context. A better metaphor for accessing different levels of data using different methods is perhaps dissecting an onion rather than a chocolate. If a survey may be said to peel off an outer layer of the onion, interviewing may peel off an inner layer. The point is, however, that the process does not end with the revelation of a kernel of something essentially more 'onion' than previous layers. In peeling, or delving, we are not automatically getting nearer to a truth. As we have seen, some of the findings from quantitative research have been both compelling *and* confirmed within qualitative studies. What the process of accessing more layers does, however, is produce a fuller, and therefore arguably more *revealing* perspective. In this sense, female participants' directly accessed accounts[4] are not qualitatively different, in terms of their truth-claim, from accounts provided by other sources; women's accounts not qualitatively different in term of their truth-claim, from men's. The trump card of qualitative techniques, however, is that they can justifiably claim to reveal *more* versions or aspects of the truths about social phenomena. In doing so, they problematise the very notion that a primary truth can exist, while, arguably, simultaneously producing a more accurate and reliable representation of the structure of complex social experience.

The aim of utilising the qualitative method of interviewing here is to identify the most significant recurring themes and accounts which emerge from girls' and women's descriptions of complex phenomena, and to offer a coherent explanation as to how and why they co-exist. It aims to identify, where possible, which accounts are generally correlated to which interests, which accounts are privileged above others in which contexts, and, ultimately, how this privileging is related to the distribution of resources, material or otherwise.

Introduction to the data presentation

The data which are presented in this book derive from a long-term[3] research project which aimed to elicit narrative accounts from women and girls about their career aspirations, interests and choices. The project comprised two 'sub-projects', with two distinct data-collection periods centred on different occupational foci. The first[4] focused on female attitudes towards the traditionally 'male' occupation of firefighting, and the second[5] on the 'female' occupation of teaching.

The entire project produced individual and focus group interviews with 186 women and girls. The participants fell into three groups. First, a large group of girls and women were interviewed to canvas opinion on their own occupational aspirations, but also in relation to these two different employment areas. They were studying either at secondary school, college or university at the time of their participation, and were therefore still formulating their occupational choices. Women and girls in full-time education were one of the key target groups of participants after a number of identified features of this group emerged from the wide-ranging literature review. It has been claimed that adolescents – young adult females (from middle-school years through to the transition to university) – live through the most critical points in their overall gender-socialisation development during this period, during which they are more likely to represent themselves at their most conservative and conformist in terms of their gender identity. The claim is that they simultaneously identify possible future occupations at this time, and begin ruling out others and/or make educational choices that circumscribe their occupational choices, and that this initial orientation towards some roles and away from others is not easily be jettisoned later on in life (Anderson 1998; Colley 1998; Lightbody & Durndell 1998; McQuaid, Bond & Robinson 2004; Miller *et al.* 2004; HMSO 2005; Woodfield 2006b).

The second group of interviewees was female firefighters and prospective firefighters, and the third group was teachers or prospective teachers at primary- or secondary-school level. These supplementary target groups were identified for interview because they represented women who had already selected either an occupation associated with men, or one associated with women, and who were in a position to provide an account of this choice retrospectively, as well as a narrative of their subsequent employment experiences.

Firefighting represented a clear example of a male-typed occupation for women, within the UK and elsewhere, and one that has strong associations with many of the characteristics commonly associated with male working environments and with men: risk, danger, the requirement of physical strength and prowess; its paramilitary internal structure, organisation and image. School teaching was selected as it is now a female-typed occupation within the UK and elsewhere, and one that is overtly associated with many of characteristics more generally linked to gender-typical work for women: a 'safe', 'clean' environment, with a role reliant on good interpersonal and/or caring skills. It was also identified by a substantial amount of those participants still in full-time education as a possible future career.

A total of 12 group interviews comprising between five and seven participants in full-time education were undertaken: four with school girls aged approximately 16, three with school girls aged between 17 and 20 and five with university students (with all but a handful aged between 18 and 22). An additional group interview was undertaken with nine students on a BTec *Public Services* course. These were supplemented with 20 individual interviews with girls and women in full-time education (total number (N) = 97). Interviewees in full-time education studied at ten different educational institutions in Sussex and the surrounding area. These varied in size, catchments and student type. Interviewees were, however, recruited on a convenience sample basis, with some conducted by teachers known to them and a former teacher turned careers development advisor[6]. Interviewees were offered small inducements to take part in the project, such as a lip gloss, some eye shadow or chocolate.

One group interview, along with 15 individual interviews, was undertaken with female firefighters. Five further individual interviews with actively prospective firefighters i.e. those in the process of the occupation's lengthy and time-consuming application procedure, and whose details as committed and known applicants were provided by the Fire Service (N = 22). These women had often applied several times to the Service and had identified the firefighter role as their primary career aim, and were dedicated to fulfilling it. Their comments are discussed alongside those of actual firefighters here, although distinctions between the two types of women are flagged where warranted. Participants in the firefighter group were recruited via Fire Service referral lists, as well as snowballing and convenience sampling. They were aged between 19 and 40, and were offered no inducements for undertaking interviews (although in the case of in-post full-time firefighters, they were offered the opportunity of undertaking them during working hours).

Thirteen group interviews with employed teachers were also undertaken. These were supplemented by ten individual interviews with teachers, and two group interviews with prospective teachers (N = 5). As with the prospective firefighter group, these latter interviewees were individuals whose commentary can be included in with the employed teachers group, due to their strong similarities and the fact that all were already working in educational roles within schools, were undergoing teacher training, and applying for teaching roles (N = 67)[7]. The group interviews for teachers comprised fewer participants, the average being four. These interviewees were recruited via snowballing and convenience sampling and from a wide range of primary and secondary schools and colleges in the Sussex area. They were aged between 24 and 62, with approximately 50 per cent being under the age of 45. Teachers were offered a bottle of wine for undertaking the interviews.

All interviews were semi-structured insofar as they were guided by a skeletal list of questions addressing areas of interest, and all designed to elicit data on key concepts around careers and career decision-making. Some interviews focused more specifically on gender-typical work and some on gender-atypical work. Example questions for those in full-time education are:

> Can you tell me what your favourite subjects are at school or college, and why?
> Can you talk to me about the kind of jobs you think you want to do? What are you looking for in a career?
> What would you like to achieve at work? What level would you like to work at?
> What factors have most influenced your choice?
> What are the typical kinds of jobs that young women your age are aiming to secure?
> What would you like to achieve from your working life?
> Can you give me your general impressions of firefighters/teachers?
> What kind of person would consider working as something like a firefighter/teacher do you think?
> What kinds of barriers, if any, do you think women would face if they wanted to do this kind of work or something similar?

The development of interviews was often, however, participant-driven, with the result that some areas identified in advance as being of interest were not fully addressed, while other areas were covered in more depth than anticipated. For the participants in full-time education, as is indicated above, guiding questions covered a range of topics including personal preferences and perceptions of personal skills, views on what particular careers involved, views on gender-typical (including teaching) and atypical work (particularly firefighting) and key influences on job choice. If deemed appropriate, participants were prompted to give some areas more consideration (such as the tasks involved in the firefighter role). For those in the firefighter or teacher groups, the interviews were also semi-structured, but were, as might be expected, more focused around the selected occupation, the attractions it held for them, and the subsequently experienced advantages and disadvantages of working within it. Guiding questions included:

> Can you tell me what your favourite subjects were at school or college, and why?
> What do you think are your best employment qualities?
> Can you talk about when you first thought about teaching/firefighting as a career?

Can you talk to me about your impressions of teachers/firefighters before you decided you wanted to become one?
Can you talk to me through how you became a teacher/firefighter?
Now you know more about the job, would you say that your initial impressions were based on reality?
What qualities does someone need to do teaching/firefighting well?

The duration of group interviews varied and was between 30 and 105 minutes. Individual interviews tended to be shorter – of between 20 and 60 minutes. It was the case that interviews with younger school-age women in the education group tended to be shorter, and often required more skill on the part of the interviewer to elicit information. All interviews were transcribed and were analysed to identify recurring themes and motifs. The themes selected for discussion and development here were identifiable across a number of informants' accounts, unless otherwise specified. Verbatim quotations are selected because they crystallise and illustrate such themes.

In the following data presentation chapters, all verbatim quotations are italicised. Those over two lines in length are indented with attached identifiers. Those under two lines in length, including 'snippets', have generally been kept within the text, and do not have identifiers attached, unless several over one line in length are cited together, in which case they are indented as multiple extracts, and do have identifiers. In the case of participants in full-time education, identifiers indicate whether the comment was derived from an individual interview (II) or group interview (GI), and the type of educational institution attended by the individual whose words are quoted (PS = primary school, SS = secondary school, C = college, HE = university[8]). In the case of teachers, the same system is used, although with the added identifier for teacher (T) and (TT) for trainee teacher interpolated between interview type and institution type. In the case of firefighters, identifiers indicate type of originating interview and whether the interviewee is a prospective firefighter (PFF), retained firefighter (RFF) or in-post firefighter (FF)[9]. In the case of teachers, Interviewers comments are always in bold. In the case of extracts with multiple speakers, each is allocated an alphabetical letter to indicate the chronology of their comments.

Extracts are as they were spoken, with omissions and editorial comments clearly indicated in the usual manner. The exception to this is the editing out of phrases such as *'I know'*, *'I mean'*, *'sort of'*, *'kind of'* and so on, of which there were many. No information about the occupations being discussed was provided by interviewers to participants during the course of the interviews.

It remains to be said that, as a consequence of the sampling strategies deployed, it is possible that participants are unrepresentative. In the case of those in full-time education, although they were recruited through a range of educational institutions, the very act of agreeing to be interviewed may indicate something unknown but significant about their background. In the case of participants in the teacher and fire-fighter groups, their class background, where it was mentioned, would seem to have been varied, but, as it was not the focus of discussion for the purposes of the project, data that did emerge were not utilised. It could further be argued that the selection of occupational roles examined in detail – firefighters and teachers – is odd inasmuch as they are asymmetrically placed on the Standard Occupational Classification scale (firefighting being classified as an Associate Professional and technical occupation and teaching a Professional occupation). Certainly, awareness of this difference should be borne in mind when reading the rest of this book. It is hoped, however, that this asymmetry has proved to be a fruitful one for exploring several themes identified in the literature review, and that it produces some interesting findings of its own.

4
Women and Non-Traditional Work: A Case Study of Firefighting

Introduction

The chapter presents issues and themes that arose from the data relating to girls' and women's expressed attitudes to undertaking an atypical, or non-traditional occupational role. Although some generic commentary on atypical employment will be discussed, the chapter will focus on the views and feelings about such employment through the lens of commentary on the specific case study occupation of firefighters. The views of participants in full-time education will be explored first within each section, before moving on to the views of prospective firefighters or those already in a firefighter post. The chapter provides an initial context for assessing how the commentary of participants relates to externally verified 'facts' about the firefighter role.

Firefighting – official statistics

Firefighters are employed in either a 'wholetime' or 'retained' role. 'Wholetime' firefighters are employed on a full-time basis, and 'retained', or 'retained duty system' (RDS), firefighters are those who are contracted by the Fire Service to be available for duty for agreed periods of time, but can otherwise take full-time or part-time employment elsewhere (DCLG 2006:35). There are 33,515 wholetime firefighters in England and Wales, and over 14,029 retained firefighters (DCLG 2006: Appendix 2). Firefighters are overwhelmingly male, and largely white. The first female firefighter in the UK joined East Sussex Brigade in 1976. In 2003, however, men still accounted for 98.3 per cent of wholetime firefighters and 97 per cent of retained in 2003, and 97.8 per cent of wholetime and 96.7 per cent of retained in 2005. Although these figures signal a small increase in the proportions of women in the firefighter role, the Service are working towards a Home Office established target set in 2000, which asked that the percentage of women firefighters rise to 15 per cent by 2009 in the context of a general request for the Service to 'modernise' following the 'Bain Report' (2002). Ethnic minorities accounted for 3 per cent of wholetime firefighters in 2005 and 0.5 per cent of retained posts (DCLG 2006: 14).

The salary level of a wholetime trainee firefighter is currently £19,918, rising to £26,548[1] once they are fully qualified and competent (after four years). Retained salaries are roughly 10 per cent of these rates (Fire Service 2006). This pay, once achieved, does not rise further without promotion – there are no further increments to the scale. Firefighters can make themselves available for overtime. These rates follow a long pay dispute and review which ended in 2003, and during which some of the interview data was collected. Before the end of the dispute, the rate of pay was approximately £21,500 for a fully qualified firefighter (Hansard 2002; Fire Service 2005). The salary level of an Area Manager who is fully competent is £50,775.

No formal educational qualifications are required to join the Fire Service as a firefighter, although passing written and practical tests forms part of a battery of entrance requirements, the most stringent of which are the physical tests. These include: the shuttle run/bleep test, ladder tests, dead weight tests, breathing apparatus tests, hose running tests.[2] These tests are designed to screen out vertigo and claustrophobia, and ensure manual dexterity, basic fitness and strength, co-ordination and stamina (Fire Service 2005).

The Fire Service targets the following personal qualities and attributes: commitment to diversity and integrity, openness to change, confidence and resilience, ability to work with others, effective communication, commitment to development, problem solving, situational awareness and commitment to excellence (Fire Service 2005).

In 2004–2005, there were 20 applicants for every firefighter post that became available (DCLG 2006: 12). Successful applicants attend a training school for an initial 20 weeks of intensive instruction, but the Service sees training as an ongoing issue, and there are now Integrated and Personal Development Systems in place for each firefighter to explore opportunities for career development and promotion. Wholetime firefighters work a 42-hour week and their shift system comprises two day shifts, followed by two night shifts, followed by four days without working. This means that each working week starts a day later than was the case in the previous week. Home Office attempts to 'modernise' the Service have also targeted the shift system as not family-friendly and have asked individual Fire and Rescue Services to consider offering alternatives, although there is some strong resistance to this among firefighters, as there is against other key Bain recommendations.

In 2004–2005, 2590 injuries were sustained by firefighters in the course of duty, of which 41 injuries were 'major' (DCLG 2006: 29). There were five deaths as a result of operational duties, representing 0.01 per cent of firefighters. Just over 1 per cent of firefighting personnel retired on grounds of ill health (ibid.: 13). The shift days lost to sickness are around 10 per annum per wholetime firefighter (ibid.: 25). Firefighting has been ranked the 23rd most hazardous occupation (in terms of mortality figures) in the UK, with fishing, seafaring, forestry work, window cleaning, lorry driving and some railway and construction work substantially ahead of it (Roberts 2002).

Senior fire officers are classified in the top category of the Standard Occupational Classification system,[3] 'Managers and Senior Officials' (major group one). The standard firefighter role is classified as an 'Associate professional and technical occupation' (major group three). Also classified within this category are building and civil engineering technicians, draughtspersons, architectural technologists and town planning technicians, nurses, midwives, medical radiographers, occupational therapists, speech and language therapists, artists, journalists, dancers, musicians, producers, directors, sports coaches, personnel officers and marketing associated professionals.

Participants' accounts

Choosing gender-atypical employment

Education group

Very few girls and women in the education group proactively indicated that they had targeted what they identified as gender-atypical employment as a possible career direction. Commonly, we remember, gender-atypical areas for women are those with a male to female ratio that is equal or greater than 3:1. The nine interviewees who were undertaking a Business and Technology Education Council (BTEC) qualification course in Public Services nearly all proactively indicated a willingness to consider gender-atypical careers, and were generally positive about doing so. This course was designed to cater to 'intelligent students with a practical/physical outlook' who are considering a career in one of the Public Services, and tends to be physical in orientation (Woodfield 2003), and so these students' positive view of atypical work was unsurprising. Only three other participants indicated such work as probable, or even possible, choices – and these indications were all in relation to firefighting. One came at the start of an interview, with two more coming at the end of interviews, and as a direct result of the preceding discussion.

Gender-atypical employment was otherwise almost always understood among girls under the age of 18 to mean employment at the lower end of the occupational scale, and to denote manual, comparatively unskilled work: *'so you mean plumbing or something?'*; *'like a car mechanic or a builder?'* Work that is male-dominated at the top end of the occupational scale, such as senior posts in the financial services sector, managers, scientists, engineers and so on, was rarely independently raised, and related commentary indicated a lack of awareness of what such roles might involve:

> A: *I've got a friend who wants to be an engineer. I think it's quite impressive because, I don't want to sound patronising, but she is a girl, and I don't think they will have many female applicants, I don't know.*
>
> B: *What exactly do engineers do?*
>
> A: *Mechanical, civil*
>
> B: [with sarcasm] *Oh right, that's what confused me!* [laughter].
>
> A: *Anyway, I think it's good, going against the grain.* (GI, C)

This was less the case with students on degree programmes, but discussion of areas of more skilled work that were gender-atypical were only introduced by female students reading atypical subjects, such as physics or artificial intelligence.

Many participants were clear that the male-dominated environment of gender-atypical work raised issues for them. Many indicated a belief in their ability, if not a willingness, to undertake male-dominated work when specifically asked, and some indicated that this might present *'another sort of challenge to rise to, to prove that I could do it'*; *'I think I would want to succeed for the girls'*. The characterisation of gender-atypical employment as work that was not skilled or aspirational enough was a barrier for many, however:

Extract 1:

> *More boys seem to go straight from compulsory education into what they want to do, so they're more, like, 'manual' and they are happy with, have a clear idea about what they want to do and what they're good at . . . I don't*

actually know any girls considering manual though . . . I could never do a job like [that] *. . . that doesn't involve quite a lot of thinking. I get bored very easily and I couldn't do the same thing everyday or do boring things . . . I want to go quite far in life and I definitely don't want a job that leads to a dead end . . . Once you leave compulsory education, there's nowhere else to go and then you get your money at the end of the month and it's quite nice and that's it, so if you haven't got education, very much of it, then it puts an end to your career.* (II, C)

Extract 2:

I could never consider manual, menial work. (II, SS)

By contrast with themselves, boys were characterised as being more likely to have a *'laid-back'* attitude to their studies, to be less academic overall and to have a different set of life priorities, all of which meant they were more likely to end up in manual occupations. It was suggested that some areas of work, such as plumbing and building, had become male-dominated because boys were more likely to have *'settled'* for it, and on the basis of their different employment priorities, which were to *'earn money'*, and gain independence from parents at an earlier age.

Partcipants' commentary on girls and women who had targeted such employment was somewhat negative in nature:

I've got a friend who wants to join the army. She is really determined. She's not very academic or intelligent so she's very different, but really wants to do that. (GI, SS)

Another strong theme to emerge, however, was the anticipation that participants would not be willing to withstand discrimination on the basis of their gender, and that this might be more likely to occur in male-dominated occupations. Although some participants said that they found men *'more straightforward to get along with'*, and women more *'catty'*, *'bitchy'* and *'harder'*, this was very much a secondary observation in this group, and the fear of discrimination from men was far more dominant:

Extract 1:

There's no way that I could put up with prejudice and I think I'd be more likely to have it in a job with lots of men, so that would put me off. (GI, SS)

Extract 2:

> *As long as I didn't feel I was being discriminated against I could work in a male-dominated world. I wouldn't want to feel that I couldn't get promoted because I was a woman. I definitely couldn't work in a position like that.* (II, C)

In relation to discussions on the subject of male-dominated environments and discrimination, participants were more likely to introduce the idea that men might occupy senior positions within the workplace, although not that they were disproportionately likely to do so:

Extract 1:

> *My aunt used to be in a really high-powered position . . . just then this new man boss came in and it became much more sexually discriminatory and I really wouldn't want to think that men had put an end to my climb up the career ladder.* (II, C)

Firefighter group

This entire group shared a keen interest in physical activity. Without exception, all reported being physically very active and taking formal exercise regularly. They also reported that they had been keen from a young age to incorporate physical activity into their working lives if this were possible. Physical Education was cited as one of their favourite subjects at school, with most citing it as *the* favourite. Other subjects favoured were usually those not traditionally associated with girls: principally maths, but additionally geography and the sciences.

The clear trend was for most of this group to have hankered after a career with a significant component of physical activity, but also of public service and 'outside' work. Many had considered the armed forces to meet their desire for *'activity and action'*, although they also often stressed an antipathy for working for organisations whose core business was *'warfare'*; *'killing people'*. Others had considered the emergency services, with the occupation of choice usually being that of paramedic.

This group described their emerging possible range of occupations before orientating to the firefighter role as developing largely through social networks and by *'chance'* encounters, but also as matching pre-existing preferences for atypical work on their part. All knew a number of individuals in strongly male-dominated occupational roles, even if these were not women. Some saw television programmes or advertisements focused on a particular occupation that they then identified as possibilities. Others heard about possible careers via family or friends, who reportedly already understood their preferences.

The firefighter group claimed that their career decision-making was open to the possibility of non-traditional work as they were sure from a young age that they did not want to do something *'very traditional or girly'*, or *'something a bit rebellious'*, career-wise. They remembered being unhappy with expectations placed upon them that *'dictated'* they would follow a path into a work role associated with, and dominated by, women, and wanted *'a challenge'* that suited their history and persona:

> *I was raised to never to be afraid to have a go at anything, that everything was open to me. I had that confidence, self-reliance, to not be afraid and to have a go at everything. If I see a barrier I want to have a go at it.* (II, FF)

These interviewees were very comfortable with the idea of working in male-dominated environments, and many reported a positive preference for them. They cited problematic previous experiences with contrasting female-dominated environments, and female *'ways of interacting'* as the main reason, with the most common adjectives used to describe the latter being *'catty, bitchy'*:

> I *had worked as a chef and I found that really good because there were loads of men in the kitchen. I found I liked it and preferred it to areas where there were more women.* (GI, FF)

General images of firefighters and firefighting

Education group

The participants still in full-time education were asked to talk about their general impressions of firefighters, what images and words the role evoked. Strong, recurring themes emerged from the interviews. The most obvious of these focused on the *maleness* of firefighters, their physicality and sexuality:

What are your immediate impressions of firefighters?

Extract 1:

A: *Men*

B: *Men in uniform*

C: *Big strapping lads*

D: *They are well fit and wear uniforms* [laughter] *and it's the uniforms.*

E: *They have a lot of power to them.* (GI, S)

Extract 2:

Macho . . . strong. . . lads. (II, C)

Extract 3:

A: Gorgeous. Macho.

B: Big men, sexy. (GI, S)

Extract 4:

One of my friends had a sexual fantasies birthday party for her 16th and fireman was what everyone wanted to go as so everyone had to dress up as firemen. (GI, S)

Male firefighters were far more sexualised than men in other areas of uniformed work discussed. All but three of the group interviews, and several of the individual interviews, saw a mention of 'The Fireman's Calendar'[4] in connection with this theme.

This focus on firefighters' attractiveness formed part of a more general focus on their physical nature and on their physically based skills. The suggestion was repeatedly made that such skills, within the firefighter role, were possessed to the exclusion of non-physical, intellectual strengths, with the exception of the ability for '*quick*' and '*instinctive*' thinking:

Extract 1:

Brawn not brain. (GI, SS)

Extract 2:

None of them are particularly intellectual or educated. (GI, SS)

Extract 3:

Firefighters are not very academic. (GI, HE)

Further general images retained a focus on the physical, but also stressed the levels of commitment and altruism that the role required:

Extract 1:

Safety, security, manly, big and strong. Exciting, courageous and strong and have a nice big heart. (GI, SS)

Extract 2:

Sexy, do a good job, hardworking. (GI, SS)

The desire and ability of Firefighters to provide a major public service was admired by most commentary produced in the interviews. They were described as *'Knights in shining armour'* and *'self-sacrificing'*. In this respect, firefighters were viewed by the majority of participants as different to themselves, and from many other types of worker. Firefighters were presented as following a strong vocation, a key part of which was a demonstrable willingness to give and risk more of themselves in the course of their work than the average person:

Extract 1:

They are this amazing type of person. That they do the opposite of what you naturally want to do when you see a fire, a burning house. You naturally want to run away and they do the opposite for someone else. (II, SS)

Extract 2:

I see it attracting maybe different people actually. Maybe if it's the police force they are more, well, it is such a gross generalisation but maybe they are a bit more authoritarian, and maybe more conservative. I don't know what kind of person would be attracted to the fire service but I do see them as quite distinct. (GI, HE)

There was some ambivalence about this aspect of the firefighter role, however, with a few dissenting remarks within most group interviews. In these instances, the heroism of firefighters was viewed more cynically, and their 'calling' viewed as more instrumental.

Extract 1:

A: *Do you think about them being heroes? Do you think they join because they want to look like heroes or join because they are heroes?*

B: *I think probably want to look like heroes. That is probably a gross over-generalisation. I don't know.* (GI, HE)

Extract 2:

I don't get the impression that firemen do it because they think it's worthwhile . . . I think it's people who like to be active and they like the image of it . . . I don't really think of them as being caring that much. (GI, HE)

Extract 3:

> *Someone arrogant because they believe they've got the skills needed. They put themselves above other people. They've got to go in and save us. I suppose you need to be that arrogant. Maybe arrogance is not quite the right word. Sure of yourself.* (GI, C)

Participants held very exaggerated beliefs about the risks involved in firefighting, with some estimating mortality rates to be *'low, say around 30 per cent'*, and many estimating it to be *'around 10 per cent'*. They also estimated the amount of time spent on fighting fires to be substantial. There was, however, a significant awareness of 'backroom work' associated with the role. Participants used descriptive terms, such as *'mundane'*, *'menial'*, *'quite bland'*, *'uninteresting'* in their initial discussions of these non-firefighting aspects of the occupation.

An interwoven strand of commentary focused on the amount of 'leisure' or 'down' time that was built into firefighters' working day:

Extract 1:

> *They can't actually be out all the time so there must be a lot of time sitting round, drinking cups of tea* [laughter] *Ready to dash out.* (GI, SS)

Extract 2:

> *They spend a lot of time playing snooker, fitness.* (GI, HE)

Extract 3:

> *They sit in a room, don't they? Watching the telly.* (GI, SS)

The perceived amount of 'empty' time was linked in participants' comments to the lack of intellectual stimulation they associated with the role: *'Lots of time sitting round doing nothing and sleeping. They must be so bored'*; *'It's not very intellectually stimulating, well I can't imagine it can be'*. This was matched by the perception of a surfeit of physical activity of both healthy (*'lots of keep fit . . . all fire stations have a gym'*) and less healthy (*'they cook and eat a lot'*; *'they eat a lot of donuts'*) kinds.

As indicated above, all participants claimed firefighters were overwhelmingly male, with common estimates of female presence being around 1 per cent. The majority of commentary on firefighters' background also claimed that they came from 'manual', or 'working' class backgrounds, with some stress on the job presenting an opportunity for those from non-professional social backgrounds to do something *'respectable'*: *'Maybe from a poorer background and want to establish themselves in a profession'* (GI, HE). There was certainly a consensus that firefighters did not come from the middle classes as a rule, although some participants suggested that they could come from the *'lower middle'* classes. A variety of sub-themes emerged to underpin these general impressions. The first, again, echoed the comment on firefighters' physicality, and linked this to observations of likely class background and concomitant levels of education. Firefighters were said to come from state schools only, and to have left school at the earliest opportunity:

Extract 1:

> *Working class. It's to do with the activeness of it, if you like, that you don't do much paperwork.* (GI, SS)

Extract 2:

> *Well, if people have had that level of education, I might be wrong, would they want to go into that profession? I don't know. I suppose it brings me back to what I was thinking about maybe pay but also, I might be wrong, but more brawn than brain in that job. If you have someone highly educated, would they be attracted to a very physical job like that or would they want to do a job where they could get better pennies, education, use their brain more?* (GI, HE)

Extract 3:

> *Often middle class people come from families who are more academic, getting an education and going to university or something.* (II, S)

A further sub-theme to emerge in relation to the imputed origins of firefighters was the suggestion that the middle classes did not have to 'resort' to a job that involved risks, as they had the liberty to select something safer: *'I can't imagine someone middle class . . . because they've got money and can do what they want. They don't have to take that risk'*.

Just as a distinction had been made between 'intelligence' and 'quick wit' in the commentary, a further distinction was drawn between firefighters being *'trained'* rather than *'educated'*. It was overwhelmingly the case that physical skills were usually represented as basic and given. The level of training itself was therefore the subject of some discussion, with some participants comparing the role to what they perceived to be more 'skilled' occupations in this regard:

> *They get far less training than paramedics. You can be a firefighter in a number of weeks . . . I think it is really quite short . . . But you have to train for years to be a paramedic, I think.* (GI, HE)

From the 92 females interviewed who were still in full-time education, only two participants mentioned the possibilities of promotion with the Fire Service, and both of these bucked the general trend in saying they thought firefighters could be from any background, although both also confirmed the general expectation that people from different broad class positions would most likely be mapped onto different future occupational levels:

Extract 1:

> *That's the thing, you could be someone superior couldn't you? So I think . . . I thought firefighters came from every kind of background because I thought . . . maybe if you have more educated people, maybe they would go for the more senior jobs.* (GI, SS)

Extract 2:

> *Maybe . . . in the fire service there's not just one job. Isn't there different ranks you can have? . . . So there might be class differences between the jobs. Presumably there's a chief man, I don't know really!* (GI, C)

As well as explicit associations with class, participants also talked about their images of firefighters' families during these discussions. It was suggested that firefighters were likely to come from a *'big family so they always work as a unit'*, and that the occupation *'ran in families'*, with male children following in a male family member's footsteps.

A striking feature of the interview data on firefighters from the *education group* was the extent to which themes emerged in a decidedly uniform manner, indicating a degree of cultural prevalence, while, at the same time, the information on which they were based appeared to have no clear origin. Some participants proactively noted the lack of clarity around their information sources. Most did not, however, and needed prompting for commentary on this issue. The most common response to such prompts was baffled silence, more often than not followed by references to media imagery:

Extract 1:

Where do your general impressions come from?

A: *Exactly, I was thinking that.*

B: London's Burning, *television* stuff [laughter].

A: *Exactly.*

Has everyone seen this?

Several voices: *Yes*

B: *No ... Its ... ER for me. Carrie's girlfriend was a firefighter in ER.*

Where has yours come from?

D: London's Burning. *It's pure cultural stereotype because I know very little about how the Fire Service works.*

E: *I know nothing.* (GI, HE)

Extract 2:

My ideas would be based on what I see on TV. I don't know any firemen so it's purely what I see on TV – images what I see in newspapers, on TV. (GI, SS)

Extract 3:

I am saying this but I don't actually know anything about the Fire Service other than what I've seen on TV! (GI, C)

Extract 4:

A: London's Burning

B: *Although they do say that's really realistic.* (GI, SS)

As well as fictional portrayals, participants cited media coverage of firefighters involved in both a major global event and an important national event as key sources of information: The US World Trade Centre attacks, and the UK Firefighters' pay dispute.

Many remarked that they had not consciously thought about the role of the firefighter before 2001. Most indicated that their subsequent reflections had helped shape a very positive image of the role, but also underscored the risks firefighters took in the course of undertaking a crucial public service:

Extract 1:

> *I never actually thought about it before. Very brave. (GI, SS)*

Extract 2:

> *Just so heroic. (II, SS)*

Extract 3:

> *A lot of confusion, a lot of people died. Smoke, everything . . . people running away and while they were doing that – running away – the fire crews and ambulance crews were running towards it, so like, while everyone was running away, the fire crews were running towards it. . . . They were going that way and everyone else was going that way . . . they never gave up. (GI, C)*

Some participants emphasised again at this point that they felt firefighters were highly committed to their role, that it was not simply a job to most of them but represented a central part of their identity, and something they were unlikely to '*clock off*' from:

Extract 1:

> *I think of September 11th and them being really brave and even if they weren't at work or scheduled to work they came and helped. (GI, SS)*

Extract 2:

> *It's like that one that was out in Bali . . . He was on holiday and a bomb happened and he spent his holiday helping save people's lives and he saved an Australian woman by massaging her heart for two hours while they were waiting for medical help to arrive. (GI, C)*

Extract 3:

> *It's not the same as another job. They are being paid to risk their lives and if there is something like that they go into the building knowing they are not going to come out. (GI, HE)*

Again, however, there was a countertrend in the commentary, albeit from a minority. Some participants suggested in particular that too much had been made of the role of firefighters in the September 11th rescue operation:

Extract 1:

> *I don't mean to demean it but it was their job. (GI, SS)*

Extract 2:

I thought the media neglected the ambulance and police service in the coverage. (GI, HE)

Extract 3:

I got fed up of all the hero worship . . . it linked them [firefighters] in my head with all that horrible . . . bless America stuff . . . all American nice boys. (GI, HE)

Extract 4:

Did most of the Firefighters not lose their lives because they went against orders or something? (GI, SS)

The coverage of September 11th was also, for some, a reinforcer of images of the Service as male-dominated: 'Weren't they all men again?. . . I didn't see any women'; 'Weren't there any women firefighters?' 'There were no women on programmes I watched'.

Information and images relating to the UK firefighters' pay dispute was also a source of divided impressions and opinion, with the majority again voicing positive support. Despite the coverage, participants under the age of 18 provided estimates suggesting that firefighters' annual salary fell between £11,000 and £22,000, with the majority of estimates falling at the lower end of this scale. Most of these participants however, professed complete ignorance of the occupation's salary levels:

A: *I think they should get paid more.*

You think they should get paid more?

B: *Hmm . . . Yes*

C: *But we don't actually know how much they DO get paid!* (GI, SS)

The legitimacy of the firefighters' pay claim was frequently linked to the public service nature of their role and the legitimacy of more generous pay offers to all public sector workers. For those viewing firefighters more cynically, however, the pay dispute proved a source of negative images that clashed with expectations of what the provision of a public service should involve, specifically *not* taking industrial action:

You hold society . . . If you take firemen out, if they go on strike, what are we going to do? We are going to come to a standstill . . . It's like, 'If you don't give me what I want, I will bring the country to a standstill'. I believe they should get a pay rise, but I don't like the timing that they used – September 11. (GI, HE)

Firefighter group

When asked about their general impressions of firefighters before settling on the role, interviewees within the firefighter group produced commentary that had some overlaps with the education interviewees, but also some significant differences. These differences were manifest in both prospective and in-post firefighters. As might be expected, these interviewees delineated far less ambiguous and ambivalent images of firefighters and their role. In-post firefighters acknowledged the retrospective draw of the heroic image, and especially the built-in altruism, and prospective firefighters emphasised this even more so:

Extract 1:

I love helping people. I always stop and help if I see someone in distress. As a family we are always out and about and helping people. We will help anyone. That's the way I was brought up and it's why the job appeals to me so much. (II, PFF)

Extract 2:

Saving lives is the key. It fits with my values. They are just the bravest and best people that there could ever be. (II, PFF)

Neither firefighters nor prospective firefighters reported having any negative images of the work.

Firefighter interviewees were far more likely to say that they had had a firefighter in their immediate family, or circle of close friends, before orienting to the role, although also that they knew very little indeed about what its main tasks and duties were. Prospective firefighters were no less likely than education interviewees to over-estimate on-the-job mortality rates associated with the work:

Extract 1:

It's a very risky job. There is not hiding from that. It's very dangerous.

How many firefighters lose their lives in the course of duty?

Oh, I don't know, but there are injuries as well. I guess it might be as low as 1 in 10. (II, PFF)

Extract 2:

How many firefighters do you think lose their lives in the course of duty?

Gosh. Let me see. Over their whole life time? Maybe 30 per cent. (II, PFF)

The sexualised aspects of the firefighter images were not proactively mentioned at all by this group, and, when prompted, interviewees were likely to say that, when they considered applying for the role, they did have a low-level awareness that firefighters were perceived as sex symbols by others, but that they had not held this view themselves. All these interviewees also claimed to have been fully cognisant of the fact that the firefighting working environment was male-dominated, but also, in line with general orientation to such contexts, that they had found this inviting rather than off-putting. As with the education group, this was partly because of the challenge it posed:

I love a challenge and it's male-oriented isn't it? And I quite like that challenge as well. I work better with men anyway . . . I was brought up by my dad and have had a lot of male influence, so that aspect attracted me. (II, PFF)

It was also, however, because of the anticipated *'straight-forwardness'* and *'friendliness'* of the firefighting environment's interpersonal-communication style.

Some participants indicated that they were not even aware that women could be firefighters until the possibility came to their attention after they had already begun working towards another career, which they were less committed to. This included an interviewee whose own father had been a long-serving firefighter. Once in possession of the information, however, they reported being instantly and firmly dedicated to the occupation: *'There was nothing else then. Once I knew women could do it, I knew it was for me'.*

Several interviewees said they had looked at the Army, Police and the Paramedic role, as well as firefighting, when thinking about future careers. They were all clear, however, that they considered the Fire Service to offer a perfect occupation for someone wanting to undertake an important public service. The Police, by contrast, was associated with less public regard and gratitude, and a higher likelihood of aggression:

Extract 1:

I didn't want people to look at me with no respect and that job is not respected anymore in this country. (II, FF)

Extract 2:

I don't mean to be rude but police work is not respected. People don't think the police are on their side. Firefighters are seen as on their side. (II, FF)

The association of the armed services with '*killing rather than rescuing people*', and with discipline, ruled them out for the majority. The ambulance service was considered the most similar occupational environment as:

Extract 1:

You are on the scene when the thing happens, you can help people more directly, at the time things are happening. (GI, FF)

Extract 2:

It's out and about and never the same thing twice. (II, FF)

Extract 3:

It's got all the right features and it's local. You don't get shipped to other countries without your say-so. It's an exciting job you can stay at home to do. (II, FF)

Perhaps the most significant difference in the firefighter group's commentary was in relation to the balance of skills and attributes they had associated with firefighting prior to their definitively deciding upon it as a career. As well as recognizing the requirement for physical fitness and ability, these interviewees were far more likely to report that they perceived a substantial, if not equal, requirement for mental skills:

Extract 1:

I could see it was a multi-disciplinary role. As well as sort of academic skills, you need to be physically very able, and I liked that it included

both. You can't be thick. No-one can afford to be the weakest link.
(II, PFF)

Extract 2:

I thought it was somewhere where I could possibly use my education because having an education is important when you're dealing with the public in such a variety of roles. (II, FF)

Extract 3:

It needed to be stimulating mentally as well as physically as I get bored very easily. I understood that you have to keep on your toes in the Service and that attracted me. (II, FF)

Beyond initial impressions

Further discussion of firefighters' employment skills, interests and dispositions

Education group

Following discussion of their initial impressions of firefighters, education participants were asked to talk in more depth about what they believed the firefighter's role to consist of, and what kinds of tasks firefighters spent their time undertaking. Fighting fires was the most common and immediate response. Further prompting and discussion, however, brought out a surprising amount of detail regarding other tasks that the role might involve. Respondents cited *'work with car crashes'*, *'rescuing cats'*, *'floods'* and *'breaking down doors'*, as well as educational work, *'doing safety checks'*, *'telling people "you can't put that there"'*, *'giving demonstrations outside schools'*, *'campaigns – open days'*. They also showed an awareness of preparatory and maintenance work that firefighters might be involved in, including: *'cleaning things'*, *'working on their truck'*, keeping *'everything maintained'* *'running through drills'*, *'lots of training'*.

When specifically asked what kind of employee was best suited to the firefighter role, and the tasks associated with it, the most common response from the education interviewees was someone with general and specific social skills, for liaising with members of the public, but also for working with other firefighters:

Extract 1:

Good with people, good at calming them down, because it's not all actually putting out a fire, it's managing the situation as well. (GI, SS)

Extract 2:

> *You have to be able to work with other people, work in a team as well. . . .*
> *That would be a key aspect I would imagine.* (GI, HE)

Firefighters were also said to require confidence, patience, empathy and the ability to stay calm in stressful situations. A basic tolerance of fire was seen as key to firefighters' predisposition to the role, and there was some, albeit infrequent, acknowledgement that the training firefighters undertook would counteract many of the dangerous aspects of dealing with the element:

Extract 1:

> *You have to be trained how to deal with it because there are different types*
> *of fire and different things to look for. It's smoke that's the biggest killer*
> *anyway isn't it? I think if you have the skills and you are properly trained*
> *then you should feel that you have the confidence to do it. It's like any job*
> *as long as you are properly trained, you have the knowledge and the skills*
> *and you can deal with it.* (GI, HE)

Extract 2:

> *It must be pretty traumatic. . . . Wow! How do you do that? But then they*
> *have this drill; it's their job.* (GI, SS)

In connection with the risks associated with their role, firefighters were very often characterised as having very low boredom thresholds. They were *'people not interested in routine work'; 'people who get bored easily and need the unpredictable'.* There were suggestions that some of them actively thrived in situations characterised by risk and danger:

Extract 1:

> *Yeah maybe that's why guys do it. Some people thrive in it, the thrill of it.*
> (GI, SS)

Extract 2:

> *Never doing the same thing again, never knowing what you are going to get*
> *or when you are going to get it and I suppose they must get a buzz out of*
> *the fact that 'hey I am doing something to save people's lives'. I don't know,*
> *it's appealing, like 'I am a hero'.* (GI, C)

Firefighters were characterised as requiring a particularly robust form of mental strength in order to deal with dangerous situations that did not end well. The role's *'responsibility to others'* was a recurring theme, and the ability to deal with this responsibility was seen as something that distinguished firefighters: *'And there is also going to be the days when you don't get them out. So there is enormous stress in there as well which would be tough to deal with'; 'This enormous responsibility to colleagues and to your family and to people you're meant to be rescuing'.*

The mental strength and duty of firefighters were also linked to the requirement for physical prowess: *'If you get it wrong, potentially people will die, so you would physically have to be on top of it'.* Unsurprisingly given the emphasis on physical prowess in the general stereotype, physically based skills were understood as required across a wide spectrum of the role's tasks, from carrying unconscious people, to *'driving that big fire engine'.* The role of technique and training was mentioned in relation to this aspect of the role, but, again, quite infrequently.

Firefighter group [5]

> It takes all different sorts. There are so many different characters in the Brigade. You can't say 'Oh, you've got to be strong and you've got to be outgoing and all this. It doesn't work like that. Even the blokes, some are stronger, some are weaker, smaller, bigger. Different characters – quiet ones, outrageous people. It takes all sorts I think to build a good watch.
> (II, FF)

When asked to comment on the employment skills and interests of firefighters, participants from the firefighter group cited some areas that overlapped with the education participants, such as the ability to stay calm, and social skills. As was the case in relation to general impressions, however, there were significant differences in their commentary. Firstly, as the quotation above indicates, they were far more likely to stress the diversity in the type of person suited to the firefighter role, as well as in the role itself. Somewhat unsurprisingly, this group also emphasised competencies and characteristics not mentioned by the education group, and they provided far more detail about what applicability certain characteristics would have in concrete situations. They also more strongly emphasised the skilled nature of the firefighter role, and the extensive, and ongoing, training that underpinned it.

In terms of specific skills, firefighters were said to require confidence, stability and the capacity to stay calm in stressful situations. They were further described as requiring *'quietness'*, *'gentleness'*, *'patience'* and *'empathy'*, traits not associated with the role at all by the education group. Although altruism was highlighted in the latter group's commentary, here it was described more frequently as *'caring'*, and as a *'strong desire to help others'* in an immediate and concrete way. The 'heroic' aspects of the role were not commented upon. Social skills were reportedly required to liaise with the public and *'say the right thing to traumatised victims'*: *'You have to get this right. . . . It's so important and you need a lot of skill'*.

As has been suggested, the emphasis on the mental, as opposed to physical, aspects of the firefighter role was very strong in this commentary. Intellectual skills were required for paperwork, to understand complex information related to fire, flood and accident dangers – *'about how fire works, how chemicals react . . . how people behave'* – and mental agility needed to assess very dangerous situations accurately and with speed: *'You need a bright head on your shoulders, need to be able to think quickly'*; *'you need excellent judgement'*. Such skills were also deemed necessary for the substantial educational aspects of the role, where mental skills were required to ensure *'very important information about safety can be communicated to people from all kinds of backgrounds'*.

The emphasis on teamwork was also echoed in this group, with a clear association between working in a team and safety issues: *'You're never on your own. I would never go into a situation on my own'*; *'There's always someone with you who you have to have complete trust in, and vice versa'*.

The physical demands of the job were highlighted here, as they were in the education group's commentary, but the role of training and technique in developing physical competency was far more prominent. Firefighters required a *'good basis in strength and fitness'*, which they needed to *'work hard to maintain'*, but their initial firefighting education, ongoing instruction and practice sessions, along with *'so many procedures'*, was understood as comprising a *'highly trained'*, *'highly skilled'* role, within which risks were minimised.

This group confirmed the education interviewees' view that they were intolerant of routine work: *'I could never work in an office. I would go mad'*; *'I couldn't have done anything boring'*; *'Part of the reason that we are all here is because we needed something more stimulating'*. Some firefighter interviewees further confirmed that some in the role were not averse to finding *'the danger quite exciting'*. They were also far more likely to report direct experience of fire from a young age, such as supervised bonfire building, and helping with open fires. Moreover, they were far were more likely to describe pleasurable feelings about fire. Although they were clear on the associated dangers, they reported being attracted by it and used positive adjectives to describe it: *'hypnotic'; 'fascinating'; 'pretty'; 'beautiful and powerful'*.

Although the 'heroic' aspects of the firefighter role were not directly commented on by the firefighters themselves, the 'public service' element was. The willingness to countenance self-sacrifice was mentioned on several occasions:

Extract 1:

> *My instinct is to go in where people are running out and the fact is that if things were really bad, if say, there were biological weapons or something, we couldn't wear the suits because nobody would be able to hear us, and I know that, and my instinct would still be to go in . . . The public would look to us and we would have to stand there with buckets and bleach and reassure them. They would look to us.* (GI, FF)

Extract 2:

> *It [September 11th] made me think twice . . . but then I thought, at the end of the day, they've saved so many people so it's actually worthwhile in the end. It would devastate my family and friends and stuff but if, at the end of the day, if I manage to save as many people as they did, then it's worth it.* (II, PFF)

Extract 3:

> *I'm aware that my life doesn't come first. If there's kids burning in a house. But there's no point in jeopardising everything if there's really no hope . . . that's where the training comes in I suppose.* (II, FF)

Firefighting and domestic commitments, roles and expectations

Education group

The few older participants within the HE education interviews repeatedly raised the conflict between what they understood the firefighter's role to involve, and other aspects of women's role. This issue was also raised in some interviews with participants under 18, but to a much less extent. Among the HE interviewees, there were some women who already had children, and they were quick to move discussion onto the incompatibility between motherhood and firefighting. The firefighter role was characterised as one for women who did not want children or were as yet childless:

Extract 1:

> *Can't really have children if you are a firefighter . . . by the time they've established their career they must be too old to have children.* (GI, HE)

Extract 2:

> *I find it quite difficult to picture a firewoman* [laughter] *as a mother. I would find it quite difficult to picture because it's just not your average stereotype. You wouldn't think that someone with such physical strength because you always think a mother as being nurturing, feminine.* (GI, HE)

Extract 3:

> *I think the whole kid thing does put a stop to going out and doing really outside jobs.* (GI, HE)

Practical problems were raised in relation to attempts to combine the role with pregnancy:

Extract 1:

> *And what would happen to a pregnant Firefighter? Would she get flack? She couldn't do something really active?* (GI, HE)

Extract 2:

> *Wouldn't your pregnancy be affected by all the smoke? Wouldn't you just be kicked out straight away while you were pregnant because it would just be harmful?* (GI, C)

As with other aspects of the role, it was clear that commentary from the education group was based on limited information. There was a very low level of awareness of the firefighter shift system, or what provisions there might be for women with children: '*I suppose the fire service has its own crèche service, I am not sure*'. Where there was knowledge of the shift pattern, it was clear that this was considered a significant barrier for women with children:

> A: *But if you were a mother doing shift work it would be impossible to try and organise a family life around shift work.*

B: *It would depend what the father was doing.*

C: *Lots of nurses are mothers.*

A: *I say this because I know this woman who is a paramedic and she is on nights on, nights off and it's hideous, always phoning around to see if someone could collect the children. She finds it very tricky, organising the mothering bit.*

B: *I am sure it is. It would certainly put me off personally but then women do lots of work that is shift work.* (GI, HE)

The assumption of fundamental differences between male and female psyches marked the discussion of firefighting and domestic roles, with few dissenting voices:

Extract 1:

I think women would probably like it [firefighting] but know it's not really applicable to them. I think the way we are socialised from when we are young, you have all the domestic side drilled into you that that's what you are meant to do and then to fit in that you would have a 9–5 job so that you could come home, cook the dinner, put the kids to bed and go to sleep. (GI, HE)

Extract 2:

A: *But if you have children would you ever want to do something like that where you sometimes feel nervous of driving somewhere because you want your children to have a mother. So if you have children or potentially want to have children, is it a clever thing to do?*

B: *But then men are fathers as well, but I guess I don't see that women being a mum is . . . the same thing.*

C: *But to me I think the dad can be as much as the mum. I know he doesn't give birth but I think nowadays the dad has a more of a dad role. It's a traditional thing to think that the father is not as involved.*

B: *I am not talking about involvement. I am talking about the psychology. Would you say that you would worry if your life were in danger would you worry about your children?*

A: *Me personally? Oh absolutely. I would not be a firefighter because I wouldn't want to die and leave my children. I worry about crossing the road. That's a very motherly thing to do.* (GI, HE)

Firefighter group

There was only one mother within this group of interviewees, a retained firefighter. This was partly because many of the interviewees were under 35. The mother interviewee, who was 40, reported joining the Service in this part-time role because of its flexibility, and in the context of family commitments. She distinguished between retained and whole-time firefighting in relation to the possibility of having a family, stating that the part-time option was viable whereas the full-time one was very difficult to manage. She did not, however, experience the retained role, in terms of work satisfaction, as wholly positive, and claimed that she *'would not advise the retained route. It takes a very high level of commitment and is life-changing. You can't just switch off . . . it's constantly there, and yet you aren't really into the full job'* (II, RFF).

Other interviewees in the firefighter group often did not raise the issue of parenting in relation to their decision to join the service, or their subsequent experience of it. In the few instances where the subject was raised, the commentary chimed with that of the firefighter above insofar as it stressed the difficulty of undertaking the role with parenting responsibilities: *'Of course, families come along. You can do it then, but you can't really call up and say "Oh, the baby's sick" because it's a team'*; *'The shift system does make it very difficult'*. It was suggested by two interviewees that having children with another firefighter was one possible route to making parenting responsibilities easier, and that they were aware this model had been successful for firefighter couples on separate watches. It was stressed that all female firefighters *'had the choice'* to try to combine motherhood with their work, but that it was *'their responsibility to make it work'*, and that they would do this most successfully, in terms of their career, if it did not involve challenges to the work environment, such as changes to the shift system.

Becoming a firefighter: barriers and facilitators

The requirements of the role

Education group

Can you imagine yourself doing that kind of work?

All: *No, no.*

Some of you?

All: *No.*

Why not?

A: *Because it's too physical.*

B: *I wouldn't want to risk my life, that's why I wouldn't do it.*

C: *I really hate exercise and that . . . rules it out . . . I need something more intellectually stimulating.* (GI, SS)

For those in the education group, there was a significant amount of commentary pointing to the fact that women on the whole were probably not as able to undertake the firefighter role as were men, although a minority of interviewees claimed that women were just as able in this regard. When asked about their individual abilities and interests in relation to the role, however, the commentary differed slightly. As we have seen, less than a handful of education interviewees indicated a willingness to consider firefighting as an option. While many indicated that their main reason was their own lack of relevant abilities, a significant number indicated an unwillingness to consider the role on the grounds that it did not interest them, regardless of ability issues. In all, six key barriers were offered within the discussions as explanation for why participants would not want to become a firefighter, and why women as a whole were less able to undertake this role successfully. These were: the physical hardship and danger; the emotional hardship; the conflict with domestic commitments and expectations; the male-dominated culture; economic and status issues; and last, but not least, the perceived lack of a calling.

Participants often raised their own feelings about fire, and the dangers associated with it, when discussing why they could not consider the role. About half the commentary on this subject indicated that participants were specifically scared of fire – more scared of it than other threats: '*Terrified*'; '*You feel like it's going to take you over*'. Most of the commentary from this group centred on the unpredictability of fire:

Extract 1:

> *Fire is pretty unpredictable, isn't it? You could go into something and in a split second the situation could change.* (GI, SS)

Extract 2:

> *It's always the unexpected that can happen, you know, crawling into a tiny space to get somebody and it's all blazing around you.* (GI, HE)

In this context, again, the key source of imagery was the media, from fictional portrayals, such as that provided in the film *Backdraft*, and the drama *London's Burning*, to disaster coverage. Images also originated from fire prevention advertising campaigns, which were repeatedly mentioned: '*I find those adverts so terrifying. They work. They make you very scared of fire and NOT want to be a fireman!*'

A key point that emerged from these discussions was the lack of direct contact most participants had had with fire in their past:

Extract 1:

> *I never really come into contact with fire that often, other than oven and microwave.* (GI, HE)

Extract 2:

> *I don't have a fire at home so I don't really know where I would really come into contact with fire. It doesn't happen that often now.* (GI, SS)

Those who reported being particularly fearful of fire had either no direct contact in their history, or, had traumatic contact: '*I have not been around fire. I just remember my brother running in from the garden and his hands were really burnt*'. It was suggested that this the lack of direct familiarity with fire, as well as the associated fear of it, was perhaps a particularly female problem, as fire was an element with cultural associations with men, and male activities:

Extract 1:

> *You know, when you have bonfires, it's mainly blokes who get into poking it, and it's really annoying, like 'stand back love, I'll handle that'.* (GI, HE)

Extract 2:

> *I think probably lots of men are as frightened of fire as women, they just won't admit it. But then, they spend more time with it, playing with it, so maybe the feel differently about it.* (II, SS)

Extract 3:

> *Aren't all arsonists men, young men? I don't think I've heard of a woman arsonist. It's a male thing, fire. Camping, barbecues.* (II, HE)

Another identified concern related to the viability of women becoming firefighters was evident in participants' commentary focused on their comparative bodily limitations, especially in a context in which lives might depend on physical abilities:

Extract 1:

> *You would have to do it well . . . I wouldn't be able to go into a burning building the same as a bloke. I wouldn't be able to drag them out.* (GI, HE)

Extract 2:

> *I'm not saying women are less strong than men but I wouldn't be able to do it . . . and you can't afford an off day.* (GI, SS)

Extract 3:

> *I can't see myself doing that. Even if I had masses of training I am just not built for that.* (GI, HE)

There were some isolated instances of participants arguing that the physical aspects of the role could be learned, and were more about technique than basic strength, and that the more strenuous tasks could actually be competently undertaken by women:

Extract 1:

> *I'd say it's a technique . . . Blokes are generally stronger than us but it doesn't mean they are automatically strong enough to carry someone over their shoulder.* (GI, HE)

Extract 2:

> *My six-year-old daughter can pick my twelve-year-old son up and that's not about strength, that's because she has it down to a fine art. . . . It's the same thing.* (GI, HE)

These interjections were very infrequent, however, and were muted in comparison with the emphasis on fundamental physical differences between men and women underpinning the male-domination of the firefighter role. For the majority, women could not be as effective as men when it came to the most physically demanding tasks. It is notable that this was even the case among those undertaking the BTEC in Public Services, who equally stressed the physical demands of the job as an obstacle to their orienting to firefighting:

Extract 1:

> *Because we are not as physically strong as them. We may be quite good socially, getting cats out of trees, talking to people who were barely alive, but going out of a building and carrying someone down on your shoulder?* (GI, C)

Extract 2:

A: *We obviously have the physical boundary because women on the whole are not as strong as men and that's just fact. They can train but . . . [in] the general population there is no way that women are as strong as men, but I think they could do the job. Isn't it the case that you are meant to be able to carry a person?*

B: Yes, *that rings a bell with me. Coming down a ladder with someone over your shoulder.*

C: *I can't imagine women being able to do that.* (GI, C)

This is of particular interest as these students reported signing up for their course due to their desire for a physically active occupational role, and because the course specification focused on students with a practical and physical outlook. These students also recorded their disappointment, however, that, during the first year of their course, the single hour of exercise that had been initially timetabled into their programme, had subsequently been dropped. Moreover, Seven of the Nine interviewees were seen to be smoking with their course teacher immediately after the interview.

Education participants also generally distinguished themselves from firefighters in terms of their capacity to '*separate myself off*' from the emotional trauma associated with the role, to manage their fear, and to achieve the optimal result in the event of a crisis: '*I could never go to an accident and see someone mangled up in a car. I'd just be sick*'; '*the emotional side would be too hard*'; '*too much responsibility for me*':

There is another aspect to do with the people who are burning or are in a car crash if I think about having to deal with someone who is extremely heavily injured in huge distress, in huge pain, possibly on the verge of dying, I would find that emotionally very taxing and, if it was children, I would find it even harder. (GI, HE)

Once again, these participants generalised this comparative limitation to other women. Echoing comments made as part of their general impressions, it was suggested that the 'female psyche' may be more prone to fear, but also to think through the implications of dangerous situations:

Extract 1:

A: *But women . . . go mountain climbing, bungee jumping, women are involved in race cars* [laughter]. *There are women involved in exciting, dangerous activities. Leisure activities.*

B: *I don't know about facing it every day.* (GI HE)

Extract 2:

I think women are more likely to stand back and think about what can go wrong and who will be affected if it does go wrong. (GI, HE)

The issue of family reaction was raised in relation to the danger associated with the role. Many participants indicated that their mothers and fathers would be 'shocked' if they said they were considering becoming a firefighter, and that the main reason would be concern for their safety.

Given the above, it is unsurprising that education participants did not express the view that women should expect to have equal access to firefighting. Indeed, equalities issues were low on their agenda throughout the commentary, but where they were discussed, it was more often than not to highlight the difference between men and women, and therefore the essential difficulty of expecting equal outcomes in the workplace:

Extract 1:

She should be as strong, as broad, as brave, and then she can do it. (GI, SS)

Extract 2:

This is how I get really irritated by this trend that we have in society today – it's got to be the same. In my books it doesn't have to be the same. Only because a man wants to do something doesn't mean that a woman also has to.

The majority of the commentary on this subject sought to highlight the undesirability of achieving equal opportunities in this context. It was rare that education participants focused on any positive contribution to the firefighter role that women could bring. Instead, their entry into the Service was portrayed to be at the risk of diminishing its quality:

Extract 1:

I am not being funny but if my house was on fire and my kids and I were in the top bedrooms, I would not want to see a woman's head pop over the top of the ladder. I would not want a woman to come and try and get us out. I would not care about equal opportunities at a time like that. Sorry,

> *I'm just being honest. I don't think anyone would be as happy about see-ing a woman as a man then.* (GI, HE)

Extract 2:

> *The fireman will go saving the woman rather than the person in the fire building* [laughter] *Get out of the way! If you are in a wheelchair you can't be a fireman, end of story, same thing.* (GI, SS)

Extract 3:

> *I think in this world we are getting too afraid of having this stereotypes and being labelled racist or sexist or whatever. But, unfortunately, to do certain jobs you need to be a certain way. There is not point if you are puny and not fit to even think you could go into that service. You have to be of a cer-tain build.* (GI, SS)

The suggestion that the attempt to increase female entry into atypical work may represent something of questionable fairness in relation to men and society in general was also a noticeable theme: '*I think it's a male job and it works in a certain way and I personally don't see why it shouldn't stay like that*'; '*Can you imagine the hassle, the cost to society as well? Are they so desperate to do this fire fighting?*'.

Firefighter group

As has been mentioned, all of the interviewees in the firefighter group reported a significant interest in, and commitment to, physical exercise before even considering the role as a possible future career. Nonetheless, for most, the physical requirements of the role were still reported to have been a barrier that they had to overcome. All of these participants reported having to '*step up*' their training and fitness levels substantially once they had begun the process of applying to the Service in order to maximise the chances of passing the notoriously difficult physical entrance tests. Many reported having to work for long periods to mas-ter a particular part of the test battery, such as hose running or the bleep test.

Most interviewees suggested that the Fire Service could do more in terms of the provision of help with training for the physical side of the applica-tion process. Although all readily admitted that achieving and maintain-ing the required levels of fitness was primarily their responsibility, it was also suggested that aspects of the fitness tests required specific techniques that were hard to train for alone, without guidance and equipment:

I failed the ladder bit . . . I did go down to the station a couple of times . . . but unfortunately for insurance purposes they said they can't allow me [to practice] . . . They let me have a go at the hose run and stuff but . . .

And would that have helped if you could go and practice?

Oh definitely. I would love to go up there and practice. I'd be up there every weekend if I could . . . it's not just my strength that I've failed on, it's my technique and I can't just find a bit of rope and a 60 kilo ladder to practice with. (II, PFF)

In-post firefighters reported that the motivation to maintain their fitness levels, once appointed, was unproblematic, because physical activity was part of their core life interests. What they did report, however, was less easy access than male peers to gym equipment with appropriate changing facilities. Three firefighters reported having to travel away from their stations to use a gym with adequate female facilities.

These interviewees were fully cognisant with the physical risk to themselves but, as has been indicated before, generally did not cite this as a barrier to the career, stressing the training and teamwork as significant risk-minimising features. Moreover, in direct contrast to the education interviewees' commentary, the emotional pressures associated with the firefighter role were rarely mentioned by those in-post.

Parental influence on career decision was reportedly no less strong in this group. Indeed, this group's commentary often emphasised the facilitating effects of their parents' influence, that they had, for instance, been raised in families willing to support gender atypical behaviour in girls:

Extract 1:

What's important is . . . the way you are raised by parents – what they show you . . . not afraid to have a go. (GI, FF)

Extract 2:

I was brought up by my dad and he's very outgoing. We're a very outgoing family, always doing loads of hobbies and mad jobs and things and a very compassionate family. That's why I see myself going into the rescue service . . . that's perfect . . . everyone in our family is doing a nice dangerous job. (II, PFF)

Despite this support, parents' reaction to daughters' selection of the firefighter's role was reported to have been initially mixed. Firefighters described in equal measure reports of *'shock'* and *'bewilderment'*, on the one hand, and *'pride'* and *'encouragement'* on the other. It was, nevertheless, further reported that even those parents in the former camp quickly began to encourage daughters with their plans once firefighting had been identified as a desired occupation. Parents were also reported as often knowing firefighters in advance of their daughters' choice, and as viewing firefighting as *'the lesser of evils'*, given that many of their daughters had given consideration to the armed forces.

Participants' views on women in the firefighter's role echoed some of those articulated within the education group, although here they ran alongside a more informed view of the contribution women bring to the position, and of the Service's diverse needs. Some suggested that the physical entrance tests needed further development to allow more women to pass them. Others, however, were vociferous in their defence of the established standards, claiming that the gender balance of the firefighting role was correct, given the propensity of men to be physically stronger than women, and women's lesser interest in physical skills: *'If women wanted to do it, they could. There are enough that are capable. Women just aren't interested in it though. They don't want to get dirty and cold . . . and all the rest of it'*. Some remained strongly anti-pathetic to the idea of positive discrimination as a route to balancing the occupation. Others to any attempt at changing the gender balance:

Extract 1:

> *Every year they seem to take the standard down slightly for whatever reason, whether it's because they've got to employ people of certain heights or women whatever and I disagree with that entirely. I think the standards should stay the same and if women or short people can't do it then they don't get it . . . they are making too many allowances for these people to get in. It's got to be tough to get in.* (II, FF)

Cultural issues

Education group

The culture for me. I couldn't hack the culture, if my stereotype is right. (GI, SS)

The data showed a very low level of awareness of the quasi-militaristic culture traditionally associated with the firefighting occupation.

As has been noted, however, there was a widespread perception that the role was male-dominated, and many anticipated knock-on effects for the culture of the working environment. A few lone voices thought this might be a context in which they could feel comfortable, but the majority anticipated it to be marred by a masculine gender regime. Some of the participants' general high regard for firefighters was challenged by suspicion and resentment of this environment, and it was cited as an obstacle to their considering the job. Although the team-based nature of firefighting was talked about in positive terms by these interviewees, it was also consistently suggested that this aspect of the occupation augmented the projected maleness of the working context:

Extract 1:

> *They spend a lot of time together, don't they? Waiting for fires and that's why people think of them as quite laddie because they spend a lot of time together . . . in a team. It's the one thing that really put me off even considering the fire service, it just nags.* (GI, HE)

Extract 2:

> *If I think about it in terms of motivation, one of the things that really appeals to me is . . . you can actually truly help people and get them out of a difficult situations and have that really hands-on kind of helping and that really appeals to me as an idea. Making a difference to people's lives. That aspect really appeals to me. And I think it's the idea of the macho environment . . . that I imagine it to be, that would put me off. I want an environment where there is team spirit, where I feel valued, confident rather than being undermined and the butt of jokes. The token woman.* (GI, C)

It was common for interviewees to hypothesise that they might be victims of 'locker room' humour in this context: '*They probably do their blokey things together. Maybe there is that certain type of bloke who has that immature thing going on*'. Their own, and their parents', concerns about '*the possibility of happiness*' in such a situation were raised as an issue.

It was clear that fictional portrayals were a key source of negative images of this aspect of the Fire Service too:

> *I wouldn't feel happy working in a team where I was the only female. It's like London's Burning . . . one female working there and she is treated like one of the blokes, but in a derogatory way. They are really sexist towards*

her but then she can do the job as well. She has been through so much; one of the Firefighters raped her or sexually abused her or something. (GI, SS)

Despite references to media portrayals of female mistreatment in their more general commentary, however, the education interviewees did not cite fear of sexualised harassment as a reason for not considering fire-fighting themselves. The quote above presents the exception to this rule. Elsewhere, one or two other school-age interviewees intimated that fear of sexualised mistreatment was a concern of their parents: *'I think my mum and dad would be a bit worried because there are a lot of men and you see women getting treated badly'.*

The sexualised stereotype of the Firefighter was cited specifically as a problem in relation to the unfettered development of the imagined fire-fighter culture: *'That might be part of the problem its so 'male drive',' male sexuality', it's not seen as connected with women at all'.* What interviewees were clearly most fearful about in connection with this, however, was the possibility of discrimination within their working environment. The potentially discriminatory attitudes of the public were also cited as a possible barrier in this regard, although infrequently. Anticipated discrimination from working colleagues was seen as the biggest problem:

Extract 1:

I would not want to be . . . constantly struggling, never being at home, settled there. Out of place. (GI, C)

Extract 2:

Prejudice against women and ethnic minorities . . . would put me off . . . there was that thing about that woman who was too short for the equipment . . . she got depressed and left. It was in the papers. (GI, C)

Extract 3:

A: *Fire fighters are quite macho and they wouldn't really want more women to join the force and women are aware of that and that might be why a lot of women wouldn't join.*

B: *Get teased.*

C: *Yeah, or just excluded or just thought of as inferior because it is a man's job. . . . I wouldn't want to be discriminated against.* (GI, SS)

Throughout the interviews education participants indicated that they found it hard to conceive of a female firefighter in even the most basic sense. This difficulty was echoed here, with commentary focusing on female incumbents facing the choice of being marginalised or being absorbed into the masculine culture of the service: *'In* London's Burning . . . *usually they get a hard time and they get treated like a man'; 'I think you'd have to become one of them to survive, wouldn't you? That's a big sacrifice'.*

It is notable that there was no difference in the commentary of mainstream educational interviewees and those of the BTEC Public Service participants on the subject of the culture of firefighting, and the barrier it presented to them personally. Fear of discrimination was cited as a concrete reason for deselecting the occupation, and the avoidance of discrimination was part of these students' orientation to police work:

You've been studying Public Services for a year, which is the most attractive one?

A: *Police*

Why?

. . .

A: *You see more police ladies . . . It's much less physically demanding too . . . there's also a high percentage of women already there so there's not the stereotypical stuff going on.*

B: *You wouldn't have people thinking you weren't capable.* (GI, C)

Firefighter group

Barring the issue of insufficient support for training for the entrance tests, the firefighter group was clear in their belief that the Service, and their line managers, were *'doing everything they could'* to attract more women into the ranks, and to best accommodate those already in-post. There was a unanimous acknowledgement, however, that the 'male' culture of the Service presented challenges even for those who had sought out a job characterised by just such a culture.

In-post firefighters described being *'genuinely shocked'* by the paramilitary nature of the Service once their training had begun: *'I didn't realise about that. You don't question anything you are told to do by a supervisor'; 'I wasn't prepared for the discipline at all'.* This wasn't perceived to be a barrier to their enjoyment of the work, however, and, given their own ignorance of this feature prior to joining, was not considered as a possible barrier to anyone else.

The legacy expectation that firefighters are all male was noted to be a problem in terms of the lack of women's facilities in some stations. Some firefighters reported that they still had no separate shower, toilet and adequate sleeping areas for women at their stations. Even where separate facilities were available, the default assumption of one sex in one location was acknowledged to be a problem, so much so that the best option was to '*just muck in with everyone else*' where possible:

> *I haven't got separate facilities. It started off at training school. They put me in a separate locker room on my own. And I was the only girl with 15 or 16 men and they were all in their locker room communicating and gelling and me in my separate locked room and I hated it. I used to come out in the wrong kit as I wasn't told what the next step was and they were all told in their little group, or it somehow got round. I went through three days and said 'It's not on. I want to be in the main locker room. That's what I will be expected to do on a station – which I am here by the way – and I don't want to be separate now. There are separate shower and toilets but I am in with them for everything else.* (II, FF)

Once they completed training, in-post firefighters described feeling a little marginalised within the culture at first, and being aware that some of the '*old guard would rather not have women in the Brigade*'. They saw this as a challenge, however, and reported having been keen to prove themselves. Commentary related to this issue could be particularly arresting insofar as it clearly implied that participants were happier to be viewed as having been assimilated within the pre-existing Service culture rather than being seen as introducing an element of diversity:

Extract 1:

> *They've given me a chance and seen that I am willing to just be one of them rather than a woman in the Brigade.* (II, FF)

Extract 2:

> *They have been too nice to me if anything. I was on my own* [only woman] *for four years so they made an extra effort to be nice and I had to push not to be treated differently.* (II, FF)

Extract 3:

> *There are no barriers once you are in. I think, as long as you keep your head down and just do the job and don't go 'Oh, I am a woman in the Fire Service. Look at me! Aren't I special?'. If you just join in with the men and*

you're one of them and they can see that you're one of them I don't think
there are any barriers. (II, FF)

A salient female identity made '*you stick out more. Do something right,
and it gets noticed, there is sometimes resentment. Do something wrong,
everyone knows about it*'. The search for interviewees reflected this anxiety.
About half the female firefighters approached in one Brigade declined
the offer, despite the fact that the Fire Service was funding the research,
had been sanctioned by their popular and respected Fire Chief, and the
interviews could be undertaken in working hours. The nature of the
responses declining an interview indicated that female firefighters were
sensitive to being asked to step forward to any task purely on the grounds
of their gender. Some asked why they, and not a male colleague, had been
selected.

Female firefighters were often asked to take on paid duties to highlight their presence, in lieu, or on top of, their normal work. They were
asked, for instance, to attend a Labour Party conference, to take a day
away from 'normal' duties to attend the annual 'Women in the Fire
Service conference', and to be interviewed and featured in the local
press. Interviewees from this group made it clear, however, that this
highlighting of their gender was very unpopular and ran against their
desire to be seen as no different to other firefighters:

Extract 1:

> I am quite happy about being asked to be interviewed by you, but the
> Watch all want to know why I can sit with my feet up and a cup of tea for
> a couple of hours and talk to you while they have to clean the engine.
> They're saying 'Why you and not me? It's not equal opportunities, it's the
> other way now . . . and it goes against us in the end. (II, FF)

Extract 2:

> I have spent a fair while proving I'm just like them, not special and not
> looking for excuses to work alongside them and then I'm asked to take time
> out of my routine to talk about being a woman in the fire service while they
> work together. (II, FF)

Although, therefore, there was an appreciation that enhancing their
visibility would perhaps improve gender ratios within the role, a keen
sense of token fatigue was expressed by nearly all in-post interviewees as
gender salience ran directly against their assimilation efforts.

The strong assimilation theme dovetailed with their claims that they found the male-dominated culture of firefighting preferable to female-dominated ones. The majority confirmed that their anticipation of the working environment as friendly and straightforward, with low levels of competitiveness and conflict, was confirmed by experience. Many participants were, nonetheless, also likely to state that the maleness of the working environment was '*too much at times*' – they reported having to '*take time out by myself every now and again*'. Interestingly, the language used to describe this experience did not draw on images of masculine excess, but again, on images of problematic feminine interaction modes that interviewees had counterposed to the Service when supporting their preferences for male environments:

Extract 1:

> *I think I lighten the atmosphere. Blokes can be real women actually and you need a woman to break them up a bit and you need the caring side of things to calm them down . . . I like everyone to live in this pink, fluffy world and get on.* (II, FF)

Extract 2:

> *The men can be amazingly bitchy sometimes and I think we lighten things up. Guys can be quite juvenile and get this silly competitiveness going.* (GI, FF)

Somewhat paradoxically, therefore, and in contrast with the alleged preference for male environments, and for assimilation over diversity, in-post firefighters often described their presence as having introduced a positive female element into the workplace which it had lacked without them, and that some gender difference had improved the atmosphere. They also spoke about other aspects of the role that they might more easily and better undertake than men:

Extract 1:

> *If a mother is locked outside and her baby or kiddie's inside, which happens a lot, I can go in and be more acceptable to the kiddie. Or a female RTA* [Road Traffic Accident] *may be more comforted by a woman and I am smaller and can get through little gaps and tiny little windows.* (II, FF)

Extract 2:

I think women can be better at the educational side, and at speaking to the public and informing them in the right way. (II, FF)

Economic and status issues

Education group

Only two interviewees from the education group specifically said that firefighters' remuneration would be a barrier to their being interested in the role, and these were from the HE interviewees. As has been noted, there was little clarity on the pay rates of firefighters, which might partially explain this finding. On the whole, participants produced very little coherent comment on what they would consider a desirable, or even fair, wage. This will be discussed further in Chapter 6.

Participants were far clearer, however, about their anxieties regarding the social status attached to firefighting as an occupation. In one or two cases, parental preferences were invoked again to indicate a resistance to daughters adopting atypical occupational roles in general: '*Telling people you are a firefighter, your parents . . . Might be a bit like, "Oh, I don't want you to do that, can't you be a secretary instead?"'*. Most often, however, both individual and parental preferences for what was perceived to be a 'superior' occupation to firefighting surfaced. Some of the general commentary on the physicality associated with the firefighter role, as well as that on related class and education levels, found echoes here:

Extract 1:

They'd let me do it; they just think that I should probably find something that would stretch my mind a bit more. (GI, SS)

Extract 2:

I don't think mine would be too impressed.

Why is that?

I don't know. I suppose because of their professional background they wouldn't. I suppose maybe because people see that being a firefighter as needing less qualifications. (GI, HE)

In relation to this, and in contrast to the commentary about the physical and emotional barriers to the role, it was suggested that for many women, firefighting did not present *too* much of a challenge, but was *not enough* of one. There was a clear continuation of the theme that saw academic and mental skills and physical skills as suggesting mutually exclusive career trajectories:

Extract 1:

> *Most women aim higher now, whereas men are happy to settle for less.* (GI, SS)

Extract 2:

> *We are the educated class now, aren't we? I think that is something that would appeal to boys. We're more academic and the boys are more into physical aspects and you don't usually get both together in the same person.* (GI, SS)

Extract 3:

> *I don't really know* [what future occupation], *but it wouldn't be something practical like that.* (GI, HE)

Extract 4:

> *I'm quite academic so . . . I don't know, definitely nothing physical, and somewhere where you can sit down!* (GI, C)

The fact that the public status of firefighters was often characterised very positively overall in the interviews suggested that the failure of participants to identify with the role was not a function of overwhelmingly negative feelings towards it. Their fear of being an outsider, and of discrimination, has already been noted, along with the fear of risk, the emotional rigours and failure. Their lack of identification was also, however, a function of the strong association drawn between occupations requiring physical skills and routine, unchallenging occupations, with occupations suitable for those whose educational levels and intellectual skills and interests were weaker than their own. That this is the case is attested to by participants' attitudes to police work. This work was characterised as similar in important respects – it is male-dominated, and an emergency service with paramilitary elements – although the overall impressions of the occupation were far more negative. This occupation was, nonetheless, perceived as one within which education and intelligence played a more central role, and, on this basis, it was deemed a *'far more likely career'* for some women, and a *'more professional'* role: *'It's got so many different units you can join and the job's more equal – women can do the job too'*.

Firefighter group

The firefighter interviewees did not provide much commentary on their salary levels. Indeed, only one proactively suggested that the *'crap pay'* was something that may pose a barrier to more women joining the Service. As has been indicated before, the firefighter's role was positively reviewed by all the members of this group, and this was an important reason for their orientation towards it. They were sensitive to its generally positive status with the outside world, and a handful of participants indicated concern that the threat of industrial action relating to the pay dispute might have damaged this, but the overall perception was that firefighters were secure in the public eye. Other status issues were not raised beyond these points. As we have seen, participants were keen to assimilate themselves to the male-dominated environment of firefighting. Moreover, they were not concerned about status issues relating to the presentation of themselves as *female* firefighters to the rest of the world. Some pointed out that the nature of the uniform meant that members of the public could often not detect whether a firefighter was male or female, and credited this with their experience of less discrimination in their hands, as compared to women in the police. Echoing their desire to be a little 'rebellious' in relation to certain gender-role expectations, they reported themselves to be unconcerned by any work/life conflicts that being a woman in a male occupation might bring: *'People are always shocked* [that I am a firefighter] *and I quite like that, I like being out of the ordinary'.*

The 'calling', or the lack of it

Education group

Another major reason that was put forward for not considering firefighting was the lack of *'a calling'*. As we have seen, the role was very much characterised as a vocation, and participants were clear that it was not something you fell into, or could countenance after years of never previously considering it:

Extract 1:

> *You have to have ambition to be a firefighter; you want to do it from young age.* (GI, SS)

Extract 2:

> *Unless you've got your mind set on wanting to do that type of career you wouldn't go into it. Out of all the jobs you wouldn't go, 'Oh, I'll be a firefighter!'* (GI, SS)

Extract 3:

> *I don't think people become firefighters because there's nothing else for them to do, I think they want to become firefighters.* (GI, HE)

Some participants suggested that, because female children were traditionally raised differently to male children, and because the prevailing stereotypes of firefighters remained resolutely male, it would be more difficult for female children to have travelled along the same projected career path towards firefighting in their childhoods, and to consequently see the occupation as a possible 'choice':

> *Thinking about it now if there was a recruitment stand for firewomen I don't think I would approach it because I never thought about it, you never think about it. If you are not brought up with that role in mind – 'Oh I could do this' – it just doesn't seem to be an option to women because you always think 'firemen'. I probably wouldn't go to a stand like that. There isn't much they could say to influence me to go for that option.* (GI, C)

Others, however, stated that 'natural' gender differences would predispose more men than women to hear the call, and that this was to be expected.

There was a considerable amount of commentary dealing with participants' impressions of the kind of woman who *would* consider firefighting. The same themes that arose elsewhere in the discussion recurred here. First, participants noted that any woman willing to be a firefighter would most likely be physically fit and focused on their physical selves: *'They'd be into exercise; 'definitely be into exercise'; 'athletic'.* Some participants expressed the view that such women would be less feminine than others:

> A: *They'd definitely be a bit butch. A little bit butch.*
>
> B: *I don't think you HAVE to be, I just think.*
>
> C: *Would perhaps be though.* (GI, C)

There were also echoes of the general suggestion that this focus would be to the exclusion of their intellectual selves:

> *Active, less intellectual . . . because they focus on other areas . . . because usually you have someone who is either really active or really intellectual . . . they don't go together.* (GI, SS)

The qualities of self-confidence and strength of character were also raised repeatedly so that any females feeling that firefighting was their vocation could *'see it through'*. They would need to be *'self-confident'*, *'open-minded to overcome the stereotype and put up with men getting promotion and stuff'*; *'strong willed'*; *'You have to think "I can do this"'*. It was also suggested that female firefighters would probably stay childless if they remained active in the Service into their 30s: *'Someone who is less orientated, who doesn't want to have children at a young age, and doesn't want to settle down and be married'*.

Echoing comments made elsewhere, participants indicated that they themselves, or other people, found it hard to think about female firefighters as 'normal' women:

Extract 1:

> *They are stereotyped – being butch, unwomanly and gay, manly and they are not women, just exceptions to the rule. They are not accepted as such.* (GI, HE)

Extract 2:

> *The thing that comes to my mind is a kind of tomboys, you know, when you are little and you are the tomboy and you love the action and you want to do boyish things and you want to play with the boys as opposed to being all girly. I think that kind of person. Someone who is physically active, physically fit. People who have had lots of problems, definitely, you don't get the real girly. You more actively grow up being that way and also learn to cope with being around men and be strong enough to put up with it.* (GI, C)

Firefighter group

In stark contrast to the education groups' characterisation of firefighters as knowing their vocation from childhood, participants from this group generally emphasised the serendipitous aspects of their own orientation towards the role:

Extract 1:

> *I saw an advert for firefighters and I hadn't considered it as a career option and the advert said 'women and ethnic minorities were welcome'. I didn't realise it was an option for women so I applied. It wasn't a particularly eye-catching advert.* (GI, FF)

Extract 2:

> *I played volley ball and played with a lot of firemen. They encouraged me.*
> *I thought I was too small so hadn't really considered it.* (GI, FF)

Although they might always have been interested in atypical work, and did report a strong desire to undertake a work role that helped others, this particular role was not identified as part of a range of possibilities in childhood.

As has been indicated above, these interviewees were of the belief that many women, from a wide range of backgrounds, could join the Service if they had a desire to, but that familial support for their attempts would be crucial. Despite arguing that their own sometimes atypical background had allowed for the possibility that they enter the Service, they also stressed that *'lots of normal women could do this. I can think of lots, but they just wouldn't want to'*.

Notwithstanding the reportedly serendipitous discovery of the firefighting role for all of the firefighter interviewees, all declared complete satisfaction with their choice of occupation. They were slow to discuss any negative aspects of the role, and described themselves as fulfilled, contented and excited by it. It defined a key part of who they were, and had, despite its late identification, become a vocation.

5
Women and 'Traditional' Work: A Case Study of Teaching

Introduction

This chapter presents a mirror image case study to that presented in Chapter 4, in which female participants' commentary on fire fighting as an occupational choice were explored, and contrasted to that of women who had already chosen fire fighting. In this chapter, discussions of teaching as an occupational choice will be explored. The same sample of participants in full-time education provide the data for those not yet in work and therefore still in the decision-making process (the 'education group'), and their commentary will be contrasted with that of teachers and prospective teachers, who have already selected the role. The chapter begins with a brief presentation of some 'facts' about the teaching role. It will then review the girls' and women's commentary on their most commonly targeted employment areas, before exploring their expressed ideas in more depth in the context of the case study occupation.

As was the case in Chapter 4, the views of participants in full-time education will be explored first within each section, before moving on to the views of those already in a teaching post, or prospective teachers.

Teaching – official statistics[1]

In 2006, the Department of Education and Skills (DfES) recorded 435,600 full-time equivalent teachers in England (DfES, 2006a). Nearly 95 per cent of these were recorded in the white ethnic groups (ibid.). Within these figures, women account for around 70 per cent of teachers overall, a proportion that is also recorded for Great Britain (EOC 2005c). Women are particularly concentrated in the Nursery and

131

Primary school sector. Within the DfES statistics, women comprise 84 per cent of all teachers at Nursery and Primary Schools in England, a proportion that has remained relatively static since 1997, when it was 83 per cent and comprised 56 per cent of all teachers at secondary level (DfES 2006b). As these figures are only based on full-time equivalence, however, they distort the picture somewhat. The General Teaching Council for England (GTC) maintains and publishes statistics on all teachers who have Qualified Teaching Status (QTS) in England, for whom registration with the Council is compulsory. This includes all teachers in the maintained sector.[2] In the Council's *Annual Digest of Statistics* for 2005–2006, 583,343 teachers were registered, representing a rise of around 147,000 on the DfES statistics. The main reason for this is that the GTC's statistics include part-time and supply teachers, groups to which women are far more likely to belong.[3] More specifically on the gender balance of the teaching workforce, the GTC's figures differ from the DfES ones, and suggest women comprise 74 per cent overall (GTC 2006: 4; see also, Hutchings *et al.* 2006). Women also currently represent over 75 per cent of newly qualified teachers (NQT), suggesting that the proportions will remain relatively stable in the foreseeable future (GTC 2006: 4). So, although teaching does not quite meet the standard threshold for a female 'gender-typical' occupation (which usually means that 75 per cent of its incumbents are female), it is very close, and is deployed as the comparator case study to fire fighting here as an occupation that has become clearly female-dominated.

Despite the concentration of women in the profession, men are far more likely to be in leadership positions. On the least worst estimates (the DfES statistics), women comprise 66 per cent of all Heads and 77 per cent of all Deputy Heads at primary level, despite making up 84 per cent of the sector's incumbents. They comprise 35 per cent of Heads and 42 per cent of Deputy Heads, despite accounting for 56 per cent of all secondary teachers (DfES 2006b: addition 5). These figures would be starker if part-time workers were taken into account. Hutchings *et al.* (2006) have pointed out that only 20 per cent of part-time teachers are promoted as against 44 per cent of full-timers (29).

Classroom teachers (those not in Deputy or Head positions) earned between £19,161 and £28,005[4] (Teachernet 2007). In 2003–2004, when much of the empirical work for this book was undertaken, this scale was set between £18,105 and £26,460 per annum. Teachers receive an annual increment to the next pay scale point, subject to satisfactory performance, and they may be recommended for a second increment if they perform exceptionally well. Qualified teachers who reach the top of the main pay scale may apply for other performance-based increments. They may, for example, apply for 'threshold' payments accessible within an upper pay band, to have their specialist skills recognised, or apply for a management allowance if they have taken on substantial extra duties. The pay of Head teachers and other school leaders is determined by a 43-point leadership pay scale, extending from £33,249 to £93,297, and is dependent on school size and type. Deputies and Assistant Heads are paid on a five-point range below that of the Head teacher (ibid.).

Teachers require either an undergraduate Bachelor degree in education, or a degree in another subject that provides them with Qualified Teacher Status. Either usually requires three or four years of full-time study. Alternatively, anyone with an undergraduate degree can take a Post-Graduate Certificate in Education (PGCE) that qualifies graduates for teaching. Taken full-time, this is a year-long course. There are also schemes designed to train graduates within the school context that generally take one or two years. Qualified Teacher Status requires applicants to conform to a set of standards stipulating the knowledge, skills and characteristics a trainee teacher is expected to possess. These standards fall under three headings: professional values and practice; knowledge and understanding; and teaching. They include specific targets: treating pupils and students consistently; communicating sensitively and effectively; to be confident and authoritative in the subject taught; to be clear about all pupils' progression goals; understanding what colleagues expect them to achieve; to be able to plan, monitor and manage lessons and classes; to pass numeracy, literacy and IT skills tests (TDA 2007).

Teachers' working hours are not easily identified. They are set out in the School Teachers' Pay and Conditions Document 2006 (DfES 2006d), which stipulates that teachers must work 1265 hours per year, and be available to discharge duties on 195 days per year, as agreed by their local authority and/or Head. Above this, teachers are required to 'work such reasonable additional hours as may be needed to enable him to discharge effectively his professional duties . . . The amount of time required for this purpose beyond the 1265 hours . . . shall not be defined by the employer' (DfES: section 78.7).[5]

The proportion of teachers dying in the course of their duties is very low. Indeed, there have been no reported fatalities since 2000 (Hansard 2007). Only injuries resulting in three or more days' absence from work are reported to the Health and Safety Executive. The Executive recently published statistics indicating that there were 40 'non-fatal major injuries' to teachers reported between 2004 and 2005, and 30 between

2005 and 2006. There were also 191 and 140 further reported injuries described as 'over 3-day injuries' in these respective years (Hansard 2007). The British Crime Survey (BCS), in its 'risk of violence at work' statistics ranks 'teaching and research professionals'[6] 11th with 1.3 per cent of workers reporting assaults, injuries or threats, and 2045 such incidents being reported overall (BCS 2005). If the ranking were allocated on actual assaults alone, then 0.8 per cent of all workers in this category reported an assault, and it would be joint 6th in terms of its risk ranking.

More in-depth research has questioned these figures, however, and claimed that there are far more violent incidents against teaching staff, many of which go unreported, or are not adequately centrally collated (NUT 2007). These figures produce an unclear picture of the extent of risk, but point to it being much larger than those published in available government digests. Eighteen per cent of secondary school teachers in a survey of Scottish schools indicated that pupil violence against teachers was a problem (Munn, Johnstone & Sharp 2004: 26), with 8 per cent of teachers and 17 per cent of Heads indicating that they had experienced physical aggression by pupils and against themselves in one sampled week in 2004 (ibid.: 8). In a survey of teachers in Wales, 11 per cent reported having been physically assaulted by a pupil during the past 12 months (NASUWT 2005), and UK-wide estimates with regard to violence experienced have suggested that 3.2 per cent of primary teachers and 4.2 per cent of secondary teachers have been victims of violence in the course of duty, mainly from pupils and parents, with 2.2 per cent of secondary school teachers actually experiencing assault (Cowie, Jennifer & Sharp 2001). Some surveys of self-selecting respondents have estimated that nearly half of all teachers (49 per cent) have been physically assaulted by pupils (NUT 2007).

Moreover, according to Workstress (2005), 30 per cent of all teachers in England and Wales were absent due to work-related stress in 2004 (see also, Bowers & McIver 2000). In terms of their absence rates, teachers generally fare well against other similar groups of workers such as social services workers and government employees, although it should be remembered that their contracted days are lower, and absences would only be calculated upon these. They averaged only 5.2 absence days each in 2005 (DfES 2006a; see also Bowers & McIver 2000). Retirement on grounds of ill health is low according to official statistics, at 0.3 per cent (DfES 2006c), although survey estimates of the type of illness leading to this status put 'psychiatric disorders' as the top condition, accounting for 47 per cent of ill-health retirements (Bowers & McIver 2000: 1; see also Brown, Gilmour & Macdonald 2006). Indeed, more than 50 per cent of surveyed teachers taking early retirement on ill-health grounds have claimed that their work had contributed to their condition (ibid.).

Education teaching professionals, including primary, secondary, further and higher education professionals, are in major group two of the Standard Occupational Classification system, a category that they share with psychologists, vets, civil engineers, scientists, solicitors, judges and coroners, social workers, the clergy and curators (ONS 2000).

'Choosing' gender-typical and gender-balanced[7] employment

Participants' accounts

Education group

The majority of the education participants reported themselves to be still very much in the process of making decisions about their eventual careers, with many indicating a strong personal desire to keep their options open, often with parental, particularly maternal, support: *'I'm too young to be making hard choices and sticking to them – I want to keep my options open'; 'my mum really wants me to keep my options open, she wants me to go through the whole of my education before deciding'.*

Despite this resistance to making definitive decisions, participants talked freely and fully about the range of possibilities that held interest for them and which they had begun to 'shortlist'. With the exception of the participants undertaking the BTEC Public Service course, who identified police work and the armed forces in their range of possibilities, the overwhelming majority identified possible future occupations that were either female-dominated, or in areas with a more balanced gender distribution than 'gender-atypical' work, as identified by the participants themselves, or as traditionally defined. Very little commentary, however, explicitly indicated an awareness of the gender balance of the favoured occupations, or that this balance was influencing any decision-making.

One striking finding was the small pool of possible career choices that participants mentioned that they were considering, or would be willing to consider. Frequently cited occupations – the collective 'shortlist' – and work areas were:

Artist/designer/photographer/dancer
Lawyer/Solicitor
Teaching
Childcare
Public relations

Marketing and advertising
Psychologist
Therapist/Counsellor
'Caring' professions – sometimes unspecified, but included under this
heading were: social worker, youth work
Working in the media – mostly journalism, TV presenting, film pro-
duction.

Notwithstanding the lack of decisiveness in relation to target careers,
those under consideration were nearly always identified as 'professional'. Possible exceptions to this rule included childcare work, which
was reasonably well cited, and hairdressing and beauty work, which was
not. Even in relation to these cases, however, participants indicated that
they wanted to work at a particular level: *'to be a childcare professional'*;
'to run my own nursery'; *'to have my own hairdressing business'*. Nearly all
participants volunteered that they were definitely intending to take an
undergraduate degree at university.

The theme identified within the commentary in Chapter 4, wherein
participants provided fairly robust explanations for why they could not
countenance work characterised as 'menial' or 'routine' or work that
was physically based, was further developed in relation to discussions of
their short listed choices:

> *I wouldn't be able to deal with jobs where it's just the same thing everyday –*
> *day in, day out, like basic things, menial jobs, I could never do anything like*
> *that, and I think people would be very disappointed for me if I did.* (II, C)

Given the reluctance to countenance gender-atypical work, the greatest
risk areas for such low-skilled and boring work were identified as direct
sales and office-work. A clear distinction operated between work that
was anticipated to be interesting and stimulating, and work in these
areas, especially in offices:

Extract 1:

> *Don't want to be stuck in an office all day.* (II, SS)

Extract 2:

> *I wouldn't like to be in an office, stuck in an office.* (II, C)

Extract 3:

> *I don't want to end up doing the same thing everyday, like serving in a*
> *shop. That would kill me.* (II, SS)

The dichotomisation of work types into physical (and less skilled) and not physical (and skilled) was repeated here, along with the routine/stimulating dichotomy. One respondent, who was considering journalism and sports coaching, and who cited both PE and English as favourite school subjects claimed:

> *I've been pushed into the academic route and stuff. The PE route, well I'm not really looking to go into that as much as journalism because of that. . . . I've been pushed more into academic thinking. Some people see it as a waste if you're academic and then you suddenly go into something that isn't academic. A waste of ability.* (II, C)

Despite the general ambition for a university education and graduate-level employment, most participants had minimal knowledge of what precise qualifications and particular characteristics applicants for their targeted jobs would have to possess to maximise the chances of success. It was not uncommon for participants to indicate that they would be most likely to 'fall into' their future line of work:

Extract 1:

> *Counselling, teaching, that sort of thing. I haven't really decided what I want to do. I don't think you ever do. I just hope I will fall into something I enjoy and I get a reasonable amount of money out or it and if not I will marry someone rich* [laughter]. (GI, HE)

Extract 2:

> *Something will come along. Artistic, creative.* (GI, HE)

Even where individuals were very certain about what particular job they wanted to do, their commentary indicated a lack of awareness of the educational steps that might be available, or necessary, for this goal to be realised:

Extract 1:

> *I want to be a journalist so I need to do English at uni' or there might be a degree in something more specific to do with journalism, but I'm not sure yet. I haven't looked into it properly.* (II, C)

Extract 2:

> *I really want to be a counsellor. I think you probably have to take a course, need a qualification in something. Although I read an interview*

with Jeremy Kyle [Television counsellor] and apparently he is not a psychologist or anything at all, for counselling . . . He's just a really, really nice guy. (II, C)

HE students indicated slightly more strategic thinking, but still often a low level of awareness of what might be required to achieve their employment desires. Despite the wish to keep career options open, this lack of information and planning meant that participants often reported having inadvertently closed off possible trajectories:

Extract 1:

[When selecting A level subjects] *I wanted to keep my options really open. I did what I was reasonably good at and then I realised afterwards that I have actually closed off some doors . . . I don't think I've had much careers advice at all. I haven't been told what careers need in terms of qualifications or anything really, and I didn't know . . . also, in my English A level, because it's got English Literature and Language combined, I can't do just one of them* [English Language or Literature] *at university and no-one told me that when I chose it so . . . obviously I wasn't very impressed with that actually.* (II, C)

Extract 2:

I really wanted to keep a balance in my A levels and not shut off any options, so I kept a science in and then did a language, Media and English, but apparently it was the wrong science as I've found out that there are lots of things I can't now do. It should have been Chemistry I think. (II, C)

The lack of awareness about what some of the target jobs involved was also conspicuous. It was particularly clear, for instance, that very few respondents understood what was involved in 'marketing', or 'public relations' work, even though these were both well cited as a possible future career routes. Commentary was confused around the issue of what role *'office work'* or *'being in an office'* would play in such occupations, and much of it seemed hide-bound by the simultaneous characterisation of office work as routine and boring, and of marketing and public relations as *'stimulating'* and *'rewarding'*. Participants often resisted attempts to explore what tasks might be involved in such work in more detail, and those who did offer further comment provided very uncertain descriptions, where the role of desk-work remained unclear:

Extract 1:

> *I am drawn to a more caring job, not nursing because I don't want to do shift work. I couldn't see myself in an office, but in a more caring environment. I don't think I could do with the stress of saving people's lives . . . [like paramedics]. I just don't think it's in my capacity to do it. I would like to be out in the field or such like, working with people like research, marketing, advertising, something like that, that isn't supervised. (GI, SS)*

Extract 2:

> *Journalism is quite office based so that would be 9-5 in an office . . . this is quite important as I don't want to be stuck in an office all day but am really interested in journalism. I suppose I could go out sometimes to research it. (II, C)*

Sometimes the discussion of participants' target work seemed to bear no relationship to even the most basic understanding of what particular work roles would involve, or had a largely random relationship with their stipulated work satisfaction criteria:

Extract 1:

> *Definitely doing something to do with PR and in the City . . . because I like being around people and I'd like to get well paid. You see I like History but I don't want to be a Historian . . . I don't really know. I don't really know what to do and that's partly why I'm doing History and not, sort of, Law or something like that because that's a lot more specialised. Because last year I did History of Art AS but it's AS only and I really like it, and it kind of works for History, and I might do something with that because I really like History of Art . . . I love travelling and seeing all the Arts. Maybe I'll just travel and do that. (GI, SS)*

Following on from this, it was not uncommon for participants to acknowledge how little they knew about possible target careers:

Extract 1:

> **A: Why advertising?**
>
> B: *I don't really know.*
>
> A: *Do you know someone in advertising?*
>
> B: *No, I don't. I did pick up some sheets on it, but I don't know whether there is a course on it anywhere. I must look into it. (II, C)*

Participants did provide some key rationalisations for their own short-listed occupations, or broad areas that they were interested in. The most common were that the work was stimulating and rewarding, which has been touched on above, and that it would allow them to 'work with people'. Sometimes this requirement was perceived to be a necessary condition for guaranteeing that work would maintain their interest:

Extract 1:

> *I would like to work with people . . . I've been told that I've got good skills at communicating with people. I wouldn't like to not be able to communicate with someone. I have to have, you know, some sort of interaction within my job.* (II, C)

Extract 2:

> *I am not sure. I think something like a counsellor or something along those lines. Possibly teaching, something like secondary school teaching. I have to be working with people because otherwise I get very bored.* (GI, SS)

Working with people was also identified as a necessary condition for the substantial group of participants who wanted to '*help others*' in their work:

Extract 1:

> *I would like to be a Youth worker and work with young children and take them around projects. . . . I like helping people.* (GI, SS)

Extract 2:

> *I would not want to look back on my career and think I had not done anything to change people's lives for the better. I don't think you can do that stuck in an office somewhere, so I think it will be something out and about, working with people.* (II, SS)

Extract 3:

> *Drama therapist, because I have always wanted to do acting since I was little but I got into this by listening to my friend talking about it and it sounded quite like acting and you get to help people.* (GI, SS)

Some explicitly linked this to gendered needs that they identified in themselves and other women. Jobs viewed as having a clearly altruistic content were also often viewed as *'girlie jobs . . . the more socially-oriented ones . . . caring jobs'*:

> *I think girls want to work with people more, and do more work with social interaction because they are more caring. They are more social. That's why I want to work in this area.* (GI, HE)

There was some comment associating the desire to work with children with women's alleged greater propensity for caring. Occasionally, someone challenged this view, but such challenges were far more likely to come from the HE student groups, and they were uncommon even here:

> *I don't like this big divide between men and women. I think some people can be very realistic no matter what sex they are and go for it and others can be very caring even if they are male. So it depends on the individual.* (GI, HE)

Money was mentioned a few times in relation to the desire for particular working roles, but usually as an equal priority with job satisfaction, or as a far less important criterion. This will be discussed in more detail in Chapter 6. The desire for fame, or, at the very least, significant recognition from occupational peers, was surprisingly widespread, with recognition frequently being seen by some as an important part of job satisfaction:

Extract 1:

> *I would like to be in the West End performing, acting, musical dance, that kind of thing. I know it's very hard to break into, so I would also like to do marketing and advertising.* (GI, SS)

Extract 2:

> *Well, journalism seems quite professional and some of them get quite famous, even if it's just in the journalism world. I don't want to, like, be doing anything that is seen by other people as unimportant really. I really would like to make an influence on what people think. One of my mum's friends is a journalist and I've seen she's got her own column and stuff and I would really like to put my own ideas out and everything. I've always quite liked to have an influence on people. It's quite nice to feel important sometimes.* (II, C)

Extract 3:

> *It might take until I'm much older, but I would want to be very well known in my area, for people to know my name.* (II, HE)

The influence of the media was very evident in the participants' identification of some of the target occupations, and in their reported deselection of others:

Extract 1:

> *I did want to be a lawyer but I'm finding the A level quite hard so not anymore . . . when I was younger I always used to like it – I always used to see it on TV and it looked really cool and really sophisticated and I loved it.* (II, C)

Extract 2:

> *I would like to be a children's TV presented, on Blue Peter or Newsround.*
>
> **Why is that?**
>
> *I don't know. I think that I quite like the idea of working with the BBC and communicating with children . . . It looks like it's an interesting job.* (GI, SS)

Extract 3:

> *ER made me want to be a doctor for a while, but then I saw, like, how little sleep they got.* (GI, C)

Extract 4:

> *You just look at a lot of advertising and you think, 'well that's really good, it really sells the product' and I think I would be able to come up with ideas for that . . . and the money is good'* (GI, SS)

The other main influence on job identification appeared to be direct or indirect contact with someone in such a role. Some participants reported actively wanting to follow their parents' career, but this was unusual, and it was more common for them to report the 'discovery' of a possible career via a non-family member:

Extract 1:

> *My teacher's daughter did this job with charities; she travelled to Africa, sort of fundraising. She didn't tell me about it. I don't know how she got involved with it but it did sound very interesting because I want to help people.* (GI, HE)

Extract 2:

> *I always wanted to be a dancer, but it's very tough . . . but then someone who knows my mum works as a dance teacher for adults, which I didn't realise you could do.* (II, SS)

Some participants underscored the importance of at least some direct or indirect contact specifically with a female in a particular occupational role:

Extract 1:

> *I wanted to be a firefighter when I was quite young but I've never seen a female firefighter, so then, I wanted to be a dancer.* (II, C)

The final, common rationalisation for target work areas was that previous, and future, academic subject choices had channelled participants into particular trajectories. As has been seen, there was awareness that this could go wrong in some cases, but there was also a general, and often relaxed, acceptance that such channelling was inevitable. Participants rationalised this attitude because their subject choices had nearly always been made on the basis of '*what I am good at and most interested in*':

> *I want to do psychology at university and that probably limits me but I am really interested in it . . . the job I do will probably be related to it and that's cool as I find it fascinating.* (II, C)

This did not always seem to be the case. One participant, for instance, had selected social science A levels over mathematics because of fears about her future performance, and associations drawn between the subject and particular types of people:

> *I liked maths. I like logic better than all these argument-based subject. 'Just tell me the right answer! I need right or wrong!' I like algebra. I decided against it at A level though as I thought I wasn't good enough and I don't want to be sat next to some spotty, long-haired, greasy boy with Harry Potter glasses. I thought there'd be brainier people and I didn't want to struggle.* (II, C)

For some, there was an exaggerated sense of how particular degree subjects restricted possible career range:

> *But I really want to do a History degree, so that's going to be sort of research or solicitor or something.* (GI, SS)

Perhaps with such restrictions in mind, some participants reported preferring, or deliberately selecting, academic subjects that had no obvious correlative career choices:

Extract 1:

> *Well I'm honestly not sure, I mean I want to do Sociology and Psychology at university and I think there's not one specific career than comes out of that is there? . . . I don't know which one yet anyway! And I think that's a good thing.* (GI, SS)

Extract 2:

> *I picked Sociology . . . because I heard it's a good mixer and . . . can lead onto lots of different things.* (II, C)

Extract 3:

> *I don't know what I want to do. I hate saying things about the future. I don't even know what I am doing tomorrow. Because I am doing a Sociology degree, people assume 'Oh, you're going to be a Social Worker'. 'No!' Why would I?* (GI, HE)

There were only a few mentions of the role played by careers tutors or teachers in shaping career decisions. With some exceptions, it was generally the case that education group participants felt that they had not had adequate access to, or advice from, careers tutors regarding their subject choices at school, college and university, and in relation to their possible future careers: *'I've had no advice'*; *'no-one helped'*; *'careers advice was not really helpful'*; *'They just keep saying "keeping doing the things you most enjoy doing"'*. Teachers' influence was most pronounced in relation to *'making a subject interesting and so encouraging you to carry on with it'*. Some lamented this and the work routes it may have closed for them. Others did not seem overly concerned, stressing the importance of their autonomy when it came to career choice:

Extract 1:

> *It* [careers advice] *hasn't been that good, but it's up to me anyway, so it's not that important. I won't blame anyone if it doesn't work out, except me.* (II, SS)

Extract 2:

> *I wouldn't let anyone tell me what to do, but I would let them advise me.* (II, C)

Teacher group

The commentary within this group chimed with that in the education group insofar as participants stressed that their career hopes and aspirations prior to entering teaching had frequently centred around the avoidance of boredom: *'I couldn't think of anything worse than working in a job where I was bored'*. Most also equated these efforts with the avoidance of *'office work'*. There was an exception to this. One participant in her 30s described actively wanting to do secretarial work:

> *I went into hotels and I learnt to type and I wanted to be a medical secretary. And it never, ever, ever, ever occurred to me* [to be a teacher]. *Well I liked typing. I thought 'that's a nice thing', and . . . my mum and dad kept saying, 'Well you know, you ought to do something with yourself', so medical secretary was the, like, top of the secretarial things, so that was what I was going to do.* (GI, T, PS)

The general trend of comment, however, indicated that these participants were as keen to *'avoid being stuck in an office'* as all the other interviewees:

Extract 1:

> *I did office jobs, fairly sort of high profile things, like I worked for the Foreign Office, but I mean it was utter boredom, it was shuffling pieces of paper.* (GI, T, SS)

Extract 2:

> *I was sort of doing horrible stuff in offices and loathed and detested it.* (GI, T, SS)

Beyond this shared ambition, the commentary within this group of participants differed by age. Interviewees from their mid-40s and older described having felt constrained in terms of their career options, and considerably influenced by social expectations regarding suitable jobs for women. Teaching was cited as one of only a handful of occupations they felt was available to them:

Extract 1:

> *It was kind of, that sort of, 1950s concept on the woman, either as an artist or they go into nursing or they go into teaching. My older* [sister] *. . . went into nursing – didn't last – the second one went into art. Because she'd done*

> that I thought, 'Well I can't, I'll have to do something else', so teaching seemed the only thing, and then I happened to be going out with a teacher, so that kind of, I just sort of drifted into it. (GI, T, PS)

Extract 2:

> I couldn't think of what I wanted to do, and there was no really imaginative careers advice at that time, you know, . . . 'Oh well. Try teaching!' and so I ended up teaching. (GI, T, PS)

Extract 3:

> I remember my dad saying, 'Oh, what do you want to do when you grow up?', and I used to come up with whacky ideas, and he used to say, 'Well, what about a secretary, or . . . ?' you know. And as he recognised that I was quite . . . able, he . . . changed his . . . aspirations for me, and he kept . . . throwing in teachers, so it seemed to be quite a good job for a girl. (GI, T, SS)

The younger participants in this group described growing up with similar aspirations to those in the education group. Although some reported being interested in careers such as medicine and hotel management, in the main they cited interest in law, media work, advertising, marketing and so on:

> When I was at school . . . I wanted to be a hot-shot lawyer, I wanted to be living in the City, going out for boozy lunches, wearing snappy clothes, doing all those kind of things. And then I did work experience in a law firm and it was fun, but it wasn't that much fun, and I didn't really think that was that great, and I've worked in supermarkets, I've had loads of jobs where you've had to follow . . . you've just been a cog who's got to follow what everyone else says to get any results. (II, T, PS)

A strong theme in the commentary was the desire for a career that '*gave something back*', '*helped people*'. For those with experience of working within a '*business culture*', such work was very clearly counterposed to '*making a proper contribution*':

> I worked first in business and I just found it completely meaningless and despicable and corrupting the kind of values that I think mattered in the world. (GI, T, SS)

Images of teaching and teachers

Education

A particularly noticeable finding from the education group data was that participants' commentary on teachers rarely stayed at the level of general impressions, and instead quickly became particularised around their own experience or knowledge of specific teachers. They did, however, express some general thoughts on the occupation's incumbents in answer to questions designed to elicit these. These were primarily that teachers were conscientious and committed. They were dedicated, caring people on the whole, with few rewards other than the intrinsic value of the work:

Extract 1:

They work really hard. Long hours and it's stressful. (II, S)

Extract 2:

An important job. Public servants again. Hard-working and under-paid probably. (GI, HE)

Extract 3:

I think they are really into what they are doing, and are not there because of what they can get out of it in terms of money. They really care about the kids. (GI, SS)

The kind of person attracted by teaching was *'dedicated'*, *'nice'*, *'energetic'*, *'patient'* and *'caring'*, *'quite selfless'*. As with the commentary on firefighters, a note of dissent was set against these generally positive impressions, with some few participants suggesting that the kinds of people that could be attracted to teaching could be *'controlling'*, *'into authority'* and sometimes *'boring'*.

By contrast with the firefighter discussions, the class background of teachers was not a prominent theme. There was, however, a consensus that teaching was a professional role, attractive to *'people with a good level of education'*. There was some suggestion that the majority of teachers are from middle-class backgrounds, but it was not uncommon for this to be countered with alternative examples: *'Although I know teachers who are from completely ordinary backgrounds'*; *'. . . from a whole mixture of backgrounds'*. Also at odds with the firefighter commentary was the fact that teachers were not immediately or independently 'gendered' by participants.

Beyond these initial broad impressions, participants nearly always reverted to particularised comment, even if this was used as a vehicle to confirm the same themes. This was the case for both negative and positive commentary:

Extract 1:

> *I had this one teacher – I've liked all my teachers – but I had this one who was an amazing person. He just caught everyone up in what we were learning and we did this fantastic project and, like, we were all into it and working at home and stuff. He had really good skills at understanding what we wanted and communicating.* (II, HE)

Extract 2:

> *My parents were both teachers and they both really hated it. My mum left because she was ill and my dad retired, but they both really hated it and I'd see them go in and come home and moan about it. . . . That has influenced me.* (GI, HE)

It is of interest that a disproportionate amount of fondly remembered and inspirational teachers were male. Furthermore, by stark contrast with discussions of fire fighting, interviewees did not invoke media images in their discussions of teachers.

Teacher group

The general impressions of teachers from participants in the teacher group chimed with those in the education group. They reported feeling that their occupation was an *'honourable'* and *'worthwhile'* one before they joined it:

Extract 1:

> *I think maybe my own images . . . my own thoughts about teachers, I mean, I remember really looking up to teachers and holding them in great esteem, and . . . one of my favourite games when I was a kid was playing 'schools' with toys.* (GI, T, PS)

Extract 2:

> *I thought it was a really kind of good job, I mean that was my view of what it was, it was . . . a safe, steady, good, job.* (GI, T, SS)

Teaching matched the strong desire in many to undertake a public service. Participants reported identifying it as *'a useful job'*, and a job that *'contributed something'*, which was an important criterion for both their own personal satisfaction, but also for a realising a socially useful working life:

Extract 1:

> I wanted to help people and I thought about medicine, but medicine could help individual people, but actually you have quite an impact being a teacher, so that was my justification, to start with. (GI, T, HE)

Extract 2:

> Mine's an old cliché I'm afraid – I really wanted to make a difference, and doing my degree I did a lot of work on poverty and how that effects young people's opportunities in education, and I really wanted to get into teaching to try and work with, kind of, less advantaged kids. (GI, T, SS)

Extract 3:

> For me . . . the issue was inclusion. I'd worked with adults with physical disabilities and just was always frustrated at how hard life was, how excluded from society in general you could be as an adult, and how much worse it was for a child . . . I'm passionate about inclusion and that's what I want to work for, that's what I want to do in school. (GI, T, SS)

Extract 4:

> I think people do have respect for teachers actually, and I think . . . one of the reasons probably that made me go into teaching was . . . coming from a family where . . . you kind of had to give something to society. (GI, T, SS)

Other positive perceptions of teaching that were mentioned far less frequently included the work's sociability, its basis in interaction, and its flexibility. Teaching was perceived to be a job where *'you worked with people'*, which was a benefit. It was further believed to be an occupation *'that you could travel with'*, and that *'could be picked up and put down and picked up again'* as the need or desire arose.

Very few negative general perceptions of the role were reported. There was a little commentary suggesting that, prior to becoming teachers themselves, these participants believed teachers were prone to exaggerate their workload:

> *I mean, I remember laughing at my girlfriend who's a primary school teacher. Every Friday night we would go out to the pub and she would fall asleep. And I'd say, . . . 'For goodness sake . . ., pathetic. We all have hard jobs, get a grip!' And when I started teaching I'd never been so tired in my entire life.* (GI, T, SS)

As the previous extract indicates, and as was the case with the education commentary, the impressions of teaching held by these participants were nearly always particularised, and based on direct knowledge or experience. Only one interviewee (who oriented to teaching as a second career) reported forming an earlier opinion about the role based on media influence:

> *The only thing I remember . . . that might have influenced me about it was 'Please, Sir'. They made it look really scary, and when I was that age when I possibly could've gone and did it, I certainly didn't because, you know, at 18 or 20, there was no way I was going to do anything like that. I found it really scary . . . Yes, it did put me off.* (GI, T, SS)

Interviewees otherwise reported the same origins for their impressions as the education interviewees: teachers they had at school, and known role models who were teachers:

Extract 1:

> *I had a couple of really good teachers myself, both of whom made me think, 'Well, if I could teach like that, that would be a fantastic thing to be' . . . And I also had a couple of really dreadful teachers . . . I hated school myself, overall, generally, my own experience of school was very negative, and I did feel that I could go into school . . . [and] could actually make it a little bit better, maybe.* (GI, T, SS)

Extract 2:

> *I had a really inspiring uncle . . . who was very left wing, very. He taught in a very tough comprehensive in London, and I remember going up and seeing him and his wife teach and just being completely excited and bowled over by the idea of, I don't know, just very charismatic, committed teachers, who had always taught in London in very tough schools, one in*

Biology, one in History, and, you know, were still doing it twenty years later, and that definitely inspired me into that kind of route. (GI, T, SS)

Extract 3:

> *I got my interest in teaching because I had very good experiences of it myself, I really did enjoy my education and it had a huge impact on me because my teachers appeared to be young, enthusiastic, on-the–ball teachers and I wanted to be like that and I thought I could be like that. That's why I wanted to do it.* (GI, T, SS)

A fair few of the interviewees had parents and family members who were teachers, and reported feeling that they *'knew what the job involved'* as a consequence, in terms of both its positive and negative elements. They could *'see the enormous satisfaction'*, as well as *'the huge amount of work'*, that the role required. As one participant put it: *'I thought that there were no real surprises.'*

A very commonly cited motivation for orienting towards the occupation was the perception that it allowed them to continue to stay with a particularly much-loved academic subject, or with academics in general. This was especially salient in teachers with post-primary experience:

Extract 1:

> *Well, I wanted to teach not so much particularly because I wanted to teach but because I was very interested in Biology and I was interested in all the areas of Biology, and I didn't want to go down one narrow area. I still wanted to be able to do it all, and get lots of other people interested as well.* (GI, T, SS)

Extract 2:

> *Yeah. I never wanted to teach, I wanted to be . . . I wanted to keep up with the subject Geography, that was what I wanted to do, so I ended up wanting a job with people and geography and there aren't many job openings that way, so that's why I ended up in education.* (GI, T, C)

Notwithstanding all of this commentary, the vast majority of participants within the teacher group were very clear that they had no long-standing designs on the role before they *'fell into it'*. To be sure, many held generally positive impressions of the profession, and teaching was a *'kind of familiar'* occupation that they were *'open to as a possibility*', but they reported their actual path towards becoming a teacher as nearly always serendipitous, rather than the outcome of careful planning:

Extract 1:

> *I didn't really make a conscious decision. My first choice was Law and I wanted to go I into that but then I messed up my A-Levels and went through clearing to Brighton and it was Law with Accountancy and so I didn't excel at that at all. I looked around at what other courses were available to me and teaching was the other one that appealed to me, because I thought . . . it was more vocational and I'd come out of it with a skill and a job. And my mum and dad are both teachers as well, although if anything I specifically didn't consider teaching until the opportunity arose at university, purely because I didn't want . . . to be seen to follow in their footsteps. And so I then started at university and I did teaching and for the first year I didn't even think it was that brilliant, and then I did my second placement and I loved it, and so it wasn't really until then that I really wanted to be a teacher. (II, T, PS)*

Extract 2:

> *Long story I suppose in a way, convoluted story. Well, when I did my Psychology degree I was interested in Psychopathology and mental health work and so I went into that for a few years, and did a bit of TEFL [Teaching English as a Foreign Language], just so I could travel, quite liked the teaching aspect, but had never considered teaching as a career. Always saw it as a bit of an opt-out and my friends who'd gone into teaching did because they couldn't think of anything else to do. And then I decided I was going to be a Clinical Psychologist so I did my Masters degree and applied but had left it too late, was considered a bit too old by that point, and couldn't face the sort of competition involved, so I thought, 'I know, I'll teach Psychology A-Level', so I went off, did the training, and really it was, because I couldn't think of anything else to do, and I needed to get away from Mental Health work for a while because I was finding it quite draining, and was astonished to find that I really, really loved doing it, I really enjoyed it. But . . . it wasn't a sort of deep desire in me from an early age to become a teacher, so I guess I fell into it in a way. (GI SS, T)*

Extract 3:

> *But in terms of why I decided to teach, I'm really not sure, because I never wanted to teach, it wasn't anything I ever had an ambition to do. When I*

*was at university, I always envisaged myself and wanted to work like in the
Media or in Advertising or Marketing one of those areas. I just think . . .
after a couple of friends went into teaching I actually decided to give that
a shot.* (II, T, PS)

A significant number of interviewees claimed that they *'definitely
never wanted to be a teacher'*, and in these cases, the role of chance was
highlighted in their narratives. It was not uncommon for participants to
report that the route to teaching was taken after the path towards a previously preferred occupation had been disrupted by forces external to
themselves:

Extract 1:

A: *I was in Sixth Form in a small grammar school in Cornwall, where
they weren't exactly aspirational at all, and I wanted to go to university . . . I was the first, would have been the first person in my family
to have gone, except that I sat in the exam room for my A-Levels and
found that I couldn't do a single question in English because I'd been
given the wrong syllabus, so that kind of slammed that idea. Although
I passed by some miracle, I didn't do very well, and at that time in
Cornwall, if you didn't get three lots of grade Cs or above, you couldn't
get a grant, so there was no way for me to go to university, even though
I had at least the minimum requirements for at least one of them, so the
only thing that was left in Higher Education was a teacher training college . . . I mean, who knows, I might still have been a teacher but it
would have been a different route. Of course, I always wanted to be
Kate Adie!* (GI, T, SS)

Extract 2:

*It wasn't something that I chose to do, and . . . I didn't really know then
anything else that I'd like to do apart from maybe Architecture, and at my
school I wasn't allowed to study Physics and Art at A-Level. You couldn't
do both, you could do one or the other.* (GI, T, SS)

Even in these cases, for younger participants, the favoured explanatory mode of accounting for their move into teaching involved emphasising the role of chance. Older participants were also likely to provide
accounts stressing the serendipitous aspects of their trajectories into
the role, but were also more likely to provide commentary more
strongly suggestive of the role of external pressures or expectations. As
we have seen, older teachers were more likely to report feeling that

they did not have the opportunity to consider anything but a small range of career options, within which teaching was prominent. They were also more likely to link this restriction to their gender politics, however obliquely, and to query the idea that they had been completely free in their choices:

Extract 1:

A: *So you mean being female influenced your decision to come into education?*

B: *Unwittingly for me, yes. It was only as I sort of matured and realised that I was, you know, following a stereotype thing, that I realised. Yeah, unwittingly, definitely.* (GI, T, SS)

Extract 2:

There was a period in the middle where I got very frustrated with it, because I think I could see I could've done other things. And I think it was related to the fact that my children, my girls, were growing up and they'd got all these things that they could choose from to do, and then that sort of opened my eyes more, and it makes you question, you know, the choices that you made. (GI, T, PS)

Extract 3:

Looking back, there was just nothing in my way. It all went so smoothly and was so easy. For something I didn't want to do, it was a remarkably smooth entry! (II, T, PS)

In the context of this emphasis on luck and, to a far lesser extent, elements of external restriction, teachers were, nonetheless, at pains to underscore that their motives for first beginning to teach, as well as for continuing to undertake the job, were worthy ones, that the role may not have been actively chosen at first, but that they were continuously making the choice to stay with it, and that they had not *'settled for second best'*.

A: *'Awful conditions, terrible money. Why on Earth would you want to do that? Surely you could do something better?' One of my friends said to me the other week, she's an IT contractor, and she said, 'Oh . . . you know, you read Law . . . you're obviously clever . . . you could do anything. Why, why have you chosen* [teaching]*?'*

B: *Get that impression, like you've settled for teaching.*

A: *Settled, yes.*

C: *Yes. I felt that. And I think that was partly why I went and sort of explored other things to see whether or not I did feel that, whether that was true.*

A: *Because you've explored something else, it's like, you can say with confidence can't you 'Well actually, I teach'* (GI, T, C)

Given these themes in the data, it is unsurprising that the majority of participants also reported that their orientation to teaching had little or nothing to do with a perception that it was an occupation well-suited to women with children. They insisted that such considerations were irrelevant to them at the time they began teaching, with some finding the suggestion *'offensive'*, and many seeing it as belying their professional motivations:

A: *I wasn't going to have a family!*

B: *Ironically, at 35, haven't got kids, but it was part of mine!* [laughter] *Sort of, you know, I think again, my mum probably said, 'And when you have children'.*

C: *Hmmm, I don't know. I think when I decided to be a teacher I had no thoughts.*

D: *I definitely was committed. I mean I did definitely in my . . . twenties or something, I definitely didn't want children. Ambitious, you know, you're kind of ambitious and intrigued and I really genuinely had no* [thoughts about children].

. . .

A: *I just saw it as my career and my job.* (GI, SS, S & HE, T)

As indicated here, there were some exceptions to this rule. Several interviewees described how their mothers had pointed out that a career in teaching could be combined with domestic responsibilities, allowing for part-time work, job shares, long holidays that overlapped with children's breaks, and easy return to work when one's own children were of school-age. Some mothers were credited with advising that teaching was *'a very good career for a woman'*, *'well-paid for a woman's job'*.

Women who already had children prior to starting teaching also bucked the general trend in this regard. These individuals claimed that their belief that the job was something they could combine with their existing family commitments played a large part in their decision-making. This was a sizeable group, containing several single mothers, and all were likely to emphasise the perceived impossibility of working full-time in other occupations given their parental status. Teaching, although involving a good deal of commitment and work, presented itself to them as *'an area where I could just about juggle parenthood with a profession'*:

> *The sole reason for my choice has been that it's a career that fits in with my family, the children's holidays and hours . . . Otherwise I could not have worked in a professional occupation. It just wouldn't be possible for me to manage the family.* (GI, TT)

Beyond initial impressions

Further discussions of teachers' employment skills, interests and dispositions

Education group

When asked to flesh out their general impressions, education participants were able to provide a good amount of detail on the main tasks associated with the teaching role: *'making sure the curriculum is covered'*; *'marking assessments'*; *'keeping discipline'*; *'making the atmosphere relaxed, but not too relaxed'*; *keeping everyone safe'*; *'making sure everyone understands what's going on'*; *'communicating with parents'*; *'communicating with students'*; *keeping everyone enthusiastic'*; *'being organised'*; *'ensuring everyone is reaching their potential'*; *'spotting when someone isn't happy'*. Again, they were quick to particularise their commentary:

Extract 1:

> *I think they stay long after we go. I'm tired after a school day, but I've seen that they stay and get it all ready for the next day, and then go home and mark work sometimes, I know. It takes a lot of organisation and they must be tired, but they keep smiling mostly* [laughter]. (GI, SS)

Extract 2:

> *With my mum it's a lot of hard work. She gets lots of abuse with the kids she works with and it's hard – a lot of hard work and a lot of planning and discipline.* (II, C)

Extract 3:

> *They are meant to make sure there's not bullying. I have seen some just look the other way, but that is part of their job.* (II, C)

Participants were also able to contribute commentary of the differences between teaching roles at varying levels of education:

Extract 1:

> *Well, primary get to cover all the subjects, it's not just focused on one. And you can just be more creative and at that age you can bring in a lot more other arty and all creative things, whereas at secondary it's more academic.* (GI, SS)

Extract 2:

> *At our level, teachers can be more relaxed because we are there because we want to do it. There is no uniform and it's very relaxed. It's up to us really now. There can be less emphasis on discipline and behaviour and more concentration on teaching the subject.* (II, C)

Additionally, there was some discussion of the different requirements of the role of Head and Deputy positions, stressing that people in these positions were responsible for the overall vision, direction, targets and morale of schools, as well as for discipline. They were contrasted with classroom teaching staff that was viewed as responsible for the day-to-day work of schools and for the delivery of learning. As a result of the tendency to particularise, the difference between the 'general impressions' commentary on teaching from the education group, and commentary elicited by more detailed and specific prompting, was minimal.

Teacher group

The wide variety of tasks associated with their role was underscored repeatedly by teacher participants, as was the variety between different jobs in the sector: '*It's never the same, not from day to day or in terms of tasks, there's always a new idea*'; '*Every teaching job I've had has been really different*'. Participants cited this feature as a key reason why the occupation was so '*stimulating*', '*challenging*', '*exciting*', '*interesting*', and associated it with the necessity for teachers to be highly flexible, and to have the ability to multi-task.

A long, but uniform, list emerged from this group's participants in terms of the other traits and skills that they suggested were required for the teaching role. It included patience, the ability to build and sustain relationships, enthusiasm and the ability to enthuse, interest and the ability to be interesting, mental strength, self-esteem, confidence, authority, self-reliance, humour, good communication skills, including the ability to explain things logically, aspects of extraversion, patience, organisational and time-management skills, adaptability, common sense and conscientiousness. Most also cited *'a love of children'*; *'a desire to be around children'*, and *'a strong desire to help people'*, or provide a public service. What was not cited, and was notable by its absence, was intellectual ability. Knowledge of area being taught was also very infrequently cited.

A further, very commonly cited trait was energy. Interviewees described needing *'huge amounts of physical energy'*, as well as *'serious mental reserves'* to maintain the pace, unpredictability and pressure of work: *'Nothing stands still'*; *'it's full-on all day every day and you need to keep that positive momentum going'*. As well as the variety in the role, and the workload, participants stressed that the performative aspects of teaching required such reserves. They talked about needing to project a *'knowing'* image, and *'an authoritative'* persona, especially when first in the occupation:

> *'I know things, and you are learning things!'* . . . *quite difficult really. But now, with experience, I think you don't have to put on that persona so much. You don't have to put that on as a mask when you go in, it's just a natural part of who you are, and therefore it's less stressful. But when you first start, I really felt I had to gear myself up to be that person.* (GI, T, SS)

Some participants also talked about the need for commitment, and for an underlying moral energy to sustain the commitment. These interviewees claimed that they could never *'work in a private school'*, even though the conditions would be more favourable to them, because of their strong belief in equal educational opportunities for all.

Despite their pre-entry beliefs that there were to be few surprises within the teaching role, most participants did identify unanticipated elements. In particular they reported being unaware of the full extent of the workload, and its attendant pressures: *'It was harder than I ever could have possibly imagined'*. The majority described working intensively all day during school hours and beyond, often to five o'clock, and then every evening until late, and at least one half day on a weekend:

> *I think you have this kind of . . . vision of what teaching's going to be like, that it's going to be in a classroom, and although obviously that's a huge*

chunk, I think it's all the extra stuff you don't realise when you're not teaching, the paperwork, the report writing the open evenings. You know, all of that stuff that comes with it . . . I just don't think you have any idea unless you're actually amongst that. . . . the workload. . . . time, the preparation, the marking, and all that. I mean, you know you have to do that before you get into it, but you don't realise just how much that involves your time and your spare time and your private time as well I suppose. (GI, T, SS)

The fact that this pace was unrelenting was also frequently mentioned, and the comparison made to many other jobs *'where you can have a bad day'*:

Extract 1:

And also having worked in business, the amount of actual real work that you can do some days working in an office, I mean, my God, you can really skive. Whereas teaching, it's full-on, the minute you're in the classroom to the minute you leave. (GI, T, PS)

Extract 2:

People who don't teach don't realise that, you know. I get very cross because my friends – I love them dearly – but they work in sort of social services or health trusts, and they say, 'Oh, I've got a presentation tomorrow'. And you think, 'Well, excuse me I've got three'. (GI, T, SS)

Connected to this, some individuals also commented that they had not been aware of how significant the *'control element'* was in teaching. They were surprised both by how much self-discipline they needed, and how much disciplining of students they had to undertake to ensure that all the tasks associated with their workload was executed. Although some lamented this latter aspect of their role, most recognised it was necessary, especially those at secondary school:

And one of my first experiences of going into the classroom was some of the students tore up my handouts, others made them into paper aeroplanes, and there's another student threatening to jump out the window! And everybody took it as a matter of course, this kind of unruliness, and, you know, it's just awful. So it was, you know, when you came out that kind of teaching environment into the staffroom, if you managed to survive, you were seen to have had a good lesson. . . . here it's different and so much better. (GI, T, SS)

And, although there were some benefits to schools and colleges with laxer regimes, no interviewees suggested that the trade-off was worth it:

Extract 1:

> *I worked before where we could take breaks and stand around having a cup of tea and chatting, but the whole environment was geared to under-performance. We have not time here and it's because we're doing it properly.* (II, T, SS)

Extract 2:

> [Referring to a less disciplined school] *You weren't expected to do well, you were expected to cope.* (GI, T, SS)

Another aspect of the role that was reportedly unexpected, but which was also welcome, was the autonomy. Despite an *'endless stream'* of government and school policies and targets, participants often described their enjoyment of having their own classroom and class, and the relative freedom accorded to them in relation to the style and format of teaching:

> *You're your own manager, yeah, you look after kids and you've got people supporting you, but you can try out your own ideas and stuff, and everyone's really supportive. So it's kind of changing into that culture of, 'Look, we are actually professionals now'.* (GI, T, C)

On top of all of the individual skills and traits cited as pre-requisites for teaching, it was sometimes suggested that there was something ineffable about the role, and that some people could have all the correct skills, and yet still not be a good teachers:

> *It's like learning to drive isn't it? . . . You can say 'do this, this, and this' but then there's more in being able to drive. To be able to teach, to work in education, there's a whole range of things that you have to be able to get through, but there's something else as well.* (GI, TT)

Around half of the participants declared that they thought women, on the whole, were more suited to teaching than men, as they possessed more of the traits and skills required for the job. There was some linkage of this claim to women's domestic roles, and this will be explored more in the next section. It is important to note here, however, that associations were drawn between the tasks teaching involved and the maternal, or simply the female, role:

Extract 1:

> *To be honest it's also a bit like being a mum as well don't you think? It's like being a mum because . . . it's the knowledge of not only your subject but . . . the psychology and child development, all that side of it that's rather complex and complicated.* (GI, T, PS)

Extract 2:

> *I think that some of the qualities that we've were talking about* [in relation to good teachers] *tend to be female, don't they?* (GI, T, PS)

Extract 3:

> *And it could be, I don't know, I may be sounding like a sexist here, but is it that men find it more difficult with lots more things to do than a woman? . . . It's a female brain sort of thing.* (II, T, PS)

There was some commentary indicating that this was a socially constructed relationship:

Extract 1:

> *I think part of it has got to go back to socialisation as well, and this idea of gender roles and what's feminine, what's masculine, and teaching is considered in our society to be a feminine role isn't it? In that nurturing, caring, teaching obviously, well, in most cases anyway, is female, rather than, you know, masculine . . .* [which is] *I don't know, working in banks . . . building sites, you know, stuff like that.* (GI, T, C)

Extract 2:

> *It just doesn't fit in well with the masculine aspect does it? And I think . . . a lot of men are probably put off by that, even thinking it might, it might have suggestions about, you know, how manly they are, or some people might just think, 'Well men can't be teachers'. . . . I think possibly that might be why more women get involved, because it's sort of an extension of what society sort of sees girls should have, you know, a motherly nature, kind, nurturing, communicative, able to deal with children who are crying, you know, that kind of thing.* (II, T, PS)

Extract 3:

> *Well the perception is that education and learning is a female pursuit.*
> (GI, T, PS)

Some participants lamented the assumption that women would be more caring and nurturing, arguing that it meant that they were often expected to take on associated additional roles within their work, such as personal tutoring roles: *'I think there are more women who see themselves as teachers of students and more men who see themselves as teachers of subjects'*. In connection with this, men were described as more *'authoritative'*, *'ambitious'*, and as having a generally more instrumental attitude to the occupation. They were sometimes presented as feeling less comfortable with the caring aspects of the role, and more likely to adopt a *'disciplining* persona'. It was also sometimes suggested that male colleagues might willingly leave the caring aspects of the role to female colleagues so that they could concentrate on their career progression or what they perceived to be *'core teaching business'*.

Despite the fact that they usually drifted into the occupation, and some of the less positive aspects of the teaching role, all participants described themselves as being quickly won over by their experiences. No participants indicated that they felt themselves to be in the wrong occupation per se, or that they had regretted joining it. A high degree of satisfaction was reported even in the case of older teachers who reported feeling that they had had less latitude in making their career choice.

Teaching and domestic commitments, roles and expectations

Education group

Once again, education group participants drew on direct experience in their commentary on this subject. Such commentary was also minimal. Those with teacher parents appreciatively recalled spending their own school holidays with one or other parent:

Extract 1:

> *We always had these long holidays together. We could disappear off for a whole month because both mum and dad had the same breaks as us. So, I mean, it worked well for us and I'm glad they were teachers.* (II, HE)

Extract 2:

> *I live with my mum and she's a teacher and we are on the same wavelength because we are doing the same things at the same time, homework,*

getting up, going out, and we are free at the same time usually. It's fine. (II, C)

No participants with teacher parents complained about feeling disadvantaged by the time their parents spent working, although some reported being aware that the stress and exhaustion levels were high. Most interviewees expressed the belief that teaching was a good career to combine with parenthood, but only when directly prompted to consider this issue:

I remember my reception teacher had a baby. She worked up until the baby was coming and then came back the next year. We had a supply teacher for a long time. I think it worked out for her. And it was ok for us. (II, C)

Only once or twice was the female-dominated nature of the occupation linked to these discussions.

Teacher group

Although it is true that the bulk of participants in the teacher group denied considering their future domestic responsibilities when finally deciding on teaching, about half of them also stressed that, once they had become parents, the occupation's good 'fit' with this status was an important advantage:

Extract 1:

For me it was something which was really handy when that happened. I thought, 'Oooh yeah! That's handy!' But I didn't actually consciously think about it at 22 actually because it was such a long way off in my mind then. (GI, T, PS)

Extract 2:

It influenced my choice to come back, because having had my child, because I'm female, having family responsibility, caring, was one of the reasons. Because when I gave up teaching before, a couple of people said to me, 'I bet you come back when you have a kid', and I was like, 'No, no way.' And low and behold I did . . . I began to see the advantages of the holidays and being able to finish, in theory . . . at half past four. (GI, T, C)

The remaining half of this group, however, stressed the difficulties that the occupation could present to those with parental responsibilities. In relation to this, participants emphasised that they continued to work for much of their holidays. Many reported working during half-term, every day for a few hours, or full-time for a couple of days, and working for at least two weeks of the summer holidays. During term-time, these participants drew attention to the inflexibility and pressures associated with their workload:

Extract 1:

> *You're teaching solidly all day long. You're marking every night. You've got meetings until about half past five everyday, marking every night, you know, working all day Sunday. It's the absolute antithesis of the kind of job that you would want if you were trying to fit children into it.* (GI, T, HE)

Extract 2:

> *It's not like many other professions when you can say, 'Oh, I'll come in earlier' or 'work at home that afternoon', or whatever it is . . . there's no flexibility at all.* (GI, T, SS)

This group of teachers lamented that they could not undertake the kinds of parental duties that women in other jobs could, and that they would like to: *'I can't see my children's school play because I'm teaching and that can't be cancelled'*. Occasionally, interviewees would describe feeling too exhausted by their school role to attend to school-related activities of their own children outside of school hours: *'The last thing I feel like doing is going home and helping with homework'*. These difficulties were reportedly alleviated by having a partner who was also a teacher and by having children in the same school.

Following on from the generally drawn association between teaching and women, many participants in the teacher group, who were also parents, described a particular kind of relationship between the latter status and their occupation. They claimed to feel that they were a *'better'*, or at any rate a *'different'*, sort of teacher after having had their own children. Some of those coming to teaching after motherhood reported that their feelings about the profession were informed by this experience:

A: *I think it's to do with being a woman and a mother.*

B: *Without a doubt, it's absolutely without a doubt.*

C: *Because we were all mothers first.* (GI, T, PS)

Motherhood was said to augment teaching skills, facilitating participants' attempts to be caring and attentive and empathetic towards parents and children: *'you kind of see children in a different light'*; *'I was a lot more sympathetic afterwards, a lot more understanding about what it feels like for the parents and how vulnerable the children can be'*.

Becoming a teacher: barriers and facilitators

Education group

Many participants declared a personal interest in teaching. Although it should be stressed that for the vast majority the occupation was not reported to be their first choice, it was often mentioned as a *possible* future career, and one that offered a range of satisfactions:

Extract 1:

> *Recently I've really started to think about it, like, with my sociology teacher, when I see it I think it would be quite interesting and you get to meet different people each year, and you're getting something out of doing the job and seeing people progress and achieve something which would be nice at the end of the day.* (II, C)

Extract 2:

> *Because I had such a good experience in my secondary school and I would like to have that amount of impact on people like the way my teachers did.* (GI, S)

Extract 3:

> *I had work experience with small children and I think I was good at it and I enjoyed it, although I hadn't really thought that I would before.* (II, SS)

It was not unusual for participants to indicate that even negative, or mixed, experiences had encouraged their own interest in the profession:

Extract 1:

> *I want to be a teacher, secondary, because I don't like school much or the school atmosphere and I didn't think I would apply to college and I have. I have a really good English teacher now and I realise it can change everything.* (GI, C)

Extract 2:

> *I had a pretty awful time at school and I would like to make sure it's different for someone else. I think it could be done so differently and much better and I would like to try. I think I could be good at it.* (GI, C)

For those participants with teaching on their 'shortlist', there were few anxieties that they would be able to undertake the role adequately, or that they may not have the desired traits. Those interviewees who did not feel they were up to the requirements of the role, however, cited both internal and external reasons. Some believed themselves to possess the wrong temperament, being *'too selfish'*, too uncaring or impatient for the role:

Extract 1:

> *I really don't have the patience at all, and I know how upset I get if teachers don't take care and time to make sure I understand everything, so I know you need to be patient.* (II, C)

Extract 2:

> *I couldn't stand it. Too needy. Too much work and not enough coming back the other way.* (II, S)

Others felt that they might not have the strength of character to be effective, citing their own poor treatment of teachers in support of a characterisation of the job as highly stressful. The need to be highly organised was also cited as off-putting. Pay and the possibilities for promotion were also given as reasons for not considering an otherwise possible job, but only by a small number of interviewees.

Although participants did not proactively mention the female-dominated nature of teaching, when asked why they thought most teachers were women, their commentary suggested that they believed women to be better suited to the role, and picked up on themes discussed in relation to why women preferred jobs with an altruistic content in general. It stressed women's allegedly stronger elements of caring and nurturing, and the fact that they were *'social'*:

Extract 1:

> *You always know that girls excel in education straight away. Women are keen to work with people too. They want to get something out of their job*

whereas a lot of men are quite happy doing plumbing or building or something like that and just getting paid. (II, C)

Extract 2:

I've never really thought about any of this before, but girls have always got that thing where they want to nurture something and the maternal instinct. They want to see someone progress and look after people whereas men don't all necessarily have that, whereas the majority of women do. (II, C)

As the first extract suggests, women were also posited as more academically able than men, and this formed part of the explanation of why more of them were teachers:

Girls work hard and probably have a very good experience of school. I think they like it better. They . . . feel positive about it and . . . of course it is normal that . . . you would want to work somewhere you feel positive about. (II, HE)

Teacher group

Teacher participants identified barriers to the profession for men. Picking up on themes explored elsewhere, they reiterated how men could feel uncomfortable, or be made to feel uncomfortable, in a school context:

Extract 1:

[It] is really horrible, people think there's something slightly suspect about a man who wants to work with young children, which is awful isn't it? (GI, T, SS)

Extract 2:

I think society as a whole's a bit suspicious of men with young children, which is terrible, but I think it's getting worse. I've talked to NQTs who've said that they find it hard with the mums sometimes when they're a young, male teacher coming in. The mums don't relate to them as well as they would a young woman teacher, and they found that actually an obstacle. (II, T, PS)

They did not, however, identify any barriers for women wanting to become teachers. Very few participants, for instance, described parental opposition to their career choice. Indeed, many described active parental support. For those that did report parental antipathy, as was the case with firefighters, this was on the basis of fears for their safety and health:

Extract 1:

Well my father said to me 'Why are you doing this? You'll be stabbed or they'll do something'. My father was actually very worried. (GI, TT)

Extract 2:

Mine wasn't at all [pleased], *because my mother's a teacher and had spent her life putting me off, so she's heartbroken at this point, obviously! But she regularly rings up, 'I can't believe you! . . . You're ok!'.* (GI, T, C)

While the majority saw no barriers to entry, most described significant barriers to their enjoyment of the role in full, or to working as effectively as they could within it. The most prominent of these was the workload pressure. Most of the participants reported that the workload had made them ill at one time or other during their career. For some it posed a physical strain, a state of exhaustion that meant that they were perpetually tired during term-time:

Yeah, you get to the point [where] *you can't get up anymore. There's some nights now . . . You sit down but you think, 'Just don't sit down', because if you sit down you know you'll never get up again!* (GI, T, PS)

Periods of constant illness were reported, and in a context where taking time off during term-time was impossible. Illness during the first few days of holidays was commonly described. Relationships were claimed to suffer as a result of the workload: *'I've found that during the teaching year I've become a lot more kind of closed off to my friends and family'*.

Another risk associated with the role was that of violence and abuse. Some teachers, especially, although not exclusively, those with secondary school experience, claimed that they had worked in *'an atmosphere of violence'* at times:

Extract 1:

There is physical risk. We have had situations. In fact . . . [we] *did a room swap . . . had to move the class upstairs because one of the class had threatened to knife us . . . it was something about not liking the way he* [the pupil] *was dealt with about a theft accusation.* (GI, S, T)

Extract 2:

> *The biggest downside is being abused, I would say, being physically abused. I've been walloped and kicked . . . I was in primary school, yeah, and by parents.* (GI, T, C)

Extract 3:

> *Verbal abuse in secondary school is routine. I think you need to learn that.* (GI, T, SS)

Extract 4:

> *From parents, you know, really serious. And a colleague of mine was physically abused, I watched her being smacked in the head . . . it is a risk factor. . . . There was one point, we had a very dodgy parent, and we had to have panic buttons in our rooms because he was coming in with knives and guns and, yeah, it wasn't great. There is a risk element.* (GI, T, C)

The other commonly perceived risk related to accusations of malpractice or child abuse. This was raised in one way or another in about half of the interviews. Although this was usually raised in relation to men, a good number of the interviewees from all educational levels made it clear that they felt personally vulnerable to *'false accusations'*:

Extract 1:

> *You're wide open if someone wants to make a wild accusation and you know that.* (GI, T, SS)

Extract 2:

> *There's also another thing . . . the potential for cases being bought against you in terms of, you know, restraining a pupil or . . . saying you've abused them in some way. That's really changed.* (GI, T, C)

Extract 3:

> *If a parent writes in a formal letter of complaint, for example, you feel totally, totally isolated and really scared, because you have no evidence, you just have this person. And it's gone to County Hall and . . . you feel like you're just standing there on your own . . . and it's very frightening, because it's your career, you could be disciplined, you could be . . . if the accusation was up held . . . I think when it happens to you the first time, you're shocked by it, although you know it's out there, you never think it's one of those things, you never think it's going to happen to you . . . it should feel like the whole school should support you, but it doesn't . . . it's not about the whole school.* (GI, T, PS)

Following on from this, a degree of not insignificant mental strain was also cited by many of the participants as a disadvantage of the job. In some cases, this was severe enough for them to consider leaving the profession, to feel unable to perform it, and to no longer enjoy it:

Extract 1:

> *I mean I actually have to say, some years ago, which is kind of when my career went wrong, I was, very . . . close to a mental breakdown and they will put on you in teaching, and put on and put on and put on, and actually I walked out of the buildings. My friends covered me. I was off site. I just walked out. And I had a row with the principal, walked off site, sat on the beach all day, and was that close. . . . And they were phoning me half hourly to make sure I was OK, and that's twice I've had people phoning me to check I'm still alive. (GI, T, C)*

Extract 2:

> A: *Actually I get panic attacks sometimes before school. I do still, and I think, since September, you know, beginning of terms, Monday mornings, just that rising anxiety – it's not really a panic attack it's more like just rising anxiousness. Once I'm up and I'm on my way then it's gone, but you wake up in the morning and you can feel it rising.*

> B: *And, you know, that's what my anxiety is all about, it's the time. 'How can I work at that pace? How can I work at it? How am I going to work all day?' (GI, T, PS)*

In this context, the holidays were not seen as a benefit but as '*essential*' for the health of the occupation, to '*keep people in it*'. It was suggestion by some that the stressors were so substantial that they could not envisage staying in the job they otherwise loved until the normal retirement age:

> A: *And I worry that then you get to retirement and you just drop dead. . . .*

> B: *Yes, I've looked into it. . . . But it goes progressively from 55 to 65, and 55 is like the optimum, 60 is sort of not too bad, but it was a massive figure if you went beyond 60 to 65, the chances were really high of you not actually enjoying your, not appreciating or having your retirement. And . . . I've got to 50 and I know I feel tired now. You know, I've been going, I went through my thirties, forties, I could cope with it, but now if I've had a particular bad term or something like that, or things are going on actually in my home life, that's the other thing – you're fine while . . . everything's easy at home, but if you've got as problem at home, people just collapse, because they can't, they can't. It really impacts on the way you work, and I've heard a lot of people who are*

hitting their fifties who are basically saying, 'I just can't do this. I can see five more years,' and that's how actually I feel. I really honestly feel that I can do it to 55 and then I want to enjoy my life. (GI, T, PS)

As well as increasing pressure from parents, pupils and line managers, teachers perceived pressures from the governments to also be increasing, and support from the same to be decreasing. Participants expressed frustration at seemingly uncoordinated policy changes and inadequate budgets. They reported feeling unable to fulfil their public service in this context. At least two teachers claimed they had actively sought other work in recent years on these grounds:

It's become a business. Those negative things have seeped in and the mentality is corrupted in the same way, and I think that's a negative at the moment. That it's about money, it's about bums on seats; saving money, making money. (GI, T, SS)

Some of the commentary acknowledged an *'outspokenness'*, and a *'moaning'* element within the teaching profession. This was linked directly to the desire to fulfil a public service within a personally valued occupational setting, but in the context of all of these increasing and countervailing pressures. Articulating anxiety and complaint was suggested to be the outcome of dedication denied, and of the need for moral support in a high-pressure context:

A: *But I think, I think the whinging culture is because when you're here, particularly like most of us are . . . almost full-time, or quite a lot of teaching hours, I think the whinging culture is just our way of just checking with ourselves and each other that, 'we all know this is really demanding don't we?', and it's just a way of,*

B: *Releasing tension.*

C: *'I'm about to start crying in a moment. Please just make sure you're on the same wavelength as me!'*

A: *And it's, it's everyone going through this because it is so demanding and when you go home and . . . someone's going, 'Do you want a cup of tea?', and you're like . . . literally can't even string a sentence together.* (GI, T, C)

Teaching was described as a *'really, really caring profession'* in this context, and many participants emphasised the value of informal support networks in maintaining morale.

In the commentary, many of the disadvantages associated with teaching were linked to the perception that teachers and teaching had an ambivalent image and status outside the occupation. Participants reported feeling, on the one hand, that their status as a respected, dedicated profession, was still identifiable, but that this sat uncomfortably alongside a different representation, within which *'its status has been sort of dragged down'*. In terms of the latter representation, they reported feeling teachers were constructed as *'lazy and leftwing'*, *'unambitious'* and *'difficult'*. Such constructions were identifiable in interactions with pupils' parents, their own friends, but also in the media, and in the occupations' relationship with politicians.

Because of this, some participants described feeling ambivalent about revealing their occupation when on holiday or when meeting new people, and felt the term 'teacher' was used against them *'not exactly as an insult'*, but in a manner which implied they were *'bossy'*, *'whingey'*, *'stick-in-the-muds'*, *'on a cushy deal'*, *'unexciting'* or *'controlling'*:

> A: *It's just being labelled . . . just to be labelled.*
>
> B: *'Just to be labelled, yes. Because you wouldn't label anyone a solicitor or a farmer or anything would you?'* (GI, T, C)

The representation of teachers as having joined the occupation after *'having failed to do something more exciting'* was very keenly felt, and was revisited in relation to the profession's allegedly ambivalent image:

Extract 1:

> A: *I read a terrible . . . interview with Tim Henman, and he said something like, 'I mean, if you're not very ambitious, like a teacher . . . ' and it really . . .*
>
> B: *Oh but he's so thick, isn't he? He said about reading as well, 'I don't read.'*
>
> A: *. . . really got to me. And he sort of apologised for it almost in the sentence but I just thought, 'it really doesn't help'. Just thinking it's just what you do when you can't really think of anything else to do.* (GI, T, SS)

Extract 2:

> A: *Well the ones* [TV advertisements] *. . . where there are people who are quite successful and then when the ad says, 'Well, you got there because of a teacher', kind of points out that, it just sort of suggests that, we are kind of, lower status doesn't it?*
>
> B: *Teacher didn't do the exciting things that they went and did.* (GI, T, SS)

Programs such as *Teachers* were seen as reinforcing some of these stereo-types, although there was also some suggestion that their influence was positive as they portrayed the occupation as fun and interesting for a new generation of potential applicants.

For some participants, this perceived bifurcated status of teachers was linked to the gender distribution of the occupation's incumbents. It was claimed that if teaching wasn't *'perceived as a woman's profession'*, it might *'have a bigger voice'*. This was especially the case in relation to the primary sector, which was seen as *'less important'*, partly because of the age of the children, but also because of the high concentration of women. Some interviewees complained that the skill involved in teach-ing was diminished in the public eye because of the occupation's associ-ation with women: *'and it's like, "Well you're bound to do that aren't you, because you're a woman? Nurturing"'*; *'It's because it's a female field . . . yes, I can think of a couple . . . of people, they just think it's something that any-body can do.'*

The 'calling', or the lack of it

Education group

Education participants did not represent the teaching occupation as a calling, in the same way that they did for firefighters. Although there was much overlap in the way they talked about the two sets of public servants, and the required degree of commitment and conscientious-ness to undertake the role, the representation of teaching did not involve the assumption that someone must have identified the career from early in their life, and pursued their interest in it in a devoted and exclusive way. Participants did not, therefore, rule themselves out on this basis; indeed, they described teaching as something they felt they could consider alongside a range of other options until they had definitively identified their first occupational choice, and even beyond this stage.

Teacher group

A handful of participants in the teacher group did describe themselves as having a clear, unwavering calling to the occupation, from an early age:

Extract 1:

> It's all I've ever wanted to do . . . I had no outside influences but I've never really wanted to do anything else. (II, T, PS)

Extract 2:

> *I really wanted to be a teacher right from being a child myself . . . I just really wanted to teach badly, and it was like a huge motivating factor all the way through Sixth Form and degree and everything. And I've never let go of that really, I do really like it.* (GI, T, C)

As has been suggested, however, these individuals were few and far between. The most common story of how individuals ended up being teachers relayed a route into the profession was often entirely opportunistic or circuitous at best. Some declared that they had *'fought against teaching'* when it seemed to become a real possibility. Others still suggested that they had thought about teaching when they were very young, had left these thoughts behind during adolescence and early adulthood, and then 'returned' to them in the context of a lack of any other definite direction, or when an occasion presented itself:

Extract 1:

> *And then I had a family quite young and I didn't come back into . . . full time work until 1998, which was when I came here. And having done a variety of jobs, as I say, and taking advantage of opportunities that arose along the way, found myself doing some teaching.* (GI, T, SS)

To reiterate, however, teachers were very clear that, once in the occupation, they were fulfilling a role that was more than simply a job. It was a central part of their identity and, for many, it felt like a passion and a vocation. On this basis they strongly resisted teachers being characterised as *'a failed something or other'*: *'I've loved it as a profession, even though I didn't really know that I wanted to be a teacher until I was one!'*

6
Women and Career Progression: Ambition, Success and Choice

Introduction

This chapter explores material specifically related to how participants discussed their aspirations and experiences of career progress. In each section, once again, commentary from the education group will be followed by commentary from the firefighter and the teacher groups.

What is a successful career?

This section will discuss how participants defined a successful career, for themselves and for other women, including the importance they placed on financial remuneration, recognition and prestige, as well as on other work satisfactions.

Money

Education group

Education participants' consideration of financial issues associated with all employment was minimal and indistinct. Firefighters and teachers were said to be *'low-paid'*, but there was little in the way of clarity regarding what this might mean in either absolute or relative terms. Commentary focusing on their future salary aspirations was similarly vague, and was usually only elicited by direct prompting. The most common response was along the following lines:

Extract 1:

> *I would like to earn a considerable amount to be able to buy certain things and treat myself now and again.* (II, C)

Extract 2:

> *I don't know what the average is. To me, if I get five pounds per hour, I'm happy . . . I don't have to think of a mortgage or house or children. I don't really know how much it would be in the future. Just enough to keep my house going and have that little bit extra.* (II, SS)

Further quizzing on what *'just enough'*, or *'a considerable amount'* would be produced hesitant assessments, usually expressed as an hourly wage rate: *'Five pounds'*; *'Four pounds?'*; *'perhaps a little more than I get now - six or seven pound an hour?'* Almost without exception, non-HE interviewees did not know the national minimum or average wage level; and most within HE did not.

Vagueness about anticipated financial rewards applied equally to interviewees with more overtly expressed pecuniary ambition, as well as to those who claimed not to attach much importance to such rewards.

About half of the participants who discussed remuneration said that salary level was not a priority for them when choosing their careers, instead they cited happiness in their work and other satisfactions as key to their definition of employment success.

Extract 1:

> *When we get into the real world, I do think it's not about the money. It's about what you want to do, because if you don't like your job, you don't like your job.* (GI, HE)

Extract 2:

> *Money does not mean that much to me. I need to survive, but being happy in my job is going to be far more important.* (GI, SS)

Interviewees who wanted to be 'top' journalists, or lawyers, and who expressly identified salary level as a key rationale for their choices, were also unclear as to what a satisfactory salary might be:

Extract 1:

> *I don't know what the average wage is, which is really bad, and so I don't know what a good wage would be, but I would be hoping to earn quite a lot though. I measure success in happiness but also in what you earn.* (II, C)

Extract 2:

> *A: How much would you like to be earning five years after you start work?*
>
> *B: I don't know actually. I haven't really looked into it. It takes ages to climb so probably not a huge amount. About the same as my dad is earning, although I don't exactly know what that is.*
>
> *Can you put a figure on it?*
>
> *Not really. Say thirty thousand? And then I would hope to go up as I get more experienced.* (II, SS)

Extract 3:

> *I want to earn a lot . . .*
>
> *How much is a lot in your view?*
>
> *Well, much more than I would get in other jobs, I don't know.*
>
> *Can you put a figure on it?*
>
> *Well, perhaps even as much as twenty-six or twenty-seven thousand . . . I know that won't happen until I'm much older, even 40, but that kind of figure.* (II, C)

Salary level was a commonly cited rationale for most of the target jobs that participants could provide least detail on, and which connoted glamour and a particular kind of success for them: journalism, marketing, advertising, law and so on: *'The money is good in advertising'*; *'I'd quite like the money . . . I'd like a well-paid job . . . and you can earn a lot as a lawyer if you are good at it.'* Salary level was never offered as a rationale for targeting the female-dominated occupations on the participants' shortlist of possible careers: teacher, counsellor, youth worker, psychologist (except if this was more specifically identified as a *'TV psychologist'* or a *'forensic psychologist'*) and so on. There was, therefore, at least a tacit recognition that such occupations may not bring substantial financial rewards, and, as has been noted, that teachers, for instance, *'do not get good pay'*, *'are badly paid'*. This was a deterrent for a few:

Extract 1:

> *I am quite into teaching but would like to work in a job that's quite well-paid and generally teaching isn't. But I would like it for the holidays.* (II, C)

Extract 2:

> *I don't need that much to live on but I'm not sure you get enough for a reasonable life from teaching? I would like enough to pay my bills and also have nice holidays and not worry, and I don't think they do, do get that sort of amount.* (II, HE)

There was some suggestion that women may also be attracted to teaching more than men because they were more willing to sacrifice financial remuneration for alternative benefits:

Extract 1:

> *I think it's low paid though. Women get more benefit out of it. They feel like they're doing something for other people. I'm not being horrible to men – I'm sure they do too – but I think that's why more of them go into it because they get more benefits other than just money.* (II, C)

Despite their differences, both the 'money-a-priority', and the 'money-not-a-priority', groups of participants counterposed female attitudes to occupational remuneration to male attitudes. As was seen in Chapter 4, boys were characterised as less able to defer gratification, and more likely to put their energies into earning a weekly wage than pursuing a career or education. Where it emerged, this characterisation remained regardless of whether participants believed financial reward to be a key priority for themselves or not. The 'money-a-priority' group claimed that males were different to themselves in that they were more likely to trade off a high, but deferred, wage for an immediate, middling one. The 'money-not-a-priority' group contrasted themselves to males who *only* worked for their wage, rather than for inherent job satisfaction.

Firefighters and teachers

Firefighters and teachers did not define success in terms of their salaries. Both sets of interviewees acknowledged the necessity of earning an adequate wage – only one ex-teacher indicated that they were financially secure enough to stop work. Beyond this, all were equally firm that financial reward, in and of itself, would not motivate them towards one particular kind of work over another. Moreover, they could not imagine anyone else in their occupation being motivated by money:

Extract 1:

> *Well, I can't imagine anyone coming in because of the pay. There are so many other things you could do where you earn more money straight away.* (II, FF)

Extract 2:

> *I don't think you could do this for the money, not that the money is worth doing it for. I don't think anyone comes into it for the money.* (GI, T, PS)

Indeed, in the case of both firefighting and teaching, it was suggested that salary levels were probably an active barrier to the occupation, deterring otherwise able and willing individuals from pursuing the respective roles. Those participants who had experienced employment outside these roles generally confirmed that their current salaries were considerably lower than they had earned elsewhere, but also confirmed that other occupations brought less in the way of alternative satisfactions that they deemed to be more important. As we have seen, all teacher and firefighter participants described experiencing high levels of job satisfaction from their work, and particularly, being able to fulfil a public service, *'making a difference'*, and this perspective informed their personal views on the value of financial reward. There was a common perception that many of their peers recognised both sets of workers as honourably motivated, albeit comparatively poorly paid:

Extract 1:

> *I've got one* [friend] *who works as . . . a recruitment . . . consultant. She left university at the same time as me, you know, we followed a very similar path in terms of out degree results and all the rest of it, and she loves what I do, she loves me and she thinks it's amazing. But then I look at her and I think, 'Yeah, now you've got a nine 'til five, that's it', weekends are her own, and she earns at least fifteen thousand more than me.* (GI, T, C)

Extract 2:

> *I think they are glad that someone is doing it, although there's no way that they would, especially for the money.* (II, FF)

It was suggested by some that as women they might be in a better position to accept their salary levels than men undertaking the same roles, not just because they were driven by greater altruistic impulses, as suggested by the education group, but because they did not have the responsibilities associated with a *'family wage'*. Some teachers, for instance, argued that their wages were adequate *'for a woman'*, but might not be enough for men, and that they could be more *'choosey'* as they did not face the same burdens as men with families:

Extract 1:

> *I think the money is ok really, it's fine, but my husband* [who is a teacher] *compares his to other men and then it sounds less, for him. Even though he earns more than me. He doesn't compare his to me.* (GI, T, PS)

Extract 2:

> *A: I think the money point puts men off because they're probably thinking . . . I don't know, maybe, I'm being old fashioned here.*
>
> *B: No, it does.*
>
> *A: I imagine them thinking, 'Well, I'll be providing for family . . . I'm going to do Accounting, or Law, you know, something else'.* (GI, T, C)

The comparative decline in the teaching wage, so that it could *'no longer sustain a family on its own'*, was seen as a fairly recent development. Older teachers recalled joining the profession in times when their salary level was in the top 10 per cent of women's wages, with some suggesting, again, that the subsequent deterioration was linked to its gender profile:

> *I don't think that we'll raise the kudos until we are paid a lot more and I don't think that will ever happen because there's so many women in teaching.* (GI, PS)

In the case of firefighters, a recent national pay dispute provided the context for discussions about salaries. The notion of a *'family wage'* also underpinned some of this commentary. Although cautious in their support for aspects of the dispute, some female firefighters indicated a difference between themselves and the perspective of male firefighters:

> *The pay issue is a problem. I do feel it's not enough, but many of us are uncomfortable with some tactics to increase it. But then, I'm in a different position to some of the guys who are trying to support a family on it.* (II, FF)

Level

Education group

Nearly all the participants who talked about their occupational ambitions described a desire to climb far in their chosen career, regardless of whether their expressed primary motivation for occupational areas had been financial reward or altruism:

Extract 1:

> *I definitely want to climb. I don't want special treatment or anything. I just want to progress and do well.* (II, C)

Extract 2:

> *I would like to reach the top. I know it wouldn't be automatic and might not be until I was much older . . . I would like to press on as much as I could though. If I was offered promotion, I wouldn't turn it down. I'd take it up straight away even if it meant extra work, because you know you're getting there and building yourself up, and it's a nice feeling to achieve something.* (II, C)

The rationale for seeking progression was the enhanced satisfactions it would offer – to feel a sense of self-achievement – but also the enhanced chances of recognition being at the 'top' provided. Many of the comments related to this issue indicated that participants were drawing heavily on mediatised images of successful occupations. 'Forensic Psychologist' was, for instance, not uncommonly, cited as a career of interest. The version of occupational success that dovetailed with such careers was highly individualistic: *'being considered the best in your field'; 'someone that matters and is seen as important'; 'successful enough to be completely independent of everyone'.* Some indicated that working in the higher echelons also offered greater protection against discrimination.

What being at 'the top' might mean in terms of the content of their jobs, or their workloads, was usually unformulated, and such commentary as there was, was often marked by elements of confusion. Participants were unsure as to whether individuals could stay in their target roles if they progressed in their careers, and just be on a better salary, or whether they would have to take on new tasks, such as management:

Extract 1:

> **What do you think would happen if you were promoted in that work [advertising]?**
>
> *I suppose that I would be paid more, is that what you mean?*

Do you think you would have to do anything different or extra?

Oh, yes, I probably would have to do a better job at what I was doing. And, instead of working for someone else's little project, I would have to work on my own little project. (II, HE)

Extract 2:

I would be hoping to chop and change careers if that didn't mean I was climbing up and then I'd come back down and climbing up and back down. I would rather stick with one and get quite high up in it, but if I could climb and not stick to one career, I would, because I don't think you can just choose one career and stay happy with it. (II, C).

Extract 3:

I think you just stay at the same levels for years and I would really like to climb and to have something to aim for. Not to do the same thing for years and years.

And when you climbed, what would you do then?

A different job. So if you were a lawyer, you could then be a judge. (II, SS)

As has also been suggested, a key theme for many of the education participants was that a chosen occupation should deliver intrinsic satisfaction. This included for many the desire to work with others and to help people. It should also deliver a degree of contentment. Participants certainly made it clear that their future work should not bring stress and unhappiness, and this was regardless of whether they also expressed a desire for above-average financial rewards and recognition:

Extract 1:

I think my parents have influenced me, especially my mum as she had a good job, a really good job . . . but at the end she didn't like it, she hated going. She retired quite early, at about 50 – she had a good pension – but seeing her not enjoying it makes me think, 'Oh, I don't want to do a job I don't enjoy'. (GI, HE)

Extract 2:

My mum gets so stressed and tired, but she's absolutely brilliant at what she does and loves it. I don't think I need that much stress, but I want to love my work. (II, C)

Extract 3:

> *I would like to go as far as I can, would like challenges and to push myself,
> but not push myself too much.* (II, C)

Parents were cited as touchstones in this regard, with mothers' experiences in terms of work satisfaction and happiness being more frequently cited. Participants suggested that they could not countenance staying in a career that did not add value to their lives beyond financial value, and too much stress was a detractor, regardless of their other ambitions.

The generally high level of progression ambition in girls and women was attributed to female successes within education, their conscientiousness and their academic and interpersonal skills, among other traits. As was clear from the commentary already discussed, a strong theme to emerge from the education participants' discussions focused on the claim that most girls and women would not be interested in the firefighter role because it was not skilled or professional enough. This was despite its official classification as an 'Associate Professional and Technical Occupation' (ONS 2000). In this commentary, girls and women were characterised as comprising the sunrise gender, the gender with above-average educational qualifications, grades, skills and ambition. Boys and masculinity were more closely associated with physical competencies and interests, rather than mental ones, with less ambition and with less skilled work. Conversely, the kinds of work female participants were interested in was nearly always conceived of as 'professional', despite very little forthcoming detail on what this might mean beyond it requiring primarily mental skills, and commanding a certain, though ill-defined, level of respect and recognition. As was seen in earlier chapters, these characteristics were sometimes viewed as based on natural difference, but more often, female possession of them was not explored or explained. Very infrequently, women's *'new ambition'* was linked to gender politics and their history:

Extract 1:

> *I think women want to be out more getting themselves heard because
> they have had enough of being in the background, they want to be heard.*
> (GI, HE)

Extract 2:

> *Women want their own career and job . . . I think it's only recently they've
> been allowed one and they are not going to give it up.* (GI, SS)

Again, the construction of females as more able to defer gratification was raised in relation to their attempts to orientate themselves away from *'the bottom jobs'*, and towards *'higher'* work:

Extract 1:

> *I'd say we are aiming higher than boys – more boys leave education . . . I don't know why. They just don't seem to be as bothered. They seem to be quite happy . . .* [with] *lower jobs that girls are not happy with I think.* (II, SS)

Teaching was drawn as a more professional job than firefighting – referred to, for instance, as a *profession'* rather than *'a job'*, *'an occupation'* – but was still considered less than ideal for those expressing high ambition:

Extract 1:

> *Is there a clear ladder in teaching? Isn't there just teacher and then Head and Deputy? That would worry me. And most of the Heads being men.* (GI, HE)

Somewhat surprisingly, given the vagueness of much of the education groups' commentary on their future employment, boys were also characterised as less likely to plan their careers in detail from an early age, by contrast with girls, who did. As with the commentary on financial rewards, this was the case with both girls and women who claimed to have identified a target career, and those who claimed to be determined to keep their options open.

Firefighters and teachers

With one exception, firefighter participants generally claimed that they did not have desires beyond the immediate role on first joining the Service: *'when I joined, I just wanted to be a firefighter for thirty years'*. Prospective firefighters did not mention promotion aspirations in their commentary. The exception claimed that she had joined the Service *'for a career'*:

> *I really wanted something more. You can get out what you put in. You can have a go and do well, and I could see that. You have to get on with it, but there are good opportunities.* (GI, FF)

Nearly all wholetime firefighters were positive about promotion possibilities within the Service, however, and about women's chances of securing advancement. Indeed, it was suggested that women were disproportionately more likely to be promoted within the Service. Several interviewees had been promoted comparatively quickly – in their first few years of service – and referred to other known women who had also advanced through the ranks. Some of those promoted talked about discovering that they *'wanted more from the role'* after some years in it, that *'the challenge had not been enough'*, and that they wanted to test themselves further. They claimed to have not proactively sought out promotion, however, but *'when opportunities started happening . . .* [deciding] *to try and go further'*.

Again, women's success was explained in terms of their generally having *'a higher expectation'*, and *'aiming higher'*. This attitude was contrasted with male firefighters who some argued were happier remaining as firefighters: *'There are an awful lot of guys who . . . don't want to climb because they want the easy life'*.

Besides the desire *'for at the very least a permanent job'*, the majority of the teacher participants also claimed that they had few ambitions beyond the immediate role on first entering the profession:

Extract 1:

> *I don't think I really thought that there was anything beyond being a teacher. Once you'd got offered a job as a teacher, that was it, and I remember my Head, almost on my first day here, going, 'Of course' you know, 'eventually when you're wanting to move up through the ranks . . . !' I just think that was a complete surprise to me! That people might even want to do that! But I think my ambitions are elsewhere.* (GI, T, C)

A minority reported themselves to have been *'ambitious when I was young'*, aiming to be a Head at some point in the future, but only one participant had achieved this, and she did not claim it as an earlier ambition. There was general agreement that the career ladder for teachers had historically been very truncated, although this was alleviated somewhat by the introduction of incremental points for those with specialist skills, and so on:

> A: *It's always been quite a short ladder teaching, not many rungs to go up. So you'll . . . do your first nine or seven years where you're going up the points, a tiny progression in salary, until recently, that's it, isn't it? If you*

get to nine, if you get a management point, extra thousand, but other than that, there's . . .

B: *Nothing. It's a very, again . . .*

C: *It's not a career progressive job.* (GI, T, PS)

The lack of orientation to teaching at HE level was striking in the commentary. While it is true that HE lecturers were not targeted for interviewing, it was nevertheless noticeable that a strong theme for participants' entry into teaching was a desire to pursue a subject they loved for as long as they could, and in this light, the lack of consideration of employment at this level was notable. Some participants had explored continuing to study their subject as a postgraduate, and a few had started courses, but most of these had then been abandoned before completion. Alternatives existed to which participants were '*more inclined*', or which had ultimately appeared '*the more logical thing to do*':

Extract 1:

> *I was very, very interested in English Literature and wanted to keep on working with it as much as possible, and didn't consider an academic route I suppose, so teaching was the next available option.* (GI, T, C)

Extract 2:

> *I would like to think that I kind of resisted that conditioning* [prior comments suggest women are more likely to become teachers due to social conditioning], *because when I went to university I didn't have a clue what I was going to do, so I opted for a course that would interest me and it, you know, would hold a lot of relevance for me . . . it was just fabulous, and after that I went on to do a Masters and I thought, 'Hang on, I love university so much, and academia', and the government at the time was kind of supporting my stay in education, I thought, 'I'm going to do another course'. And by then, either you had to get a scholarship, or you had to fund yourself for a PhD and I just, you know, I just didn't put in an application for a PhD so I kind of missed that, and I thought, 'Well, teaching, a teacher training course is free, so that will keep me in education, give me another year of kind of respite before I actually make the decision'.* (GI, T, SS)

The preponderance of men in HE teaching, where it was discussed, was characterised as a function of their greater focus on subject rather than students, and sometimes of their greater ability to '*study at that top level*'.

Perceived barriers to choices around progression

Education group

For most education participants, parents' views were perceived to operate as direct pressures towards progressing well, both academically and in terms of employment:

Extract 1:

> *My mum says 'just do your best', but my dad is more like, 'you'd best do your best!'* (II, C)

Extract 2:

> *There are definitely pressures . . . I don't think my parents would be happy if I did a hairdressing course and ended up as some hairdresser.* (II, SS)

Extract 3:

> *I think if I decided suddenly to become something lower down, there would be a fight- 'we haven't wasted all this energy for nothing' sort of thing.* (GI, HE)

This perception did not, however, undermine the expressed sense of individual independence when making decisions about careers for most. External pressure was acknowledged to play a part, but not an excessive one: *'There is five per cent pressure, the rest is up to me'*; *'there are people influencing me, as well as helping, but it's my decision in the end'*.

The vast majority of education participants did not proactively mention the impact of domestic commitments on their projected careers, even when asked about potential barriers to progressing within them. Exceptions comprised the few HE students already with children:

Extract 1:

> *Maybe women are limited by the fact that they have children. It's is a brilliant thing, but it is also a limitation because they have to take into account childcare and other things that men don't have to and it definitely will affect the choice of jobs during a certain time of their lives for sure.* (GI, HE)

Extract 2:

> *Whereas you are brought up with the expectation that you are free to do what you like, family life is often the thing to stop you from perhaps thinking you*

*could do that kind of job. Not so much when you are younger but maybe when you are older I think it does affect it because if you want to have kids I don't think, I don't know. **I suppose you do choose your career first** [my emphasis]. (GI, HE)*

When asked directly what possible impact that parenthood might have on the progress of their careers, education participants who were not parents were hesitant and unclear, and most indicated that it was far too early to consider such issues:

Extract 1:

I want to make sure that I'm in a decent job so that I can support a family, but then you've got to think about taking time off when they are first born so you need to take a lot into consideration before even starting to think about that. I don't think anyone is thinking about it now. You just don't think about a job, 'Oh, but it will help me in years to come when I'm starting a family'. I don't think you even begin to consider it when you're thinking of college and work. You just think 'I'm so far away from that now that I don't need to worry about it'. (II, C)

Extract 2:

I'm still quite young so that's not a concern. I don't think it is for anyone as we choose our careers first, don't we? (GI, HE)

Some indicated that, in the context of the increasingly precarious nature of parental partnerships, they would defer having children until they knew they could sustain themselves independently:

Extract 1:

I will not have a family until I'm earning a lot so that if I had a family and I was married, and something happened to the marriage, I could hold myself together, so I could hold myself up. (II, C)

Others claimed that they would only consider children if someone else could take the lion's share of the caring responsibility, as a career gap was too risky or unattractive:

Extract 1:

Not if it's going to put me back down the bottom of the ladder (II, HE)

Extract 2:

> *I will either make my husband stay at home or my children will end up in childcare because I wouldn't give up my career to stay at home.* (II, C)

Less commonly indicated were plans to stay at home parenting for any period of length, although a few indicated that they would like to follow their mother's example in this respect, '*and stay home and just have a happy, relaxed life after I'd had children*'.

As was seen in Chapter 4, education group participants were seemingly largely ignorant of the concentration of men in very senior positions and occupations, or of the gender pay gap. Even the minority who claimed some awareness provided commentary indicating its effects were patchy, and avoidable if the worker were '*choosey enough*' about where they sought employment:

Extract 1:

> *I would have thought I'd be earning the same. There are certain jobs where men just get paid more I think, aren't there? I don't know what they are, but I wouldn't choose to work in them.* (II, C)

Extract 2:

> A: *In fire fighting, do they have different wages as well or is it every occupation where you have different wages, or is there a general trend?*
> . . .
> B: *It can't be everywhere.* (GI, SS)

Extract 3:

> *Well, we've just found out in sociology about the whole glass ceiling thing and women not getting the same money as men, so I'd like to say I would* [get the same pay as men], *and up until finding that out, I would have said I would get the same, but now I think it just depends on getting in the right place where they do treat people the same, but at the moment apparently they don't always.* (II, C)

There was almost no evidence of what might be identified as 'feminist' perspectives on any gender differences in relation to employment opportunities and conditions, even when male advantage was noted:

Extract 1:

> *Isn't it the case that men earn about 25 per cent more just because of the stereotype that they pay for us? But that's just how it is.* (II, C)

Indeed, as we have seen, the only sense of collective identity was expressed in relation to girls' and women's advantage in relation to both the education and employment spheres, and in opposition to the disadvantages associated with being male. The emphasis was, therefore, overwhelmingly on their greater chance of freely taken choices, their lesser likelihood of having to '*settle for a lower career*', and their ability to control the rate of progression within their career, according to internally established success criteria.

On the rare occasion where a suggestion of male advantage did emerge, it was expressed tentatively and even apologetically:

> *I know I shouldn't be like that . . . but I can't help it because I feel it's such a man's world and I am starting to get a chip on my shoulder and I know I shouldn't. I just don't like the idea that I get a degree at university and a boy does the same degree yet they all get fourteen thousand and I will get twelve thousand just because I am a girl.* (GI, HE)

Firefighters and teachers

Confirming the evidence reviewed in Chapter 4, there was no evidence of feminist perspectives within the firefighter commentary either. Again, gender differences in employment terms were more often articulated in terms of female advantage than disadvantage; where male advantage was conceded, it was in relation to physical prowess, and was ultimately unconcerning. Even these participants, notwithstanding their own physical interests and competencies, expressed a weakened version of the identification of female with the primary half of the mental/physical binary. There were, therefore, no reportedly perceived barriers to career progression. Women described some anxiety about promotion in terms of leaving behind aspects of the role they loved, but this was not a paramount worry. Perhaps because of the comparatively young age of the firefighter participants, and the relatively recent entrance of women into the occupation, discussion of combining domestic commitments with the role was minimal, and it was certainly not discussed as presenting a barrier to progression.

There was more commentary from teachers relating to the perceived barriers to progression. Three themes of fairly equal salience emerged in relation to career progression. The first was the perceived positive discrimination in favour of men within the teaching profession, the second interviewees' personal reluctance to pursue promotion because of what it entailed in relation to their role, and the third the impact of motherhood on their own progression.

There was no discussion of men being advantaged in terms of greater financial rewards for similar work as women, either in teaching or more widely, but there was significant observation of male advantage in terms of appointment and promotion. Notwithstanding the noted preponderance of male teachers at HE level, all interviews identified the rarity of men teaching in primary school – '*which is perceived to be the bottom end of the profession*' – along with the over-representation of the same in key, senior, positions within both the primary and secondary sectors:

> . . . *But men get all the promotions, generally. I mean I know from various sources, you know, friends in primary: if you're a man in primary education . . . basically, you're bound to go up the ladder because you are a good role model et cetera to bring boys on, and I think it's just incredible, that that kind of reverse discrimination is working there, and in secondary schools where there are more men than primary, and in Sixth Form.* (GI, T, SS)

Men were perceived to be promoted, not just with more frequency than women, but with greater speed. It was claimed that they '*went straight to the top*', that it took '*about five years for a man in a primary school to make Head*'. PGCE courses were also privileging male applicants: '*Anyone who stands up to pee will get in*'; '*We had some dreadful, dreadful male students . . . and the fact that they were accepted says something*'. The dominant explanatory mode was that positive discrimination was propelling men to the top because of the perception that schools, parents, and especially boys, wanted and needed them. Men were generally perceived to be '*more authoritative*', more '*disciplining*', and schools were keen to have these traits at their disposal. Those participants who had experience of appointing or had been in management positions within education, described themselves as '*always trying to operate a positive discrimination policy*' towards male applicants, and in a context in which women's performance was nearly always as good if not better than men's. That men were promoted more readily was rarely identified as discrimination *against* women, however, even when the situations being described would seem to clearly warrant it:

Extract 1:

> *And I've been here at a time when our then principal, we had three vice-principals, he apologised because . . . when he had appointed the third,*

he said he couldn't possibly have two women because it would be unbalanced because, you know, then you might have two women and one man, but he could have three men at one point and he thought that was balanced. (GI, T, SS)

Extract 2:

And you know, you're bending over backwards to see the good in these appalling male applications, because the school needs more men. I've done it myself. (GI, T, SS)

Another key explanation offered was that men were more ambitious and instrumental in their occupational aspirations, and that promotion was higher on their agendas.

Following on from this, the second theme in relation to promotion was linked to the different characterisation of men and women within teaching. Interviewees felt strongly that, historically, key promotions in teaching had taken them away from the aspects of the role they gained most satisfaction from, and which were related to the student–pupil interaction in all its aspects. Very senior roles necessitated a cut in student contact time: Area Coordinators, Curriculum-related Managers, Deputies and Heads. Women, it was claimed, were less likely than men to be happy with this, and were, therefore, often to be found in '*donkey-work jobs*' – '*guidance leadership*' and so on – that did not involve less contact time with students, just more administration and management. Men, however, were painted as happy to trade student contact for promotion:

A: *That's probably why they rise to be Heads to quickly.*

B: *Exactly.*

C: *Because they can't do those nurturing bits.*

B: *You know, those silly bits that . . . need to be done.*

C: *Which is playground duty, which I'm sure they all love doing anyway, and then you get the man rising to the top.*

A: *I know which I'd rather!* (GI, T, PS)

The relatively recent initiatives to provide teachers with promotion possibilities while staying in the classroom were welcomed in connection with the desire to '*remain with integrity in the classroom and still get on*'. The provision of higher status for specialist teachers, recognised '*women's strengths*', and '*that you might want career progression but you shouldn't be pushed into a management position*'.

Although only a minority of women reported entering teaching with promotion beyond class teacher in mind, once in-post, one factor played a substantial part in challenging such progression ambition as there was:

> A: *I must admit, I did think I was going to be a Head very quickly, by the time I was 30 or something, when I came in. As you do!*
>
> B: *Do you wish you were?*
>
> A: *It's too late I think! . . . I don't really know . . . I suppose it's because kids come along, don't they? So I could never have done it as quickly as I thought when I was 22 . . . In fact, having* [a child] *made me ditch my management role and come back and sort of start again . . . so I sort of started all over again, but that was my choice'.* (GI, T, C)

Those participants who joined teaching after having children said they had not aspired to career progression beyond finding a job, recognising that they would almost certainly lose any benefits the school year provided to them in their capacity as primary carers. For others who had either progression ambitions, or who had been selected for promotion regardless of their personal hopes in this regard, motherhood was a role that they almost universally found impossible to combine with their elevated status and its attendant responsibilities. Indeed, the teaching role itself, on a full-time basis, as we have seen in Chapter 5, was reported by many participants to be very difficult to combine satisfactorily with parenting, especially parenting pre-school children. Nearly every teacher, who was also a mother, confirmed that they had changed their employment practices post-childbirth. Many had waited a lengthy period before returning to teaching, had taken jobs in another occupational area altogether, or had returned on a part-time basis, or on a basis that reduced their responsibilities to the minimum possible. For those in senior positions, leaving their current role was a certainty, as the workloads associated with promotion just could not be combined with parenting:

Extract 1:

> *I think that's what got me out of teaching, though . . . I loved my job and I spent one year in fact as the Head of Department and the Head of Year. I was quite happy to do all the hours it took – it was loopy – but . . . it was great, and I really enjoyed doing the Head of Year's job and felt that I was more interested in children and their whole reaction to school and*

all the issues they were going through as a whole rather than my subject. And I think then having children I realised, 'My gosh', you know, 'Why am I worried about the pastoral care of two hundred and forty of my year group, whilst leaving my own child in nursery from eight in the morning until six at night, and working evenings and weekends, when I don't have to go back to work to pay mortgage at the end of the month?' kind of scenario. I think that was a big shift, which is why I currently feel like I couldn't teach. (GI, T, SS)

Any career-breaks reportedly meant *'starting again', 'at the bottom'*, leaving participants feeling as if they had wasted years of skill-acquisition and experience: *'You've got all those skills, you've built them up, and then to go back down to that position is quite disheartening'*. This aspect of the career ladder was cited as a major cause of teacher loss. Teaching contracts with more flexibility, including part-time contracts, were perceived to be rare and characterised by low status and poor job satisfaction and promotion possibilities. Part-timers were also generally resented within the occupation, including by some of the participants themselves: *'we actually don't like part-timers in our school and try and avoid them'*. Many, nevertheless, claimed that if better and more flexible contracts, or workable job shares, could be offered, retention and satisfaction rates would be greatly improved overall, and would have positively affected their own decision-making. These were thought to be *'on the horizon'*, following legislative and policy initiatives, but some were doubtful as to how effectively changes would be adopted within their institutions. There was particular scepticism in relation to initiatives to establish flexible contracts at senior levels.

Participants were clear that the organisation of teaching made combining the role with parenthood difficult for male teachers as well:

Well it's interesting because I know two of the male teachers who've worked in our team, both very good tutors, but gave up tutoring because they became fathers again for the second time, and it was too much work. . . . It goes down the male brain idea . . . you know, you know where you stand. It doesn't kind of expand to fill the hours. . . . You know you've got Curriculum work, you know it's going to take this long, and you can predict. . . . Whereas Guidance and tutoring just sort of fills out. (GI, T, SS)

The structure of teaching was therefore perceived by many as generally unfriendly to family life, and senior positions as particularly so, but

also that it was women's different priorities, and their 'choice' to prioritise their families that essentially inhibited them:

Extract 1:

> *I know I could have been there by now, but you have to look at what you
> would lose in other ways. I enjoy the job, I'm knackered, but I do love it,
> and I've had the breaks. Heads . . . carry on through most of them. That
> may be ok for some, but I just don't want to pay the price.* (II, T, PS)

Extract 2:

> *It's been my choice though . . . I could have been in a different position, but
> it would mean absolutely no life, not sensible for family and what have
> you, and it's my decision to do things as I have.* (II, T, SS)

Linking with commentary on the intrinsic benefits of their role to
themselves and to others, some participants fundamentally queried the
idea that progression was an inherently positive step in a career, and
expressed the view that their 'choices' around promotion issues were
being challenged:

Extract 1:

> A: *Perhaps we need to challenge whether promotion's a good thing, because
> it is actually a societal thing, and actually I think that's wrong. I don't
> think people are better off being promoted. You need to recognise experience
> and stick with what you do better at. That's one thing that I wish I had
> known: promotion isn't all it's cracked up to be.*
>
> B: *Not in the sense of the sort of linear . . . growth.*
>
> C: *And job satisfaction.* (GI, T, C)

Extract 2:

> *All this scrabbling for the next level, and people think you're unambitious if
> you don't want it. What's wrong with striving to be as good as you can at
> what you do . . . just for the sake of being as good as you can be?* (II, T, SS)

There was more feminist discourse within the teacher commentary
than there was within that of the education group, or the firefighter
group. As we have seen, there was, for instance, some belief that the
occupation would have better conditions and pay if it were not female-
dominated. There was some attempt by the minority of participants to

link women's position within teaching to a generally subordinate social position to men:

Extract 1:

> *I think as well there are issues . . . and it just reminds me of all the unpaid work women do . . . housekeeping, all the things that are meant to be part of your genetic make-up because you're a woman. You know, people get paid to clean, people get paid to cook in places, but not in your own home. It's, you've got to do it, it's just part of it and I think it's a horrific repetition of that in the workplace, and the workplace . . . as we all know, is about getting paid, that's why we're here first and foremost. . . . I mean, we may be moved to a certain profession because of our love for a subject, or our love for teaching students, and shaping the minds of the future generations and stuff, but I think that's something that's a really atrocious face of teaching I have to say, particularly because most of the people affected by it are women.* (GI, T, C)

As we have also seen, there was strong suggestion that men, overall, were advantaged within the occupation. Nearly always, however, male advantage in teaching was generally explained as a function of the prevalence of positive discrimination towards men, rather than discrimination against women. For many, the possibility of the broader structure of teaching, or employment in general, being a function of discriminatory forces was not considered. This often resulted in a consequential lack of analysis that privileged any kind of gender politics perspective, and the alternative privileging of personal choice and the role of *'happenstance'*:

Extract 1:

> *There's more male Course Leaders aren't there? In the college, than there are female Course Leaders, which is . . . I don't know any reason for that really. . . . I mean, I think a lot of people when they talk about the glass ceiling and all that kind of stuff, I mean a lot of it is to do with women career's being* [kept down] *because of children and stuff. And so there's almost a kind of inevitability about that, but at this level, I wouldn't have thought it would have fit in as much, but I just don't think there any many female Course Leaders.* (GI, T, C)

Extract 2:

> *I guess women drift towards some roles and men towards others. I'm not sure I'd say it's more than just personal interest in the end.* (II, T, PS)

7
Gender as Vocation: A Sociology of Occupational Choice

Introduction

In Chapters 2 and 3, it was observed that individualist approaches to research into gendered-occupational segregation have rarely, if ever, sought to access accounts of occupational decisions from individuals directly. Instead they have assumed such decisions to be a function of underlying, comparatively fixed gender differences, innate or otherwise. Such differences are expressed at the level of the individual, via reasonably rational choices made by reasonably well-informed agents. The collective outcome of these individual choices, given the underlying differences, forms the social phenomena of both horizontal and vertical gendered-occupational segregation. As these phenomena result from such a basis, these are not often explicitly or even implicitly deemed problematic within this research approach, being far more readily understood as benign outcomes or reflections of acceptable and expected difference. Consequently, correctives to occupational segregation, and its attendant social outcomes, are more rarely proffered than solutions to the problems of accurately modelling the person-choice-career relationship. Such modelling, as we have seen, insofar as its hypothesis-testing goes, has produced somewhat confused and contradictory findings, although more generally it has also produced valuable and insightful results.

In Chapter 2, we also explored part of the research base that seeks to explain gendered-occupational patterns with primary reference to social forces that act on and through the individual. 'Choices' in this framework are shaped and constrained, and lead people to live work and home lives that they might otherwise not live. For all such researchers, segregation is, therefore, problematic. Moreover, its negative effects are asymmetrically distributed as women are more disadvantaged by the overall patterning of segregation. As was seen in Chapter 3, it is far more common for those adopting this latter set of presumptions to select methodological techniques and analytical approaches that facilitate the accessing of people's accounts directly. It is easy to see why; indeed, it is difficult to imagine how anyone cleaving to a strongly individualist approach could sustain its core assumptions if they, too, had selected the same research design. As the data presented in this book testifies, when such accounts are accessed directly, *and in sufficient numbers*, it becomes clear that social factors and forces are undeniably at play in the generation of occupational ideas and decisions, and that although individual agency is also in evidence, crucially, it is not visible to the extent that it is 'experienced' by the individuals themselves.

Representations, stereotypes and discourse

All of the themes discussed in the previous three chapters, unless otherwise stated, emerged as prominent and recurring motifs within the dataset, emanating from numerous individual and group accounts. As well as sharing these common foci, the identified themes also often demonstrated a shared linguistic currency. Strikingly similar ways of speaking were evident, with the same words, phrasing and intonation manifest across the data-set, both at the intra-group and inter-group level, and despite origins across different interview settings, and types and ages of participant. It was clear that these ways of speaking were determinations of particularly salient, discursive constructions of occupations, gender differences and of group and individual identities.

Gottfredson (1981), despite her antipathy to explanations of occupational segregation that ignore innate differences between men and women, noted the powerful effect of socially produced ways of thinking and talking about occupations on individual understanding, beliefs and action in relation to occupations. Within her framework, occupational information coalesces around universally held stereotypes of types of work and their incumbents. The concept of the 'stereotype' originates in Lippmann's *Public Opinion* (1922) and referred to ways of seeing phenomena – pictures in the head – that help us interpret them, and play a constitutive role in determining thought, feeling and action about both the phenomena and ourselves (Moyle 2004). Such interpretive tools reduce the 'cognitive load' (Rennenkampf 2004), and simultaneously facilitate and limit perception, understanding and opinion. More recent developments of the concept have expanded it and emphasised the production of stereotypes using binary constructions of in-groups and out-groups, in which the stereotypes of the out-group (hetero-stereotypes) are usually always subordinate, and those of the in-group (auto-stereotypes) positive and superior (Moyle 2004: 15–17); hetero-stereotypes and auto-stereotypes exist in a 'bilateral, photographic relationship where the auto-stereotype appears as the negative of the hetero-stereotype and vice-versa' (ibid.: 18). The concept has also been developed to allow for the more fluid production and activity of stereotypes 'according to inter-group relations, context, and the needs, values and purposes of the stereotyper' (ibid.: 15). Auto-stereotypes are one of the ways groups, and their individual members, maintain and develop their social identity. An idealised auto-stereotype indicates a perceived need by an in-group to highlight collective responsibilities 'particularly at times of change or crisis' (ibid.: 17).

Despite the obvious applicability of this concept to the data explored here, its characterisation of the relationship between language and experience would seem to fall short, however, insofar as it implies that, outside of stereotypes, language, perception and experience can be representational, and that therefore stereotyping is somehow 'optional'.

The term 'discourse' is therefore necessary here, and is used to mean systemic, systematic and consistent ways of speaking about phenomena that characterise these phenomena in particular ways, and that limits description of them in other ways; the perception of the phenomena is thus shaped by the discourse. 'Discursive practices' indicate that such ways of talking about phenomena are not independent of issues external to linguistic interchange. Instead they are determinations (in the dual sense) of non-linguistic practices, such as institutional, group and economic practices and so on (Foucault 1980; Connell 1987; Wodak 1996, 1997). Discourse is, therefore, connected to issues of power, ideology and social change and has real, material effects on social actors' lives:

> [It] is socially constituted, as well as socially conditioned – it constitutes situations, objects of knowledge, and the social identities of and relationships between people and groups of people. It is constitutive both in the sense that it helps sustain and reproduce the social status quo, and in the sense that it contributes to transforming it.
>
> (Wodak 1996: 17)

Although all perceptions, knowledge and facts are assumed here to be functions of constitutive discourses, and in this sense, nothing is 'true', objective, factual, neutral and so on, a distinction is drawn between particular forms of 'truths', so that, for example, workable distinctions can be deployed between government estimates of the mortality rates of teachers and firefighters, and the estimates of these from the education participants. It is assumed that the former are still the production of interpretive, constitutive and invested processes, but that they are, arguably rightly, accorded a different status to the latter. A further distinction between 'stereotypical' discourses, or 'stereotypes' within discourses, and non-stereotypical, linguistic practices is useful. Stereotypes are particular forms of language. Many are dominant within core cultural schemas, but they are of specific interest being at once more caricatured and contestable than other linguistic practices, but also more operationally insidious due to their effectiveness as cognitive shortcuts and bolsters to identity.

To reprise and confirm points made in literature reviewed in Chapter 2, it is clear that gender remains one of the fundamental categories of social life, 'a ubiquitous dimension of social organisation, its influence is apparent in every social encounter' (Duveen & Lloyd 1986: 222), and is salient within core overarching discourses that shape social life. The overarching gender system is produced through binary and hierarchical discursive practices focused on biological sex difference, that are determining only insofar as they are employed as signifiers in a semiotic system whereby representations of male and female are constructed and sustained (ibid.; also see Davies 1997a, 1997b). Davies states:

> The construction operates in a variety of intersecting ways, most of which are neither conscious nor intended. They are more like an effect of what we might call 'speaking-as-usual'. They are inherent in the structures of the language and the storylines through which our culture is constructed and maintained. The structure of the language and the dominant storylines combine, with powerful effect, to operate on our conscious and unconscious minds and to shape our desire.
>
> (1997a: 9)

It is also noted here that within these signifying practices, male is always the primary term, and associated traits, skills and behaviour, whatever their content, become the most culturally valued (Cucchiari 1981; Duveen & Lloyd 1986; Davies 1997a); this point is interesting in the context of some of the data explored in previous chapters and will be discussed further below.

Representing occupations and gender

Although there are important differences between the firefighter and teacher roles, some significant similarities were also notable from available statistics and literature associated with each occupation. According to 'official' documentation, similar interpersonal skills and commitment levels are required, along with a public service ethic; over and above this, salary levels are broadly comparable since the firefighters' pay dispute resolution, although early career salaries have always been so. Futhermore, from within the commentary from all the interviewees it was possible to identify considerable overlap between the imputed skills and dispositions ideally possessed by good candidates for both firefighting and teaching. Both roles were portrayed as requiring, again, a strong public service ethic, and as being unpredictable, 'non-routine', and yet demanding of consistent performance, as well as physical, mental and emotional resilience, discipline, commitment and good communication/interpersonal skills.

It is especially interesting, then, that, notwithstanding these identified overlapping features, the dominant presentation of firefighting and teaching in the commentary was of two fundamentally different occupations, one of which could not seriously be countenanced as a career by participants and another which could, even if it were not the most exciting prospect under consideration. Indeed, the leading commentary from the education group also repeatedly and clearly underscored the differences between the firefighter role and the teaching role, and on this basis, the concentration of men in the former occupation, and women in the latter, was rationalised.

Within the dominant discourse on firefighting, for instance, participants made much of the dangers, and emotional and physical rigours, associated with the role, and cited these as key reasons why they could not consider it for their own career, or as a career for women in particular. Teaching, by contrast, was dominantly portrayed as a relatively safe occupation in terms of the risk of physical and mental harm, and in terms of its prestige level, against which firefighting fared notably less well. The skill involved in the firefighter role was also primarily represented as almost entirely based on physical competence, and characterised in ways shot through with suggestions that aspects of the work were menial and routine. Teaching was characterised as a professional role, a role for unselfish, respectable and committed individuals, much like the representation of them identified by Gottfredson (1981). While it is true that teaching receives a higher Standard Occupational

Classification (SOC), and is therefore a 'higher' occupation, it is also crucial to note that many of the occupations education participants cited alongside teaching as likely future careers are in the same major skill category within the SOC as firefighters: therapists, youth workers, artistic and literary occupations, design assistant professionals, media associate professionals and marketing associate professionals, are all in SOC major group 3 (Associated Professional and Technical Occupations – see ONS 2000). It is also important to note that, although teaching is less dangerous than firefighting in terms of its overall mortality rates, for those participants entering the former occupation on the grounds of its safety, it is likely to disappoint, thus confirming that expressed preferences are often not actualised in work outcomes (Reed & Dahlquist 1994; DeLeire & Levy 2001).

The dominant form of commentary on firefighters was particularly uniform in the data from the education interviewees. In terms of sex-typing it was unvarying, but overall the consistency of collective voice obtained regardless of the bifurcated and often contradictory nature of the remarks made, so that individuals were likely to draw on cohesive images of the occupation when they spoke about it positively, and again when they spoke about it negatively. Very particular phrases and images recurred in interview data, with participants in separate settings often echoing each other remarkably closely, and underscoring the impression that interviewees were accessing set-piece discursive descriptions of the firefighter role in their explorations. Although it was clear that the education participants had little access to direct observation and experience of the role, and that there were serious gaps in their knowledge as a consequence, it was also evident that they were alive to at least some aspects of the role that might counter the stronger and more exaggerated general images, but that this awareness was usually not deployed in discussions. There was a keen reluctance to incorporate direct observations or acknowledged uncertainties into expressed descriptions and opinion so that, in many cases, there was active and conscious counterfactual stereotyping of the firefighter role: .

Extract 1:

A: *I think they're generally kind of fat. It's like the whole stereotypical thing . . .*

B: *Fat?*

A: *Yeah. It's like the whole stereotypical thing . . .*

B: *I think they're quite fit . . . did you mean fit?*

C: *You always expect them to be good looking but then you look into the truck when they drive past and they're not.*

A: *They're not really fit.*

C: *Yeah, but you do expect them to be.* (GI, C)

Extract 2:

The qualities associated with firemen are bravery, being fit. All the things that add up to the stereotype you need to do the job. (GI, SS)

Extract 3:

I think of them in that traditional outfit they don't even wear anymore! (GI, SS)

Extract 4:

A: *You would probably have to be quite bright.*

B: *That doesn't fit at all with what we've been saying.*

A: *Strike that then!* [laughter] (GI, HE)

The awareness that the images being used were not always the most accurate available was underscored in the case of two group interviews. In the first, following an interviewee's very early indication that her father was a firefighter, both the positive and negative commentary was far more subdued than it was in any other interview. In the other, an interviewee also indicated relatively early on that a close family friend was a firefighter, but simultaneously that he '*completely is such a stereotype . . . he just fulfils the stereotype obscenely*', and in this case the commentary was no more measured than it was in other interview contexts.

Despite the dominance of the discourse characterising the firefighter role as relatively unskilled and lacking prestige, secondary characterisations were interwoven with it. Here firefighters were 'superior' individuals, distinct from participants, as well as many other people by virtue of their 'superiority', and, differently again, they required many of the same skills that work deemed 'desirable' necessitated. Between the various characterisations, a number of striking contradictions were maintained, and often by the same individual participants over the period of one interview. For instance, the emphasis, on the one hand, on firefighters' low requirement for intellectual skills and education, and their reliance on 'instinct', sat oddly with the strong emphasis, on the other hand, that they were required to overcome their most 'natural' instincts of self-preservation in the face of danger; to run towards burning buildings when everyone else was running away from them. Similarly, the characterisation of firefighter work as 'manual' and 'routine' sat oddly with the description of firefighters as being unable to tolerate routine and boring work. Such contradictions were rarely identified within the commentary, and there was consequently no attempt to resolve them. Commonalities between the role and target occupations were muted, so that awareness of the physical demands, as well as the risks, associated with teaching or dancing, for example, was minimally expressed. The characterisation of 'office work' as menial, unsatisfactory and tedious is also of interest here. 'Office work' stood as the hetero-stereotyped negative of their own preferred job types. In the case of education interviewees, again, this characterisation was blithely deployed in the face of the seemingly obvious difficulties posed, for instance, by the fact that some key target occupations involved a substantial desk-work component.

In the case of the firefighter group, commentary was once more strikingly coherent in places, and stereotypes were again deployed, but to a lesser extent. The characterisation of 'office work' was strong here as well, and connoted the same negative employment features for this group as it did for the education group. The firefighter group did not use stereotypical or homogenous descriptive terms about the occupation they had oriented to, however. They were also less likely to use either highly negative or positive imagery. Instead, they added detail and diversity in lieu of generalisations, and were far more liable to acknowledge the mental and physical skills associated with the role, as well as the diversity of its requirements and personnel. In some instances, there were similarities between the commentary of in-post firefighters and prospective firefighters, but there were also differences. Prospectives were, for example, more likely to invoke the 'heroic' imagery of firefighters, while firefighters themselves did not. This may have been in part due to modesty on behalf of the latter, but it was arguably also due to their direct knowledge and experience of the work, and a furtherance of the process of disruption and ultimate redundancy of the dominant positive firefighter stereotype for their purposes. The trend away from stereotype use, in the context of greater direct contact with firefighters, is noted elsewhere (Ritchie 2000; Bucke 1994), and is a feature of stereotyping activity more generally. The tendency for stereotypes to be relied upon and deployed in the absence of direct or more detailed information, and in the absence of a motivation to challenge them, was equally evident in discussions of fire itself.

Teachers used stereotypes in their discussions of occupations, although less so again. There was the same, strong tendency to deplore 'office work', and a minor propensity to characterise non-teachers as less hard-working, although much of the commentary on other occupations was tempered by direct experience of alternative working environments, and so was less exaggerated overall.

The commentary in relation to the traits, behaviour and abilities of men and women was marked by stereotyping. The construction of women as more nurturing, caring and maternal was consistently visible in the education group, and with minimal dissent. To be sure, this characterisation sat alongside secondary constructions of women as more 'catty' and 'bitchy', or 'harder' than men, and often did so in the same interview, and even in the same person's commentary. As was the case in the commentary on firefighters, these contradictions were neither identified nor addressed.

Gender stereotyping was deployed by firefighters most strongly in relation to gender-typical work. Interviewees were again likely to use very similar phraseology. For instance, in relation to female-dominated environments, especially work environments, separate interviews produced the following extracts:

Extract 1:

> *I don't mean to be sexist but I do find women-only only environments quite bitchy, catty.* (II, FF)

Extract 2:

> *Women I can find to be very, I don't like using the word but . . . bitchy . . . catty and with men you don't really get that . . . I always find it a nice challenge.* (II, FF)

Extract 3:

> *On the whole I prefer working with all men . . . less bitchy.* (GI, FF)

The general greater detail and diversity on firefighting became confused and contradictory when competing discourses on women, and what it meant to be female, were introduced. Women could be portrayed as difficult and 'bitchy', and interpersonally more problematic than men *or* more empathetic, caring, supportive and compassionate by dint of their femaleness *or*, in terms of their reported effects on their working contexts, as more straightforward and less heavy-going and competitive interpersonally. In the case of the education group, we remember, over-all the 'bitchy' theme was eclipsed by the 'caring' motif; with the fire-fighters, the opposite was the case. For firefighter participants, the negative hetero-stereotyping of women in traditional occupations and with traditional interests, was broadly explicable in terms of their desire and need to assimilate within a male-dominated working environment, of which the auto-stereotype was very positive.

For the education group, further key assumptions were also com-monly made by this group about males – usually through strong hetero-stereotyping – and females in respect of educational skills, that males were usually less interested and able with regard to academic tasks, and less able to defer gratification more generally. While it is undoubtedly true that girls are currently outperforming boys academically, and less are selecting, or being selected, for undergraduate study (EOC 2006), these relative variations between male and female performance and interest were here augmented and amplified within discursive set pieces constructed around assumptions of absolute and categorical difference.

Education participants also often presented women as generally more willing to undertake a public service occupational role – to give more of themselves at work, for less financial reward. Although male firefighters were characterised by their willingness to risk themselves for the public good, this trait was represented as something that marked them out as dis-tinct from participants, and, indeed, as distinct from most other people. Furthermore, the discussion of the public service impetus in relation to firefighters contained frequent cynical elements that were absent from dis-cussions of women's public service motivations.

By dint of these trait and ability differences, women's suitability to teaching was assumed to be good. Their suitability to firefighting was not, despite the common characteristics ascribed at various points to both of these roles, as well as the overlap between these participants' own declared traits, motivations and aspirations, and aspects of the role. Gottfredson's description of the process of building a 'cognitive map' of occupations that individuals develop over time and which evolve inextricably with their emerging sense of identity was supported in much of the data, as was the finding that 'the social identity con-ferred by occupations is clear and of great concern to people' (ibid.: 550). Possible occupations confer and confirm status, along with a particular imagined lifestyle and persona that is compatible with the presentation of self before 'teachers, family, peers and society more gen-erally' (ibid.: 546).

Education participants were associating firefighting with danger and this was represented as off-putting for them, and ran counter to their understanding of what work best suited women (DeLeire & Levy 2002). It was also evident, however, that the actual risks associated with the work were not the beginning and end of the de-selection of firefighting. 'Risk' was also a signifier for aspects of the role not considered prestigious enough for participants themselves, and for women more generally. Despite firefighting's association with the same broad occupational classification and financial remuneration as many occupations participants were willing to consider, the role connoted a particular prestige that was lower than desired, a similar prestige as other male-dominated, 'realistic' work (Gottfredson 1981; Blackburn & Jarman 2006). Skill levels and types were drawn in particular ways in order to justify the occupational decisions of the participants themselves, as well as men and women more generally (Phillips & Taylor 1980; Henwood 1987; Woodfield 2000). At least in some cases, 'office work' was used as shorthand for traditional and routine female administrative roles such as secretary, typist and clerk, that have been identified as 'conventional' work in the past (Gottfredson 1981), and from which participants wished to distance themselves.

Between these two extremes of 'realistic' male-typed work and 'conventional' female-typed work, a small group of target occupations emerged. None was sex-typed male in keeping with much previous research (see for example, EOC 2001a; Miller *et al.* 2004). Significantly, participants did not explicitly acknowledge an awareness of this in their narratives. Confirming previous analyses, the majority of the occupations targeted were within occupational classes two and three; in other words, they were not at the very top or the very bottom, although the skew was towards moderate to high in prestige, rather than simply moderate as suggested by Gottfredson (1981; see also, Charles 2005; Blackburn & Jarman 2006). These jobs were also primarily within the 'social' and 'artistic' groupings identified by Gottfredson as signifying gender-neutrality (1981: 553).

There was a very low level of awareness of very senior occupational positions among the education participants, little explicit characterisation – sex-typing of them for instance – and very little in the way of explicit, purposeful orientation towards them. Although many indicated their desire to be promoted within their chosen area of work, there was minimal understanding of what this might mean in terms of tasks and role. The appreciation of financial remunerative levels was also markedly low. The prestige of 'recognition' was, however, key in these aspirations, underscoring the importance of prestige itself, however amorphously conceived of. Related to this, there was evidence of what Gottfredson called a 'homophily bonus' – the tendency of social group-ings to rank the occupations associated with their own social group more favourably – or the hetero-stereotyping of male-dominated occu-pations, so that women favour their own-gender stratified work, and the tasks associated with their gender. In much past research, this has meant that women have identified themselves with work that connotes traditional female skills and characteristics, and connotes the domestic sphere. In a series of conceptual and practical binaries underpinning the broad gender system, this has meant that women were cast as the 'other', the more subordinate group, and men as the primary group in the following dualisms: mind–body, mental–physical, academic–practical, skilled–manual, interesting–boring (Henwood 1987; Woodfield 2000; Francis 2002), and were identified with the foremost terms, and men with the secondary characteristics. Francis, for instance, found that, although her education participants were ambitious, they deployed gendered binaries in a relatively traditional manner and failed to recog-nise aspects of the changing labour market within which 'women's skills' might be of better utility than men's. With the education partici-pants discussed here, there were similarly articulated ambitions, but for the most part, their preferred discourse of appropriate and inappropri-ate occupations for men and women, although organised around the same series of dichotomies, drew on them in ways that at once invoked and contested the traditional mind–body dichotomy which has histor-ically underpinned rationalisations for gendered-occupational segrega-tion. Girls and women, were, therefore, the 'sunrise' gender, the gender associated with intellectually demanding, interesting and skilled work. Crucially, however, they did this while fixing on very similar occupa-tional targets as they have identified in past research.

The research here also confirmed that girls and young women imag-ine their occupational life as one that reflects their identity as individu-als, rather than 'their future roles as wives' (Francis 2002: 83; see also Aveling 2002). Except in the case of the handful of education partici-pants who were already mothers, consideration of this was suggested to be far removed from participants: *'we choose our careers first, don't we?'* Participants' mothers' experiences of managing work within the con-text of family were rarely explicitly discussed either. Mothers modelled work-related stress levels, but usually from unspecified effects, or from generally 'not liking' their job. As was seen in Chapter 2, women's occu-pational preferences for the middle-, rather than high-, ranking work is assumed in much of the literature to be a function of their basic family orientation (see, for instance, Hakim 2002), but the evidence for this here is minimal. The same descriptive discourses were seemingly not available to education participants, or any participants who were not actually mothers themselves, in this regard. Education participants seemed to have minimal information of the attempt to combined work and family life that they could meaningfully relate to their own futures.

Within the teacher participants, there was also some quite strong stereotyping of the different characteristics of men and women, and their concomitant suitability for their own role, although this was contested somewhat more than it was in the education group. Predominantly, women were characterised as more caring, sensitive and altruistic again, and men as more instrumental and authoritative. This was challenged, not by the suggestion that women were 'bitchy', but by some teacher participants' contestation of the view that men could not be as caring as women, although it was rarely suggested that men would or could take the primary caring role and responsibility in the home. As with the education commentary, the prevailing discursive descriptions of women and men produced some difficult anomalies in the commentary, when read alongside sub-themes, for example, teachers' objections to a tendency in others to assume that their natural 'nurturing' inclinations meant that their occupational roles required less skill than they actually did. Within the teachers' commentary there was a reiteration of female children's advantage in terms of academic learning, but the relationship between academic pursuits and gender was more complexly drawn for adults. Many teacher participants painted themselves as being attracted to teaching because of their love of an academic discipline, but they did not draw attention to intellectual skill in relation to their occupations. Instead men were characterised as more focused on subject, rather than students, and sometimes as being more suited to HE teaching.

Representations of choice

The default figure of a freely choosing individual taking well-informed work choices with the minimum of constraint was presumed throughout the education group commentary. The vast majority of participants conceived of their own, and others', occupational choices as individually made and occurring within a context that was fundamentally meritocratic. Family, teachers, careers advisors and other potentially significant agents were acknowledged to be supporting scaffolding for individual choice, but not to have the potential to over-ride it. Choice was not gendered in any constricting way. External obstacles could be avoided if one was canny or just plain 'choosey' enough. There was some anticipation of discrimination, but this too was very much characterised as a factor that could be overcome if the individual was determined enough to pursue her given career. Indeed, the broad assumption of meritocracy by education participants was so pervasive that absence of choice was not generally considered to be constraint, but drift and freefall. Participants who reported that they were less sure than most of the kinds of work they wanted to undertake, expressed beliefs that they would eventually 'fall into' something, or that a suitable role would 'come along'. Equally, however, emphatic choice was also alien to most. Firefighting was depicted as a difficult career to countenance partly because of the assumption that an individual would have to be strongly called to it, and to the exclusion of all other options, from early in life. Certainly, an individual *could* orient to such a role, but in doing so, they were liable to shut down other options too prematurely, before they had fully explored the wide range of what was on offer: 'keeping options open' was another key principle of choice as it was articulated here. Considering a choice of career that was gender-atypical also raised the shadowy spectre of constraint – of the possibility, for instance, of being subjected to discriminatory practices. When orientations were to gender-typical or neutral roles, 'choice', and its unfettered expression, was automatically assumed to be at play, seamlessly weaving individual preferences into suitable options. When atypical work was targeted, however, the commentary still claimed personal choice as the paramount driver of decisions. Indeed, here it was thrown into sharp relief by virtue of its sure-footedness and potentially more effortful expression in the face of possible inhibitors.

The issue of persistent areas of male-dominated work was not conceived of as a 'problem', but as the outcome of freely taken choices, sometimes based on natural ability differences, sometimes on different patterns of socialisation. Mostly the origins of different choice patterns remained unexamined. Men's orientation to male-typical work was conceived of as an orientation to manual and lower-skilled work, which, at any rate, held little interest for women for the reasons explored above. Indeed, women who were attracted to such work were sometimes characterised as less able. The majority's orientation away from atypical work, as it was conceived, was not therefore expressed as one of disadvantage but of advantage; they were destined for more 'professional', or 'skilled' work. In this sense, there was nothing to be said in relation to possible barriers to such work.

In some significant respects, the discourse of choice in the education group differed from that within the teacher group. The role of individual choice dominated again in the latter, but the alleged impact of serendipity, and 'falling into' occupations, was even more marked. Worker participants were also likely to provide accounts confirming the role of external pressures or expectations in their orientation to particular types and levels of work, however. Older teachers described having restrictive choice and being channelled towards particular 'appropriate' roles for women. Moreover, the accounts of mothers differed greatly from those without children. Mothers and non-mothers accessed different discursive dialects to narrate their significantly divergent work decisions and experiences.

Post-parent life saw many reportedly previously held attitudes and aspirations towards work being modified, and the possibility of undertaking the same work roles, to the same degree, being considerably reduced. Parenting roles were clearly gendered, with males assigned primary responsibility to guarantee financial and other support, and females assigned primary responsibility to care for children and manage the home.

The language of choice prevailed even here, however. Firefighters had few experiences of motherhood among them to draw on, and offered little in the way of commentary on the subject. Those that did comment stressed that it was possible, although difficult, to combine the role with parenting, and that it was open to every woman to choose to do so as long as the necessities of the job were not challenged overtly. Being explicitly a 'woman in the Fire Service', and expecting support or change on this basis, was not a viable or desirable option. Similarly, teachers claimed that, in the context of 'impossible' combinations of work and home, it was their own decision to 'refuse' the lure of promotion, to jettison particular work roles, or to work part-time when they became mothers.

This tendency to individualise occupational problems as well as choices reflected the overall marginalisation of discourses of collectivism. The exceptions to this rule were the expressed desire of teachers to assert their collective experience of negative aspects of the role through repeated in-group articulations and the persistent representation of females and males in terms of their basic differences between them. Within this latter discourse, women were generally advantaged or there was a strong homophily trend. To the extent that a political discourse of gendered disadvantage emerged, it was more often in the service of men than women. Not much latitude was presumed for 'choice' around gendered behaviour. As claimed earlier, mostly the relationship between a person's sex, and their interests and behaviour, was not discussed; where it was, there was minimal attention to the possibility of men and women having the freedom to adopt traits associated with each other. There is a chance that the lack of attention to this issue belied considerable appreciation of, say, the possibility of the social construction of gender differences. The various discussions that did emerge, however, would not seem to support this; and, even if this were the case, the subdued and truncated nature of much of the related commentary remains significant in itself. Gender differences were accepted rather than contested.

Like other literature deploying a similar methodological approach (Erwin & Maurutto 1998; Aveling 2002; Francis 2002), this research therefore found strong evidence that feminism did not 'speak' to the participants to anything like the degree that individualism did, nor the degree to which we might hope or expect given some of the experiences they related. There was a conspicuous lack of feminist discourse in the education group and in the firefighter group, although there was some evidence among teacher participants. As has been suggested, participants who were not oriented to atypical work perceived little or no privation in this. Indeed, there were claims that women's forays into male worlds were further disadvantaging men.

Education participants perceived discrimination as a possibly unpleasant fact of life, but one which was intermittent rather than systemic, and, again, could be avoided if they were careful in their work choices. Worker participants far more readily attributed discrimination to past attitudes and practices. Most experiences that were noted to characterise women's work in the literature review – less pay, the relative lack of seniority, discrimination in favour of men, the responsibility and difficulty of managing domestic commitments and full-time work – were articulated through a discursive framework comprising the dominant strand of individualism, choice, female superiority – the 'we can, but I don't want to' (Lightbody & Durndell 1998) dictum writ large. To the extent that there was any identifiable recognition that some experiences were disadvantaging, it was still overwhelmed by the language of choice, of individual women facing specific problems that might be avoided elsewhere, of specific structural arrangements within their particular occupational setting. For most, there were no issues that could best be addressed by collective awareness and action. The 'we' was not conceived of as empowering in this regard. Indeed, for firefighters, the interests of individuals and organisations were best pursued by denying issues that required an awareness of collective female identity. For women in teaching, similarly, the interests of the organisations they worked for were also keenly felt. Although good part-time working arrangements were desired by many participants, there was also an acknowledgement that, from the school's point of view, part-timers were 'difficult' for the institution and other workers.

Narrations of positive discrimination in favour of men within the teaching environment largely drew them as vulnerable and subordinate, and such decisions were not represented as overtly made 'against' women. Positive discrimination was also articulated as a function of 'choices' made by school and parents, and ultimately served the organisation's and pupils' best interests. Discussions of positive discrimination towards women in the firefighting context also produced strong discursive articulations of male vulnerability in this regard, and were perceived to be 'against men':

> *We shouldn't be out there trying to pull women in. It doesn't do us women in the Brigade any good at all as it's making the men feel left out and 'Why are they being pushed into the job when there are more than enough men who want to do it?' I strongly disagree, **even with advertising** [my emphasis]. I strongly disagree. If a woman really wants to do it badly enough, she will find out about it herself and take the right steps herself. (II, FF)*

It may be the case that there would have been more of a political articulation of female experience had more women who had left teaching or firefighting been included within the sample, or if it had included women with a more elevated feminist consciousness (see, for example, Wright 2005).

Sourcing representations

The role of the media in the provision of information and stereotypes about firefighters for the education group was highly significant, although often not proactively acknowledged. Many of these participants talked about the occupation while seamlessly drawing on media portrayals, along with other information sources, as if they were interchangeable in terms of their origin and status. Although Buldu (2006) suggested that media representations of occupations lost power as children entered their teenage years, the impact of such images was strong here despite the participants' age. There was a positive aspect to this reliance – it was clear that television portrayals of female firefighters ensured women knew the role was open to them, and generally raised the occupation's profile. This was outweighed by negative effects, however, as such portrayals also furnished participants with images of discomfort, discrimination and extreme danger. In the absence of a discourse of gendered disadvantage, there was little critical appraisal of how such images might impact on gendered occupational choices.

The media also played a powerful role by dint of the general allure it held for education participants. It was evident that some careers with obvious glamour, such as performing, broadcasting and journalism, and about some of which participants seemed to know very little, were no less attractive because of this, and no less attractive than well-familiarised ones, such as teaching. Moreover, even those with somewhat less obvious allure, and which seemed equally, if not more, unfamiliar, such as marketing, advertising and public relations, remained popular. The source of information about these occupations was not immediately clear, although their imputed link to television and the media more generally seemed to be more than suggestive of glamour for participants again, and, in the absence of countervailing evidence, was enough for such occupations to hold attractions.

The role played by direct experience was underscored repeatedly in the data, both in terms of orientation to and away from occupations. As we have seen, descriptions of firefighters were highly reliant on media representations, unless these were contested by direct contact. One of the most interesting findings from the interview data was that the sustained contact that education participants experienced with teachers meant that they did not seem to derive their images of the role from media representations at all. This was also in contrast to teacher's expectations that such images would be formative. Instead, direct experience and knowledge of known teachers was central to the understanding and evaluation of the role. There was a negligible amount of stereotyping in relation to teaching, and comparatively little generalised commentary. Where any did occur, it was noticeably less homogenous and florid than the commentary on firefighters, and was often challenged by counter examples, or fleshed out with particularised and detailed commentary, which allowed a far greater diversity of skills, incumbents' traits and experience. Given the role of familiarity, the size and frequent childhood contact with teaching clearly played an important role in making this a popular possible career, and especially for girls given the numbers of women modelling the occupation:

Extract 1:

> *I think it's because . . . I think it's because everybody has an experience of education and it's a common ground that everyone has whether you're a*

teacher, a parent, a child, a teenager; everyone's been to school. It's such a major part of our life isn't it? For such a long time, and I think especially, if girls have had really good experiences, and have. . . . Probably, I mean, female role models early in life are probably mum, grandma . . . teacher will come right after that, and so I think that's probably why because it is such a big influence in your early years, and if you've enjoyed that, I can imagine that you probably think, 'I'd like to be a teacher too.' (II, T, PS)

Although boys' views were not examined here, it would be interesting to explore whether the female-dominated nature of teaching produces differently configured representations for them.

Again confirming the importance of contact with role models, firefighter participants did not invoke media representations in their accounts of how they perceived the occupation before entering it. Nor did they invoke them in their accounts of their work after joining the Service, referring, for instance, to the coverage of September 11th far less often than education participants. Prospective firefighters were more likely to rely on media representations, which is unsurprising given their limited access to the day-to-day experience of the occupation, but their commentary was far less reliant on such information sources than that of the education participants. The evidence, therefore, supported only a partial acceptance of Gottfredson's claim (1981) that incumbents and individuals with no direct knowledge of occupations share the same beliefs about its workforce. While it was true that certain beliefs were shared, familiarity brought effective challenges to the shorthand cognitive interpretive mechanisms that led to stereotyping, and in doing so did not simply challenge the stereotyping process itself, but also key aspects of the stereotype. Minimal direct contact usually meant reliance on mediatised information, along with all its discursive reliance on stereotyping. Such information, somewhat paradoxically, formed a key part of the immediate social setting identified by Gottfredson and others (1981: 570; see also, for example, Hanson & Pratt 1991) as key sources from which occupational information is accepted most readily, requiring as it does minimal effort to access and use.

The de-stereotyping effect of familiarity was not a simple guarantor of education participants' orientation to, or approval of, an occupation, however. Familiarity with parents' occupations did seem to encourage orientation to a particular occupation for some, but for others it had the opposite effect. Direct contact did not produce unalloyed perception, or more positive perceptions, but in reducing the viability of relying on stereotypical imaging, it allowed for multiple, fluid and diverse interpretive frameworks within which participants could better 'understand'

and evaluate occupations, and how they related to their evaluations of themselves. Notwithstanding the role of glamour in attracting participants' attention, some familiarity was therefore a necessary, if not a sufficient, condition for producing more balanced appraisals of occupations, and more concretely imagined possibilities for participants to consider. Familiarity was also not a simple guarantor of a more diverse representation more generally however, and the most salient and important example of this lay in the persistent stereotyping of men and women by all participants despite their sustained intimacy with innumerable particular examples of men and women on a daily basis.

Where the findings discussed here clearly contradicted Gottfredson's (1981) assumptions, therefore, along with those of other individualist approaches, was in relation to the implicit supposition in their accounts of identity development towards a completed, gendered, individual which could then rationally choose an appropriate occupation, despite salient stereotypes of that occupation remaining comparatively fixed. The shifting, precarious, multiple and contradictory nature of the discourses and stereotypes around occupations and gender here instead point first to the powerful role played at any point in the life-cycle by greater exposure to alternative discourses about, and direct contact with, previously unimagined work possibilities, and that even sex-typing can be contested. As has been stated, some education participants expressed interest in firefighting as a direct result of contact with the research, and talking about it with researchers after interviews had taken place. A teacher participant in the course of a discussion about the characteristics of her work versus fire-fighting also indicated a new-found interest in the firefighter role:

> *Funnily enough, I read an article and I was thinking the other day, about fire fighting, and how similar in so many ways it is to teaching, and I talked to someone about it and . . . decided to call the Fire Service up and ask about being one of those part-time firefighters.* (GI, T, C)

Aside from direct contact, or mediatised information, what other significant sources of information and portrayals of occupations emerged from the participants' accounts? In line with much of the literature reviewed earlier in this book (see, for example, MacKenzie 1997; McQuaid *et al.* 2004), there were comparatively few mentions of the role of careers tutors in relation to the provision of occupational information, and those mentions that were forthcoming indicated an uncertain role. Participants claimed that imparted knowledge and advice could be variously positive and constructive, or bland, or even inappropriate and inaccurate. There were also few mentions of the role of teachers, or of other significant adults aside from parents, beyond the aforementioned function of such individuals modelling careers for participants. This does not, however, mean that such figures played no role in forming perceptions of occupations. The role of media presentations in constructing firefighter images was often not acknowledged until participants were asked to think beyond their initial non-committal answers to question about the origin of images. Moreover, the influence of peers was not explicitly talked about and yet it was often manifest in conspicuously similar ways of speaking. It is also noteworthy that teacher stereotyping of gendered attributes, although weaker than elsewhere, was significant, and that it is unlikely, therefore that their impact is neutral in this regard (see also Francis et al. 2005).

Parents were proactively and explicitly discussed in relation to career choice. For firefighter and teacher participants, they were acknowledged to have significant, although by no means overwhelming, influence on what careers individuals felt they could *expect support* for. Firefighter participants in particular credited parents and family with providing a context within which their range of occupational options included atypical careers, and careers that were '*out of the ordinary*', and for generally supporting the development of alternative female identities.

For education participants, there was also evidence that parents were central, in both modelling career experience and influencing subject choices, although these participants were also keen to express their ultimate autonomy from such factors. Women in general seemed to provide more guiding advice for participants than men (Hanson & Pratt 1991), and those modelling careers identified of interest for participants were nearly always female. Mothers were clearly, particularly influential in modelling career experience. Crucially, however, their modelling of the management of parenthood and work responsibilities also did not 'speak' to participants in the sense that they were as likely to project a paternal role for their own management – '*I will either make my husband stay at home or my children will end up in childcare because I wouldn't give up my career to stay at home*' – or to perceive staying at home as idealistically promising '*a happy, relaxed life* '. Experiences of gendered disadvantage did not seem to be effectively communicated to younger participants more generally. Where such issues were raised by mothers, or others, they were interpreted as 'old-fashioned', and the clearest and most consistent message from parents, but especially mothers, was reprised as an injunction for daughters to take full advantage of the unrestricted range of options that were now presented to them in a way that they were not in the past.

The role of extra-individual influence on choice

To reiterate, many of the accounts reviewed here, if read in isolation, are confirming of the findings of the more individualist literature. In the main, girls *did* represent their de-selection of male areas of work as a personal choice, and as the decisions of 'well-qualified young women as active mistresses of their occupational identity' (Sian & Callaghan 2001: 93; see also, Lightbody & Durndell 1998). Working women *did* narrate their decisions to prioritise family commitments alongside work commitments as a personal, or natural, preference within a broadly meritocratic, if demanding, occupational world (Hakim 1991, 1996, 2002). Once a critical mass of accounts was heard, however, undeniable patterns emerged that evidenced external influences facilitating particular choices, and constraining others. Moreover, particularly dominant discourses, through which experiences and opinions were formed and articulated, would seem to have an occluding effect on these patterns for the individuals themselves.

The injunction to 'keep options open', for instance, was commonly received by education participants as sensible, constructive and liberating advice. In the context of a mother's assumed work experiences, and the mixture of concern and optimism that this might bring to their understanding of daughters' life chances, this reception was undoubtedly matched by maternal belief that such advice was positive. Yet, the combined education accounts revealed that, in practice, this strategy represented a triumph of the belief in individualism over the actual structural constraints of the curriculum and beyond. It nearly always, for instance, meant selecting a range of A Levels that best prepared for a social science or humanities degree – areas which are already female-dominated – and dropping out of subjects perceived to be less '*good mixers*', such as mathematics and chemistry. Stark examples of '*a good mix*' included '*sociology, psychology and communication studies*', '*media studies, photography and drama*', both of which were chosen by young women expressing their enjoyment of these subjects, but who were also very unsure about what they wanted to study at university and about which occupations they favoured. Many careers were consequently made inaccessible for education participants, unless they were to take supplementary qualifications, or to study at less prestigious HE institutions.

'Keeping options open', and its tacit effects, also worked in conjunction with the elision of the fact that all of the 'shortlist' occupations identified as possible future careers by the education participants were either female-dominated or gender-balanced. Furthermore, although many of the most coveted positions were more gender-balanced than female-dominated, more of these participants will almost certainly end up in female-dominated work than otherwise. There is a strong likelihood that many of them will end up in teaching rather than any other occupation on the list. Many of the education respondents had identified 'preferred' occupations above teaching, but perceived it to be a viable career if first choices did not work out. In this sense they were more clearly focused on teaching as an option than many of the teacher participants reported they had been while still in full-time education. Indeed, as we have seen, most of this latter group characterised their route into teaching as entirely serendipitous, although ultimately pleasing: '*I didn't choose teaching, it sort of chose me but I'm very pleased it did*'; '*It wasn't really a career choice*'. An important reason why so many women who do not feeling a strong 'calling' to teach, nevertheless do end up in the role, is the profile of the employment market.

It is notable that some of the occupations cited most often by the education participants with the highest citation counts are comparatively small in size. There are, for instance, less than 10,000 dance professionals and choreographers in the UK, only around 28,000 psychologists, 44,000 broadcasting associate professionals and 76,000 journalists (ONS 2006). Teaching, however, accounts for over 1,300,000 employees, with nearly 800,000 in primary and secondary roles alone (ibid.). Participants therefore have a much likelier future in this occupation than some of the others targeted.

Furthermore, if we total the number of employees[1] recorded on the Labour Force Survey in areas that participants identified on their shortlist and that *are* female-dominated, and contrast this with the number of employees working in all other shortlisted areas, it is clear that female-dominated occupations account for over a million more jobs (ibid.). Teaching (all teachers), social and youth work, therapeutic work of various kinds, being a psychologist, and childcare work, between them, account for about 2.5 million employees, as against approximately 1.3 million recorded in all the other general categories that participants confirmed as target occupations (ibid.). Although it is no surprise that female-dominated occupations are on their short-list, what is important about this is that such occupations were not given clear preference priority above the others in the participants' commentary. Nonetheless, the size of the employment base of those occupations on the list that were female-dominated means that it is significantly more likely that the participants will hit these targets rather than the others listed, and that they are therefore more likely to be ultimately employed in female-dominated areas by default. Interestingly, women are also far more likely to find themselves in an occupation allocated a higher-skill classification – in SOC major group two – if they eventually find themselves appointed to one of their shortlisted occupations that *are* female-dominated, but they are also more likely to end up in an occupation with considerable wage and seniority bottlenecks.

The commentary from the teacher group on the eventual identification of their role was indicative of something more than individual serendipity and socially engineered numerical happenstance channelling women into teaching, however. Participants in the teacher group talked about having teaching *'always in my mind'*, and that *'opportunities presented themselves'* in relation to the occupation. Although many were expressly resistant to the idea that their gender may have affected their trajectories, others reflected that occupational choices may indeed have been constrained by the fact that they were women:

Extract 1:

Did your being female influence your decision at all? To your choice to come into teaching or to education in general?

A: *Consciously or not . . . ?*

B: *I don't think so. I certainly wasn't sort of planning ahead to have a family or anything like that.*

C: *I don't think I was, I thought about it. I went into teaching because I wanted to be a teacher.*

B: *X's looking very perplexed!*

A: *It depends how you look at it really doesn't it?*

C: *It's difficult to know how much you've limited your own horizons because you're female.*

D: *Yes.*

C: *Because you didn't think of yourself as being possibly . . .*

A: *Something else.*

D: *Something else.* (GI, T, SS)

Extract 2:

> *I think it did it affect me. I was kind of thinking, 'What about Social Work? What about teaching?' at one stage.* **There's a convenience which is built into your choice, was built into my choice, of teaching I think** [my emphasis]. (GI, T, SS)

Some of the older women, despite being very happy with their choice, indicated '*real regret*' that they had not had more options or experienced other careers prior to becoming a teacher; it was older teachers in general who were more likely to indicate some awareness of constraint. Of course, as with education participants' mothers, they were undoubtedly more likely to experience restrictions given the progressive legislative and social changes since the 1960s. The commentary of the younger teachers, nevertheless, did indicate that teaching presented itself to them, and was actively presented to them by others, as a possible career, even a good, respectable and suitable career for a woman; or, at the very least, that in the majority of cases, their choices would be supported by family and beyond:

Extract 1:

> *Partly it's people saying to you, 'Oh, you're a born teacher, you're a born teacher, X. And so I suppose you start to believe it. If people said it to you often enough! And I like, I really like working with children.* (GI, T, PS)

It was not, therefore, simply the fact that teaching remained an option in the heads of participants that shaped the 'drift' towards it. The evidence suggested that the familiarity and positive predisposition to the role was supported by societal processes and procedures, from the gravitational pull of unspoken gendered expectations, through to curriculum organisation at school and university and the viability of combining motherhood and paid work in many other occupational contexts. An A-Level curriculum mistake is indeed bad luck, and one could argue that it was a chance event, but the fact that a teaching degree was the only undergraduate course available at the time for an applicant with lower than expected results, is not best understood as a function of chance. Similarly, from an individual's perspective, being advised to take the wrong A Levels for medicine may be most easily perceived to be a matter of luck, as may finding work experience in a law firm to be unsatisfactory, or being allocated work experience in a classroom or nursery when such a placement had not been requested, or choosing a career in dance, along with innumerable others, when the occupation is very small and cannot incorporate more than a few hundred new entrants each year. But, examined collectively, these appear as more than fateful moments. Each individual event may not be the result of actions intended to constrict female choices, but, taken overall, they amount to something more than serendipity, or even structured serendipity.

Looking at the experiences of women once in an occupational role, and the collective pattern of their 'choices', the influence of other external, structural factors is also in evidence in the accounts. They confirm numerous findings elsewhere that emphasise the role of in-post experiences over pre-post attitudes in determining decision-making around work and family life (Kanter 1977; Padavic 1992; Halford *et al.* 1997; Risman *et al.* 1999; Crompton & Harris 1999b; Aveling 2002). Motherhood was a dominant watershed moment when women's previously held decisions were reviewed and revised. Contra preference theory research, (Hakim 1995, 2002), but confirming of Crompton and Harris (1999b) among others, women's collective accounts of their various combinations of motherhood and work, and their experience of working in various roles, indicated not different levels of commitment or satisfaction on their part, but varying degrees of success in relation to making the work-life balance manageable in a structurally driven and problematic framework, the effects of which fell asymmetrically on men and women.

Following on from this, it is also confirmed here that strong discursive links between femininity and skills associated with domesticity (communication, caring, for example), and domesticity itself, persist, and that these shape the way 'suitable' occupations emerge (see also Charles 2005; Crompton 1997). In the context of the overall structural shift towards service-sector employment, this is narrated as an advantage for women, but critical disadvantages were also evident. Female social skills are more likely to be understood as 'natural', rather than as discrete competencies that are the function of training, education and expertise. Skill ascription, in this sense, like other phenomena, emerges from socio-political processes in which men and women signify differentially on the basis of their gender, and command different responses for their competencies (Phillips & Taylor 1980; Henwood 1987; Padavic, 1992; Woodfield 2000). The greater tendency, identifiable both here and in the literature, to characterise women's public service motivations as a function of natural 'altruism' more often than men's, is a case in point, although numerous others emerged from the data.

Also evident here is the fact that women, as they have been for decades (Shinar 1975; Gottfredson, 1981), but as is even more the case now (Blackburn & Jarman 2006) given the service-shift and given women's relative educational achievements, are oriented towards moderate to moderate-to-high occupational goals, and specifically away from manual and unskilled work. The ambition of participants in the education group, most of whom were younger than the other participants, could be interpreted as indicative of their reasonable recognition that their occupational future will not hold the same constraints as it has for women in the past, for their mothers, and some of their older female teachers. The evidence here also suggests, however, substantial ignorance on their part of many features of women's employment, and of the role their ascribed gender traits play in determining what is considered a 'suitable' role. Equally evident is an overly optimistic assessment of the likelihood of experiencing discrimination. As we saw in Chapter 2, research findings in 2007 confirmed that recently three times more women graduates have ended up in low-level work than they did 10 years ago (EOC), and that many of them will stay there, suggesting that the ideation of women as the 'sunrise' gender may be misplaced. It would be difficult to argue that any of the participants interviewed here would *prefer* such work after investing time, finances, hopes and energies into completing a degree. To reiterate a point, it seems inconceivable that so many women undertake this qualification in order to work in a bottom-quartile role for the rest of their working life. This situation is certainly difficult to explain in the context of elevated ambition levels, or by utilising the framework of assumptions underpinning either rational choice or human capital theories.

If we accept that there is a pattern to the 'serendipity' that many participants here narrated into their accounts of work decisions, whose interests are served by this? And in whose interests is it that the dominant discourse of individualism overrides any discourses of collective experience of disadvantage for women? In whose interests is girls' and women's seeming ignorance of gendered pay and seniority gaps? Whose interests are served by the fact that even those girls and women who are more aware of potential pitfalls in working life, firmly believe they can avoid them, or that it is their choice if they do not? Although the concept of patriarchy has become marginalised in much sociological research, and, indeed, discoursers of male disadvantage have swamped it in popular representations, it is clear that girls and women are not the main beneficiaries of the current, complex web of relations constituting the person–choice–career nexus. Although appreciation of the diversity within the categories 'women' and 'men' is necessary, focus should be maintained on those commonalities across women that are not best understood by overly disaggregating women into analytical sub-groups.

It is not suggested here that women are victims of a male conspiracy comprising of individual men's strategic and malign intentions to dominate women and benefit from their domination, but that, contra the most salient popular discourses of gender currently in circulation, and speaking in *overall* terms, men maintain an advantage, in terms of status, prestige and other returns on their investment at and around work (see Halford *et al.* 1997). One of the findings of interest here is that women recite discourses that disadvantage them more frequently than they recite discourses that identify their disadvantage. Perhaps the multiple and contradictory viewpoints emerging from their accounts is confirming of female 'bi-modality' (Davies 1997a: 27), if not their more 'objective' (Harstock 1983; Harding 1986; Harding and Norburg 2005) standpoint, but without the inclusion of male participants, this cannot be confirmed.

Could there be a biological explanation for the overall patterning of these interlinked phenomena? Do fundamental messages and effects of discourses of femininity and masculinity in relation to work persist because they reflect their basis in nature (Govier 1998; Holdstock 1998; Kimura 2001, 2006; Gottfredson 2005)? The evidence here does not discount the claim that biological sex differences may predispose men and women towards different competencies or interests. What is asserted, however, is that such distinctions, and any limitations they may produce for men or women, are essentially unknowable, overlaid as they are by constitutive and interpretive meanings that amplify difference. How else can we understand the substantial changes that have occurred regarding which occupations are deemed male and which female over time and space? The evidence here highlights the view that, even given the possibility of innate predispositions, the amplification process is considerable, and is allied to differential interests and resource allocation; it is therefore on these that we should focus our critical attention.

The role of agency

There is substantial evidence in the literature testifying to the role of individual agency. It goes without saying that it is the cornerstone of much of the individualist literature (Hakim 1995, 2002; Lightbody & Durndell 1998; Bandura *et al.* 2001; Kimura 2002), but it is also present in the more socially focused research. A highly agential group of women have been identified (see, for instance, Proctor & Padfield 1998; Crompton & Harris 1999b; Meiskins & Whalley, 2002), individuals who seemingly have a greater capacity to override the constrictions that determine the majority of life-courses. On the other hand, it has also been suggested, again from researchers from a variety of backgrounds, that an analytical distinction should be maintained between individuals in 'high-choice' situations and those in 'low-choice' ones (Anderson 1998; Walkerdine *et al.* 2001; Hammond & Hammond 2002).

At first glance, the firefighter participants here could be characterised as highly agential, as they buck the trend for females oreinting to gender-typical work. Their collated descriptions of this orientation, however, are more suggestive of lesser, or at the very least, different, constrictions than many other participants, rather than their having higher degrees of agency. What about their expressions of agency once in post? Surely there is an irreducible difference between someone willing to '*run towards a burning building when everyone else is running away from it*'? This may be so, but we should also attend to the fact that such expressions of agency are enshrined in the firefighter stereotype and, to some extent, in the endogenous requirements of the role. Teachers, on the other hand, face often unacknowledged risks in their work, and their willingness to self-sacrifice, albeit in the face of less critical and immediate dangers, was clear in the data, but we do not readily attribute higher than average agency to them.

Where there was evidence of agency was in relation to participants' strategic deployment of the diverse series of discourses identified here. Sometimes the movement between narrative frames was ostensibly unconscious and confirmed Aveling's (2002) finding that participants may articulate firm accounts of choices that are then contradicted by others with no expressible awareness of the conflict. At other times, however, the participants here seemed to be actively and instrumentally selecting between narrative frames, so that they might, for instance, adopt a strategy of foregrounding a negative hetero-stereotype of boys and men when asked about the limits to their own ambition, and that this might cede to a more moderate discourse when discussing identified 'problems' faced by boys at school. The claim that strong auto-stereotypes, and their corresponding hetero-stereotypes, are crystallised and augmented in times of crisis, would seem to be borne out here. Girls and women, faced with the variety of fundamentally different and highly contradictory discourses of 'choice' are arguably experiencing a period of particularly precarious individual and group identity (Walkerdine *et al.* 2001), within which such stereotyping mechanisms are more functional and desirable than they otherwise might be.

The post-structuralist development within the sociology of gender allows for the experience of considerable constraint simultaneously with an active, agential subject (Davies 1997a, 1997b; Jones 1997; McNay 2003). Subjects take up discourses of gender at the same time as being subjected to them and are, therefore, not passive before constraint (Jones 1997: 262). They are 'neither determined nor free, but both simultaneously' (ibid.: 273). Although we experience ourselves as humanist subjects through the language of the 'everyday', this is the subject that should be 'deconstructed' as it is only through discourse that they come into existence (ibid.: 273; see also Davies 1997b). These discourses are multiple, contradictory and fluid, and agency is apparent within their operation; development can occur in the interstices and overlap between existing meanings.

It is not the intention here to contribute to long-standing and ongoing debates about the role of agency within discursive formations (Davies 1997a, 1997b; Jones 1997; McNay 2003), although in relation to this it is perhaps important to note that both Davies's and McNay's arguments for adequate theorisation of a more generative subject are convincing. Instead the intention is to draw attention to the fact that we cannot understand 'individuals' conceptualisations and articulations of their decisions around occupational choice unless due attention is paid to the constituting effect of the language they use, and discursive regimes that shape their 'options', but also to their latitude for meaning production within these phenomena. Davies's model of 'critical literacy' (1997a) is based on the teaching of reflexive awareness and the deconstruction of our 'speaking-as-usual constructs' (25), and is of obvious importance here: 'we learn to be transgressive, we develop the skills of critical imagination and through which we open up new possibilities, think the as yet unthinkable, beyond and outside dead language' (29). There was evidence of progressive ideation around gender, work and home in the participants' commentary, but its effects were precariously pitched between occlusion and the critical reflection of existing gender norms. The role of such educational tools in this context would appear to be vital.

Concluding Comment

The dominant place of individualism within western societies has been widely acknowledged in sociology. Giddens (1991) and Beck (1992), amongst others, have linked this social, economic and cultural force to the augmentation of individual agency. The data here suggest that the relationship between individualist discourses and individual outcomes, at least in the employment sector, may not be as linear and straightforward as it is sometimes represented. Discourses of 'choice', freedom and meritocracy permeate our societies from media representations to political policies and practices (Hughes 2002; Martell & Driver 2006), and the 'grand narratives' of structural constraint have been radically marginalised within public and private life.

In this context, women, and especially young women, have narratives at their disposal that emphasise their choices within occupational decision-making, but de-emphasise how these choices are framed, and the role of exogenous factors that decisions may interact with once they are formed. Against a backdrop of female educational successes, the service-shift within the economy, and the spectre of discrimination being confined to anachronistic pockets, parents and daughters perceive a world of unfettered employment options.

Individualist work on gendered occupational segregation has yielded some fascinating and important results, as was clear from the review in Chapter 2. The core assumptions of such work dovetail neatly with the rise of individualism, but paradoxically, rarely engage directly with individual accounts of occupational decision-making. This is not merely a nuance of methodological choice – Kanter's early warning against over-emphasising individualist models because they assume that inequalities are explicable via analysis of factors 'carried inside the individual person' (1977: 261) is as relevant today as it has ever been. As is clear from the data explored here, taking what Crompton and Harris (1999b: 132) have called a 'bottom up' approach to exploring occupational choice produces narratives that showcase both the individualist discourse, and, undeniably, the role played by extra-individual forces. As Walkerdine *et al.* (2001) have suggested, identification and articulation of the latter within the context of overarching individualism is increasingly difficult and produces particularly precarious identity politics for young women today – 'individuals are increasingly held accountable for their own fate', but in the context of 'old patterns of gender politics' remaining firmly entrenched (81).

The exploration here indicates that the effects of extra-individual factors, from socially produced ways of speaking through to organisational work patterns, structure the production of occupational decisions as well as their chances of being realised. Identifying what women *want* from work has to take place within this empirical and theoretical context, and the presumptions of equal opportunities legislation critically examined (Henwood 1998).

Although the empirical work here was confined to UK participants, both the roles of a teacher and a firefighter have broadly similar profiles – gender and otherwise – in many other countries and the findings should therefore have broader applicability. Moreover, there are striking similarities with the analysis of girls' and women's narratives of occupational decision-making elsewhere, including the US, Australia, Europe and New Zealand (Padavic 1992; Erwin and Maurutto 1998; Crompton & Harris 1999b; Aveling 2002; Walshaw 2006), pointing to the generalised nature of the gender regime, including comparable employment patterns and experiences.

It is hoped that the research will also contribute something practical to girls and women, as well as to employers, careers guidance professionals, teachers, parents and policy makers. Although it is not advocated that girls (and boys) should receive unadulterated messages of gloom about their occupational futures, what Davies (1997a) has called a 'critical literacy' would seem to be required to bolster awareness of, at the very least, the nature of the gender pay and seniority gaps, and the understanding of how personal desires might be generated by public discourses reflective of a gender system in which women are not advantaged overall. Greater direct contact with a broader range of occupations is also indicated here as a valuable tool for deconstructing the most stereotypical discourses of appropriate and inappropriate roles for men and women.

Such educational tools and practices would at least challenge the role played by abstract, mediatised images and information. Recent estimates suggest children are watching four hours of television a day (Sigman 2005) and that they glean much of their key information and opinions from this medium. The data here suggest that a significant amount of children's occupational information is based on television, magazines and advertisement. A person's occupation is one of the most important, observable and practical status differentiators, as well as the context in which they will live much of their waking hours. It is the potential source of pleasure and reward, but also of extreme dissatisfaction and disaffection. We have a responsibility to ensure our occupational education is as good as it can be.

Notes

2 Gender and Occupational Segregation – Setting the Scene

1. The validity of the *BSRI* is still considered to be robust – see Holt & Ellis (1998).
2. Although utilising both quantitative and qualitative data, and the use of Q methodology, this research is included here because of its assumption of individual agency and overall approach.
3. Bandura's origins lie in Social Learning Theory and in some ways he straddles both individualist and social approaches. The self-efficacy study discussed here, however, has more in common with the characteristics of individualist research as outlined above.
4. 'Whiston & Keller's 2004 review again provides an excellent resource for those interested in the association of family variables and occupational orientations'.

3 Accounting for Occupational Segregation – The Perspective of Girls and Women

1. The exception being some work related to the 'fear of success' phenomenon, which ascribes to women an 'internal glass ceiling' insofar as they are believed to experience limitations on their occupational ambitions because of intra-psychic needs and pressures related to nurturing, femininity and feminine roles, and for which internal resolutions must be found. Although individualist in focus, this literature is usually based upon individualised therapeutic accounts (see Pope-Fozard 2004 for a review; also Seelig, Paul & Levy 2002).
2. In some of this research, mixed-sex samples are used. In these cases, care has been taken to highlight whole-sample findings where there were no noted gender differences, as well as those findings that pertained to females only.
3. The data collection period was between 2002 and 2006.
4. This was mainly funded by East Sussex Fire and Rescue Service.
5. This was mainly funded by the British Academy.
6. Emma Fielding, Lucy Solomon and Jacqui Shepherd, respectively.
7. Three group interviews were undertaken by Jacqui Shepherd, seven by Emma Fielding and two by Wendy Bishop.
8. There was only one teacher at HE level in the sample, who taught on a PGCE course.
9. So that, for example: (II, SS) denotes the comment derives from an individual interview with a secondary school girl; (GI, T, C) denotes that the comment derives from a group interview and specifically from a teacher in a sixth form college; (II, FF) denotes the comment derives from an individual interview with a firefighter.

4 Women and Non-Traditional Work: A Case Study of Firefighting

1. Excluding those in receipt of London Weighting.
2. For a description of these tests, see the Fire Service website: http://fireservice. co.uk/recruitment.
3. SOC 2000, which classifies jobs according to the level of skill required to undertake all the tasks associated with an occupation competently, and the length of time it takes for a person to become fully competent for the role (ONS 2000).
4. An annual publication of male firefighters in sometimes provocative and scantily clad poses, published for charitable purposes by individual and national firefighter groups. Sometimes named *'Firefighters'* Calendar'.
5. All of the discussion in this section is based upon data from in-post firefighters.

5 Women and 'Traditional' Work: A Case Study of Teaching

1. These statistics relate, in the main, only to teachers in the Local Authority or publicly maintained educational institutions, and only teachers employed in this sector were interviewed. All school and college students were also from the maintained sector.
2. About one-quarter of independent sector teachers are also registered, but this is voluntary.
3. Hutchings, Smart, James & William (2006) have estimated that 97 per cent of part-timers are female (see also ONS 2006).
4. All pay figures, unless otherwise stated, based on 2006 scales, and excluding those in receipt of London weighting.
5. This stipulates teachers' duties. Their 'rights' in terms of condition are negotiated between unions and national employers and are set out in 'The Burgundy Book' – *Conditions of Service for School Teachers in England and Wales* (Teachernet 2007).
6. It is estimated that research professionals are less likely to be at risk of violence, and so this ranking may be skewed because of the amalgamation of these two occupational groups.
7. Employment where the male:female ratio is less than 75:25.

7 Gender as Vocation: A Sociology of Occupational Choice

1. This total includes both Marketing Assistant Professional and Marketing and Sales Managers, which account for 640,000 employees between them, and Advertising and Public relations Managers that account for 39,000 employees. It is notable that the education participants did not mention sales as a desirable occupation, or indeed, mention marketing management specifically. Consequently, the inclusion of this category probably introduces types of occupations not specifically targeted by them. The total does not include social services managers (N = 43,000), as this comprises a very diverse grouping, but does incorporate all categories of teacher. Although the categorical bases for these calculations are not unchallengeable, therefore, they should be robust enough for the purposes to which they are here put.

Bibliography

Agha, R. (2002) "Are women less ambitious than men?" *GKT Scientific*, 1 (5): 1–3.

Ajzen, I. & Fishbein, M. (1977) "Attitude-behaviour relations: A theoretical analysis and review of empirical research", *Psychological Bulletin*, 84: 888–914.

Allen, I. (1999) "Factors affecting career choices in medicine", *Baillière's Clinical Obstetrics and Gynaecology*, 13 (3): 323–336.

Anderson, P. (1998) "Choice: can we choose it?", in Radford, J. (ed.), *Gender and Choice in Education and Occupation* (London: Routledge), 141–161.

Atkinson, P. & Delamont, S. (1990) "Professions and powerlessness: female marginality in the learned occupations", *The Sociological Review*, 38 (1): 89–110.

Aveling, N. (2002) "'Having it all' and the discourse of equal opportunities: reflections on choice and changing perceptions", *Gender and Education*, 14 (3): 265–280.

Bain, G. (2002) *The Bain Report: Independent Review of the Fire Service* (December).

Bandura, A., Barbaranelli, C., Caprara, G. V. & Pastorelli, C. (2001) "Self-efficacy beliefs as shapers of children's aspirations and career trajectories", *Child Development*, 72 (1): 187–206.

Barak, A., Feldman, S. & Noy, A. C. (1991) "Traditionality of children's interests as related to their parents' gender stereotypes and traditionality of occupations", *Sex Roles*, 24 (7–8): 511–524.

Beck, U. (1992) *Risk Society: Towards a New Modernity* (London: Sage).

Becker, H. S. (1970) "Interviewing medical students", in Filstead, W. J. (ed.) *Qualitative Methodology: Firsthand Involvement with the Social World* (Chicago: Chicago University Press), 103–106.

Becker, G. (1985) *A Treatise on the Family* (Cambridge, MA: Harvard University Press).

Bellingham-Young, D. A. & Adamson-Macedo, E. N. (2003) "Foetal origins theory: links with adult depression and general self-efficacy", *Neuroendocrinology Letters*, 24 (6): 412–416.

Bem, S. L. (1981) *Bem Sex Role Inventory Professional Manual* (Palo Alto, CA: Consulting Psychologists Press).

Berg, B. (1995) *Qualitative Research Methods for the Social Sciences* (London: Allyn & Bacon).

**Betz, N. E. (1994) "Basic issues and concepts in career counseling for women", in Walsh, W. B. & Osipow, S. H. (eds), *Career Counseling for Women* (Hillsdale, NJ.: Lawrence Erlthaum Associates), 1–41.

Blackburn, R. M. & Jarman, J. (1997) "Occupational gender segregation", *Social Research Update*, 16 (Spring).

Blackburn, R. M. & Jarman, J. (2006) "Gendered occupations: exploring the relationship between gender segregation and inequality", *International Sociology*, 21 (2): 289–315.

Blustein, D. L., Kenna, A. C., Murphy, K. A., Devoy, J. E. & DeWine, D. B. (2005) "Qualitative research in career development: exploring the center and margins of discourse about careers and working", *Journal of Career Assessment*, 13: 351–370.

Blyton, P. & Turnbull, P. (2004) *The Dymanics of Employee Relations* (Basingstoke and New York: Palgrave Macmillan).

Bowers, T. & McIver, M. (2000) "Ill Health Retirement and Absenteeism Amongst Teachers", Department for Education and Skills/School of Education, University of Education, Cambridge, November.

Breugel, I. (1996) "Whose myths are they anyway?: a comment", *The British Journal of Sociology*, 47 (1): 175–177.

British Crime Survey (BCS) (2005) *Violence at Work: Findings from the 2003/04 and 2004/05 British Crime Survey*. Supplementary table to the online report. Table A.2.7.

Brown, D. (2002) "The role of work and cultural values in occupational choice, satisfaction and success: a theoretical statement", *Journal of Counselling and Development*, 80 (1): 48–56.

Brown, J., Gilmour, W. H. & Macdonald, E. B. (2006) "Ill health retirement in Scottish teachers: process, outcomes and re-employment", *International Archive of Occupational and Environment Health*, 79: 433–440.

Bucke, T. (1994) "Equal opportunities and the Fire Service", HMSO Research and Planning Paper 85.

Buldu, M. (2006) "Young children's perceptions of scientists: a preliminary study", *Educational Research*, 48 (1): 121–132.

Charles, M. (2005) "National skill regimes, postindustrialism and sex segregation", *Social Politics*, 12 (2): 289–316.

Colley, A. (1998) "Gender and subject choice in secondary education", in Radford, J. (ed.), *Gender and Choice in Education and Occupation* (London: Routledge), 18–36.

Connell, R. W. (1987) *Gender and Power* (Cambridge: Polity Press).

Cowie, H., Jennifer, D. & Sharp, S. (2001), *Tackling Violence in Schools: A Report from the UK*, UK Country Report for Connect UK-001.

Crompton, R. (1997) *Women and Work in Modern Britain* (Oxford: Oxford University Press).

Crompton, R. (1999) "The decline of the male breadwinner: explanations and interpretations", in Crompton, R. (ed.) *Restructuring Gender Relations and Employment: The Decline of the Male Breadwinner* (Oxford: Oxford University Press), 1–26.

Crompton, R. & Harris, F. (1998a) "Explaining women's employment patterns: 'orientations to work' revisited", *British Journal of Sociology*, 49 (1): 118–136.

Crompton, R. & Harris, F. (1998b) "A reply to Hakim", *The British Journal of Sociology*, 49 (1): 144–149.

Crompton, R. & Harris, F. (1999a) "Gender Attitudes and Domestic Labour", in Crompton (ed.) *Restructuring Gender Relations and Employment: The Decline of the Male Breadwinner* (Oxford: Oxford University Press), 105–127.

Crompton, R. & Harris, F. (1999b) "Employment, careers, and families: the significance of choice and constraint in women's lives", in Crompton, R. (ed.) *Restructuring Gender Relations and Employment: The Decline of the Male Breadwinner* (Oxford: Oxford University Press), 128–149.

Crozier, S. & Dorval, C. (2002) "The relational career values of post-secondary women students", *Canadian Journal of Career Development*, 1 (1): 1–9.

Cucchiari, S. (1981) "The gender revolution and the transition from bisexual horde to patriarchal band: The origins of gender hierarchy", in S. B. Ortner & H. Whitehead (eds), *Sexual Meanings: The Cultural Construction of Gender and Sexuality* (Cambridge: Cambridge University Press), 31–80.

Davey, F. H. (2001) "The relationship between engineering and young women's occupational priorities", *Canadian Journal of Counselling*, 35 (3): 221–228.

Davey, H. & Lalande, V. (2004) "Gender differences, values and occupational choice", *The National Consultation on Career Development*, Canada.

Davies, B. (1997a) "Constructing and deconstructing masculinities through critical literacy", *Gender and Education*, 9 (1): 9–30.

Davies, B (1997b) "The subject of post-structuralism: a reply to Alison Jones", *Gender and Education*, 9 (3): 271–283.

DeLeire, T. & Levy, H. (2001) *Gender, Occupation Choice and the Risk of Death at Work*, National Bureau of Economic Research, Working Paper 8574, (Cambridge, MA).

DCLG (Department of Communities and Local Government) (2006) "Fire and Rescue Service Operational Statistics Bulletin for England and Wales 2004/05". Code: 06 FRSD 04183.

DfES (Department of Education and Skills) (2006a) School Workforce in England (including pupil: teacher ratios and pupil: adult ratios), January 2006 (Revised). Code: SFR 37/2006.

DfES (Department of Education and Skills) (2006b) School Workforce in England (including pupil: teacher ratios and pupil: adult ratios), January 2006 (Revised). Addition 5. Code: SFR 37/2006.

DfES (Department of Education and Skills) (2006c) School Workforce in England (including pupil: teacher ratios and pupil: adult ratios), January 2006 (Revised). Addition 6. Code: SFR 37/2006.

DfES (Department of Education and Skills) (2006d). *School Teachers Pay and Conditions 2006*.

DeWine, D. B. (2005) "Qualitative research in career development: exploring the centre and margins of discourse about careers and working", *Journal of Career Assessment*, 13: 351–372.

Dryler, H. (1998) "Parental role models, gender and educational choice", *British Journal of Sociology*, 49 (3): 375–398.

Duveen, G. & Lloyd, B. (1986) "The significance of social identities", *British Journal of Social Psychology*, 25: 219–230.

Eckstein, S. (1988) "The poverty of revolution: the state and the urban poor in Mexico" by Review author(s): Peter Singelmann, *Social Forces*, 56 (4): 1278–1279.

Elder, S. & Schmidt, D. (2004) *Global Employment Trends for Women, 2004*. International Labour Office, Employment Strategy Papers, International Labour Organization, Geneva.

England, P. (2005) "Gender inequality in labor markets: the role of motherhood and segregation", *Social Politics: International Studies in Gender, State & Society*, 12 (2): 264–288.

EOC (Equal Opportunities Commission) (2001a) *Young People and Sex Stereotyping*, October.

EOC (Equal Opportunities Commission) (2001b) *The Development of Gender Roles in Young Children*.

EOC (Equal Opportunities Commission), (2002) *Women and Men in Britain: Management*. January.

EOC (Equal Opportunities Commission), (2005a) "Free to choose: tackling gender barriers to better jobs", *Great Britain Summary Report – EOC's Investigation into Workplace Segregation of Women and Men*. March.

EOC (Equal Opportunities Commission), (2005b) *Facts about Women and Men in Great Britain*. March.

EOC (Equal Opportunities Commission), (2005c) *Jobs for the Boys and the Girls (Scottish)*. February.

EOC (Equal Opportunities Commission), (2006) *Facts about women and men in Great Britain*. May.

EOC (Equal Opportunities Commission), (2007) W*orking outside of the Box*. January.

Erickson, E. (1980) *Identity and the Life Cycle* (New York: W. W. Norton and Co.).

Erwin, L. & Maurutto, P. (1998) "Beyond access: considering gender deficits in science education", *Gender and Education*, 10 (1): 51–69.

Fassinger, R. E. (1990) "Causal models of career choice in two samples of college women", *Journal of Vocationalist Behaviour*, 36: 225–248.

Fassinger, R. E. (1993) "A causal model of the career orientation and career choice of adolescent women", *Journal of Counselling Psychology*, 40 (4): 459–469.

Ferree Jr., G. D. (2003) "Gender and occupations", *Badger Poll No.6, Release No.6*, University of Wisconsin Survey Centre, 3 March.

Fire Service (2005) http://fireservice.co.uk/recruitment/pqa.php.

Fire Service (2006) http://fireservice.co.uk/recruitment/pqa.php.

Flood, S. (2005) "Making all the right connections," *Computer Weekly*, 18 (2): 10.

Foucault, M. (1980) *Truth and Power*, in Gordon, C. (ed.) *Power/Knowledge: Selected Interviews and Other Writings 1972–1977, Michel Foucault*, (Brighton: Harvester), 109–133.

Francis, B. (2000a) *Boys, Girls and Achievement: Addressing the Classroom Issues* (London: Routledge Falmer).

Francis, B. (2000b) "The gendered subject: students' subject preferences and discussions of gender and subject ability", *Oxford Review of Education*, 26: 35–48.

Francis, B. (2002) "Is the future really female? The impact and implications of gender for 14–16 year olds' career choices", *Journal of Education and Work*, 15 (1): 75–88.

Francis, B., Hutchings, M. & Archer, L. (2003) "Subject choice and occupational aspirations among pupils at girls' schools", *Pedagogy, Culture & Society*, 11 (3): 423–440.

Francis, B., Osgood, J., Dalgety, J. & Archer, L. (2005) *Gender Equality in Work Experience Placements for Young People*, Occupational Segregation Working Paper, Series no 27 (EOC).

General Teaching Council for England (GTC) (2006) *Annual Digest of Statistics 2005–6*.

Gerson, K. (1985) *Hard Choices: How Women Decide about Work, Career, and Motherhood* (Berkeley, CA: University of California Press).

Giddens, A. (1991) *Modernity and Self-Identity* (Cambridge: Polity Press).

Ginn, J., Arber, S., Brannen, J., Dale, A., Dex, S., Elias, P., Moss, P., Pahl, J., Roberts, C. & Rubery, J. (1996) "Feminist fallacies: a reply to Hakim on women's employment", *British Journal of Sociology*, 47 (1): 167–188.

Gottfredson, L. S. (1981) "Circumscription and compromise: a developmental theory of occupational aspirations", *Journal of Counselling Psychology (Monograph)*, 28 (6): 545–579.

Gottfredson, L. S. (1994) "From the ashes of affirmative action", *The World and I*, November: 365–377.

Gottfredson, L. S. (2005) *"What's Holding Women Back in Science?" Wrong Question. Presentation in the Panel "Women in Science: Are They Being Held Back?"* sponsored by The Ensemble Studio Theatre and The Alfred P. Sloan Foundation in association with The New York Academy of Sciences (Women Investigators Network, Cooper Union, New York City) April 14.

Gottfredson, L. S. (2006) "Social consquences of group differences in cognitive ability" (Consequencias sociais das diferencas de grupo em habilidade cognitiva), in C. E. Flores-Mendoza & R. Colom (eds), *Introducau a psicologia das diferencas individuais,* (Porto Allegre, Brazil: ArtMed Publishers), 433–456.

Govier, E. (1998) "Brainsex and occupation", in Radford, J. (ed.), *Gender and Choice in Education and Occupation* (London: Routledge), 1–17.

Grey, S. & Healey, G. (2004) "Women and IT contracting work—a testing process", *New Technology, Work, and Employment*, 19 (1): 30–43.

Hakim, C. (1991) "Grateful slaves and self-made women: fact and fantasy in women's work orientations," *European Sociological Review*, 7 (2): 101–121.

Hakim, C. (1995) "Five feminist myths about women's employment," *The British Journal of Sociology*, 46 (3): 429–455.

Hakim, C. (1996) "The sexual division of labour and women's heterogeneity," *The British Journal of Sociology*, 47 (1): 178–188.

Hakim, C. (2002) "Lifestyle preferences as determinants of women's differentiated labor market careers", *Work and Occupations*, 29 (4): 428–459.

Halford, S., Savage, M. & Witz, A. (1997) *Gender, Careers and Organisations. Current Developments in Banking, Nursing and Local Government* (London: Macmillan, 1997).

Hall, E. J. (1993) "Waitering/waitressing: engendering the work of table servers", *Gender and Society*, 7 (3): 329–346.

Hall, P. A. & Soskice, D. (eds) (2003) *Varieties of Capitalism: The Institutional Foundations of Comparative Advantage* (New York: Oxford University Press).

Hammond, T. & Hammond, J. (2002) *Gender-Based Underrepresentation in Computer Science and Related Disciplines,* 32nd ASEE/IEEE Frontiers in Education Conference, November 6–9, Boston MA.

Hammersley, M. (1990) *Reading Ethnographic Research. A Critical Guide* (London: Longman).

Hammersley, M. (1992) *What's Wrong with Ethnography* (London: Routledge).

Hansard (17 Dec 2002) "Written Answers: Firefighters: Rates of Pay", Column WA85.

Hansard (19 Feb 2007) "Written Answers: WORK AND PENSIONS: Physical Violence: Schools: Column 152W.

Hanson, S. & Pratt, G. (1991) "Job search and the occupational segregation of women", *Annals of the Association of American Geographers*, 81 (2), June 229–253.

Haraway, D. (1988) "Situated knowledges: the science question in feminism and the privilege of partial perspective", *Feminist studies*, 14: 575–599.

Harding, S. (1986), *The Science Question in Feminism* (Ithaca, NY: Cornell University Press).

Harding, S. (1997) "Comment on Hekman's 'Truth and Method: Feminist Standpoint Theory Revisited': Whose Standpoint Needs the Regimes of Truth and Reality?", *Signs: Journal of Women in Culture and Society*, 22 (2): 382–391.

Harding, S. & Norburg, K. (2005) "New feminist approaches to social science methodologies: an introduction", *Signs: Journal of Women in Culture and Society*, 30: 2009–2015.

Harstock, N. (1983) *Money, Sex, and Power: Towards a Feminist Historical Materialism* (New York and London: Longman).

Hartmann, H. (1981) "The unhappy marriage of Marxism and feminism: towards a more progressive union", in Sargent, L. (ed.) *Women and Revolution* (London: Pluto Press).

Hekman, S. (1997) "Truth and method: feminist standpoint theory revisited", *Signs: Journal of Women in Culture and Society*, 22: 341–365.

Hensley, L. (1998) "The influence of gender roles and gender-stereotyping on the career choice and career commitment of adolescents", http://www.samford.edu/schools/artsci/scs/hensley.html.

Henwood, F. (1987) "Microelectronics and women's employment: an international perspective", in Davidson, M. J. & Cooper, L. (eds), *Women and Information Technology* (London: John Wiley & Sons), 97–121.

Henwood, F. (1998) "Engineering difference: discourses on gender, sexuality and work in a college of technology", *Gender and Education*, 10 (1): 35–49.

Holdstock, L. (1998) "The ratio of male to female undergraduates", in Radford, J. (ed.), *Gender and Choice in Education and Occupation* (London: Routledge), 59–83.

Holland, J. L. (1973) *Making Vocational Choices: A Theory of Careers*, (Englewood Cliffs, NJ: Prentice-Hall).

Holt, C. L. & Ellis, J. B. (1998) "Assessing the current validity of the Bem Sex-Role Inventory", *Sex Roles: A Journal of Research* (December).

Holton, V. (1998) *Women Managers-Reflecting on the Glass Ceiling*, Ashridge Report, February.

Horner, M. S. (1968) "Sex difference in achievement motivation and performance in competitive and non-competitive situations", Unpublished Doctoral Dissertation, University of Michigan.

HMSO (2005) *Jobs for the girls: the effect of occupational segregation on the gender pay gap,* 16th Report of Session 2004–5, House of Commons Trade and Industry Committee (April).

Hughes, C. (2002) *Key Concepts in Feminist Theory and Research* (London: Sage).

Hutchings, M., Smart, S., James, K. & Williams, K. (2006) *General Teaching Council for England: Survey of Teachers*, Institute for Policy Studies in Education, London Metropolitan University.

Hwang, S. K. & Polacheck, S. W. (2004) *Occupational self-selection and the gender wage-gap: evidence from Korea and United States:* http://econ.binghamton.edu/wp04/WP0413.pdf.

International Labour Office (ILO) (2004) *Breaking Through the Glass Ceiling – Women in Management, Update* (Geneva: International Labour Organization).

Jacobs, J. A. & Gerson, K. (2004) *The Time Divide: Work, Family and Gender Inequality* (Cambridge Mass., Harvard University Press).

Jones, A. (1997) "Teaching post-structuralist feminist theory in education: student resistances", *Gender and Education*, 9 (3): 261–269.

Jones, C. & Goulding, A. (1999) "Is the female of the species less ambitious than the male? The career attitudes of students in departments of information and library studies", *Journal of Librarianship and Information Science*, 31 (1): 7–19.

Kanter, R. M. (1977) *Men and Women of the Corporation* (New York: Basic Books).

Kimura, D. (2000) *Sex and Cognition* (Cambridge, MA: MIT Press).

Kimura, D. (2001) "Biological constraints on parity between the sexes", *Psynopsis*, Winter, 23: 3.

Kimura, D. & Clarke, P (2002) "Women's advantage on verbal memory is not restricted to concrete words", *Psychological Reports*, 91: 1137–1142.

Kimura, D. (2006) "'Under-representation' or misrepresentation?" in Ceci, S. J. & Williams, W. (eds) *Why Aren't more Women in Science?* (Washington, DC: APA Books), 39–46.

Kirkpatrick Johnson, M. (2001) "Change in job values during the transition to adulthood", *Work and Occupations*, 28 (3): 315–345.

Kohlberg, L. A. (1966) "A cognitive-developmental analysis of children's sex-role concepts and attitudes" in Maccoby, E. (ed.), *The Development of Sex Differences* (Palo Alto, CA: Stanford University Press).

Krishnan, A. & Sweeney, C. J. (1998) "Gender differences in fear of success imagery and other achievement-related background variables among medical students", *Sex Roles*, 39 (3–4): 299–310.

Lapan, R. T., Hinkelman, J. M., Adams, A., & Turner, S. (1999). Understanding rural adolescents' interests, values, and efficacy expectations. *Journal of Career Development*, 26: 107–124.

LaPiere, R. T. (1934) "Attitudes versus actions", *Social Forces*, 13: 230–237.

Lee, J. D. (2002) "More than ability: gender and personal relationships influence science and technology involvement", *Sociology of Education*, 75 (4): 349–373.

Lightbody, P. & Durndell, A. (1998) "Using stereotypes to dispel negative perceptions of careers in science and technology" in Radford, J. (ed.), *Gender and Choice in Education and Occupation* (London: Routledge), 37–58.

Lippmann, W. (1922) *Public Opinion* (London: Allen & Unwin).

Mackenzie, J. (1997) "It's a man's job . . . class and gender in school work experience programmes" Spotlight 60, The Scottish Council for Research in Education Centre, University of Glasgow.

Marjoribanks, K. (1987) "Gender, social class, family environment and adolescents aspirations", *Austrian Journal of Education*, 31: 43–54.

Martell, L. & Driver, S. (2006) *New Labour* (2nd edn) (Cambridge: Polity Press).

McNay, L. (2003) "Agency, anticipation and indeterminancy in feminist theory", *Feminist Theory*, 4 (2): 139–148.

McQuaid, R., Bond, S. & Robinson, P. (2004) *Gender Stereotyping in Career Choice*, Careers Scotland (Scottish Enterprise).

Meiskins, P. & Whalley, P. (2002) *Putting Work in Its Place: A Quiet Revolution* (Ithaca, NY: Cornell University Press).

Messner, M. (2000) "Barbie girls versus sea monsters: children constructing gender", *Gender and Society*, 14 (6): 765–784.

Millar, J. & Jagger, N. (2001) *Women in ITEC Courses and Careers* (Brighton: Science and Technology Policy Research Unit & Institute of Employment Studies).

Miller, L., Neathey, F., Pollard, E. & Hill, D. (2004) *Occupational Segregation, Gender Gaps, and Skill Gaps* (Brighton, UK: EOC Working Paper 15).

Mills, C. W. (1940) "Situated actions and vocabularies of motive", *American Sociological Review*, 5: 904–913.

Moyle, L. R. (2004) *Drawing Conclusions: An Imagological Survey of Britain and the British and Germany and the Germans in German and British Cartoons and Caricatures, 1945–2000*, Unpublished Doctoral Thesis, Universitat Osnabruck.

Munn, P., Johnstone, M. & Sharp, S. (2004) "Discipline in Scottish schools: a comparative survey over time of teachers' and headteachers' perceptions", Final Report to SEED, September.

NASUWT (National Association of Schoolmasters Union of Women Teachers) (2005) "Workload, working conditions and work-life balance: a survey of teachers in Wales", November 2005.

NUT (National Union of Teachers) (2007) *Violence in Schools – Useful Information*.

Nauta, M. M. & Epperson, D. L. (2003) "A longitudinal examination of the social-cognitive model applied to high school girls' choices of nontraditional college majors and aspirations", *Journal of Counselling Psychology*, 50 (4): 448–457.

O'Brien, K. M. & Fassinger, R. E. (1993) "A causal model of the career orientation and career choice of adolescent women", *Journal of Counselling Psychology*, 40 (4): 459–469.

O'Brien, K. M., Friedman, S. M., Tipton, L. C. & Linn, S. G. (2000) "Attachment separation and women's vocational development: a longitudinal analysis", *Journal of Counselling Psychology*, 47 (3): 301–315.

Oakley, A (1981) "Interviewing women: a contradiction in terms", in Roberts, H. (ed.), *Doing Feminist Research* (London: Routledge and Kegan Paul), 30–62.

ONS (Office for National Statistics) (2000) Standard occupational classification 2000 Volumes 1 and 2. London: The Stationery Office.

ONS (Office for National Statistics) (2006) "Labour Force Survey (LFS): All in employment by status, occupation & sex", Quarter 2 (April–June) 2006. The Stationary Office.

O'Neil, J. & Ohlde, J. M. "Attachment, separation and women's vocational development: a longitudinal analysis", *Journal of Counselling Psychology*, 47: 301–315.

O'Reilly, J. & Fagan, C. (1998) (eds) *Part-time Prospects: International Comparisons of Part-time Work in Europe, North America and the Pacific Rim* (London and New York: Routledge).

Padavic, L. A. (1992), "White collar work values and women's interest in blue-collar work", *Gender and Society*, 6: 215–230.

Payne, J. (2003) *Choice at the end of compulsory schooling: a research review*, DfES Research Report RR414.

Phillips, A. & Taylor, B. (1980) "Sex and skill: notes towards a feminist economics", *Feminist Review*, 6: 79–83.

Pope-Fozard, F. (2004) *The Internal Glass Ceiling*, unpublished MA dissertation, Integrative Psychotherapy, The Minster Centre, London.

Proctor, I. & Padfield, M. (1998) *Young Adult Women, Work and Family. Living a Contradiction* (London: Mansell).

Radford, J. (ed.) (1998) *Gender and Choice in Education and Occupation* (London: Routledge).

Reed, R. & Dahlquist, J. (1994) "Do women prefer women's work?" *Applied Economics*, 26: 1133–1144.

Rees, T. (1998) *Mainstreaming Equality in the European Union. Education, Training and Labour Market Policies* (London: Routledge).

Reskin, B. F. & Roos, P. A. (1990) *Job Queues, Gender Queues: Explaining Women's Inroads into Male Occupations* (Philadelphia: Temple University Press).

Rennenkampff, A. V. (2004) "You look so feminine! When did you fail the last time? Social interaction following the *think manager – think male* stereotype", *Brandeis Graduate Journal*, 2: 1–4.

Risman, B. J., Atkinson, M. P. & Blackwelder, S. P. (1999), "Understanding the juggling act: gendered preferences and social structural constraints", *Sociological Forum*, 14 (2): 319–344.

Ritchie, E. (2000) "Women in the Fire Service: recruitment, culture and career structures", unpublished MSc dissertation, Manchester Institute of Science and Technology, School of Management.

Roberts, S. E. (2002) "Hazardous occupations in Great Britain", *The Lancet*, 360: 543–544.

Roger, A. & Duffield, J. (2000) "Factors underlying persistent gendered option choices in school science and technology in Scotland", *Gender and Education*, 12 (3): 367–383.

Rowe, R. & Snizek, W. (1995) "Gender differences in work values: perpetuating the myth", *Work and Occupations*, 22 (2): 215–229.

Schultheiss, D. E. P., Palma, T. V., Predragovich, K. S. & Glasscock, J. M. J. (2002) "Relational influences on career paths: siblings in context", *Journal of Counselling Psychology*, 49 (3): 302–310.

Scott, N. & Creighton, P. (1998) "Gender issues in employment selection", in Radford, J. (ed.), *Gender and Choice in Education and Occupation* (London: Routledge), 104–141.

Seelig, B. J., Paul, R. A. & Levy, C. B. (eds) (2002) *Constructing and Deconstructing Woman's Power* (London: Karnac).

Shinar, E. H. (1975) "Sexual stereotypes of occupations", *Journal of Vocational Behaviour*, 7: 99–111.

Sigman, A. (2005) *Remotely Controlled: How Television Is Damaging Our Lives and What We Can Do about It* (London: Vermillion Press).

Sian, G. & Callaghan, M. (2001) "Choices and barriers: factors influencing women's choice of higher education in science, engineering and technology", *Journal of Further and Higher Education*, 25 (1): 85–95.

Skelton, C. & Hall, E. (2001) *The Development of Gender Roles in Young Children: A Review of Policy and Literature*, Research Discussion Series EOC.

Smith, D. E. (1974) "Women's perspective as a radical critique of sociology", *Sociological Inquiry*, 44: 1–13.

Smith, C. & Lloyd, B. (1978) "Maternal behavior and perceived sex of infant: revisited" *Child Development*, 49 (4): 1263–1265.

Spender, D. (1981) *Men's Studies Modified – The Impact of Feminism on the Academic Disciplines* (Oxford: Pergamon).

Stanley, L. & Wise, S. (1983) *Breaking Out: Feminist Consciousness and Feminist Research* (Routledge & Kegan Paul).

Steitz, J. A. (1997) "Curricular track, career choice, and androgeny among adolescent females", *Adolescence Magazine*, 3/22/1997.

Super, D. E. (1957) *The Psychology of Careers* (New York: Harper & Brothers).

Teachernet (2005) *Understanding Teachers' Pay*. September 2005. http://www.teachernet.gov.uk.

Teachernet (2007) Teaching in England – *Pay and Conditions: More Detailed Information.* http://www.teachernet.gov.uk.

TDA (Training and Development Agency for Schools) (2007). *Ways into Teaching.*

Treas, J. & Widmer, E. (2000) "Married women's employment over the life course: attitudes in cross-national perspective", *Social Forces*, 78 (4): 1409–1436.

Trusty, J., Robinson, C. R., Plata, M. & Kok-Mun, N. G. (2000) "Effects of gender, socioeconomic status and early academic performance on postsecondary educational choice", *Journal of Counselling and Development*, 78 (4): 463–472.

Turner, S., Bernt, P. & Pecora, N. (2002) *Why Women Choose Information Technology Careers: Educational, Social, and Familial Influences*, paper presented at annual meeting of American Educational Research Association (April).

UWSC (University of Wisconsin Survey Center), Badger Poll #6 (2003): "Gender and Occupations", March: 1–9.

Vogel, R., Bell, V., Blumenthal, S., Neumann, N. U. & Schuttler, R. (1988) "Work and psychiatric illness: the significance of the post-hospitalisation occupational environment for the course of psychiatric illnesses", *European Archives of Psychiatry and Clinical Neuroscience*, 238 (4): 213–219.

Wacjman, J. (1998) *Managing Like a Man: Women and Men in Corporate Management* (Cambridge: Polity Press).

Walby, S. (1986) *Patriarchy at Work* (Cambridge: Polity Press).

Walby, S. (1990) *Theorising Patriarchy* (Oxford: Basil Blackwell).

Walkerdine, V., Lucey, H. & Melody, J. (2001) *Growing up Girl. Psychosocial Explorations of Gender and Class* (Basingstoke: Palgrave Macmillan).

Walshaw, M. (2006) "Girls' workplace destinations in a changed social landscape", *British Journal of Sociology of Education*, 2 (5): 555–567.

Werum, R. (2002) "Matching youth and jobs? Gender dynamics in new deal job training programs", *Social Forces*, 81 (2): 473–503.

Westmarland, N. (2001) "The quantitative/qualitative debate and feminist research: a subjective view of objectivity", *Forum for Qualitative Social Research*, 2: 1–11.

Whiston, S. C. and Keller, B., K. (2004), 'The Influences of the Family of Origin on Career Development: A Review and Analysis', *The Counseling Psychologist*, 32: 493–568.

Wodak, R. (1996) *Disorders of Discourse* (London: Longman).

Wodak, R. (1997) *Gender and Discourse* (London: Sage).

Woodfield, R. (2000) *Women, Work and Computing* (Cambridge: Cambridge University Press).

Woodfield, R. (2003) *"Female Recruitment Levels to the Fire Service"*, Report to East Sussex Fire and Rescue Service.

Woodfield, R. (2006a) "Women and professional-level IT work in the UK", in Trauth, E. M. (ed.), *Encyclopaedia of Gender and Information Technology* (Pennsylvania: Pennsylvania State University Press), 1238–1244.

Woodfield, R. (2006b) "Degrees of computing: gender, participation and performance in undergraduate computer science courses at UK universities", in Trauth, E. M. (ed.), *Encyclopaedia of Gender and Information Technology* (Pennsylvania: Pennsylvania State University Press), 365–371.

Woodfield, R. & Earl-Novell, S. (2006) "An assessment of the extent to which subject variation in relation to the award of first class degree between the arts and sciences can explain the 'gender gap'", *British Journal of Sociology of Education*, 27 (3).

Workstress (2005) The UK national workstress newsletter, Winter 2004/5. www.workstress.net.

Wright, T. (2005) *A comparison of the experiences of lesbians and heterosexual women in a non-traditionally female occupation, the fire service*, Unpublished Masters Thesis, London Metropolitan University.

Wulff, M. B. & Steitz, J. A. (1997) "Curricular track, career choice, and androgyny among adolescent females", *Adolescence*, 32 (125): 43–49.

Yeandle, S. (1999) "Gender contracts, welfare systems and 'non-standard working': diversity and change in Denmark, France, Germany, Italy and the UK", in A. Felstead & N. Jewson (eds), *Global Trends in Flexible Labour* (Basingstoke: Macmillan).

Index